KT-387-536

KA 0238102 8

Oeconomy and discipline

TO
VIVIEN AND JOE

OECONOMY
AND DISCIPLINE

Officership and administration
in the British army
1714–63

ALAN J. GUY

Manchester
University Press

KING ALFRED'S COLLEGE
WINCHESTER

02381026

Copyright 1985 © Alan James Guy

First published in 1985 by
Manchester University Press
Oxford Road, Manchester M13 9PL, U.K.
51 Washington Street, Dover, N.H. 03820, U.S.A.

British Library cataloguing in publication data

Guy, Alan J.
 Oeconomy and discipline.
 1. Great Britain. *Army*—Pay, allowances, etc.
 —History 2. Great Britain. *Army*—
 Officers—History
 I. Title
 355.6′4′0941 UC185

Library of Congress cataloging in publication data

Guy, Alan J. (Alan James)
 Oeconomy and discipline.
 Bibliography: p. 173
 Includes index.
 1. Great Britain. Army—Appropriations and
 expenditures—History—18th century. 2. Great Britain.
 Army—Officers—History—18th century. 3. Great Britain.
 Army—Management. I. Title.
 UA649.G89 1985 355.6′22′0941 85–1268

ISBN 0–7190–1099–3 *cased only*

Filmset by J & L Composition Ltd, Filey, North Yorkshire
Printed in Great Britain by Butler & Tanner Ltd, Frome

Contents

Preface and acknowledgements

War and the exigencies of world-wide military service provide the backgound to this study of the standing army of the first two Georges and its officers, but it is not concerned with officership in the sense of leadership in battle, nor with the regiment purely as a fighting unit. Instead, it deals with the mercenary and speculative dimensions of command as they were allowed to function during a critical phase of the decline of proprietary soldiering in the British army, and their replacement by a view of military service which, though far from being 'professional' in the modern sense, suggested that officership had become something quite distinct from a trade.

There were two grades of proprietary officer in the early Georgian army: a small and privileged fraternity of regimental colonels and a large but much less influential interest-group of captains of troops (of cavalry) and companies (of foot) within each regiment. At the accession of King George I in 1714, both grades derived valuable financial perquisites from their opportunities to manage the disbursement of funds voted by Parliament to maintain the soldier, but during the years up to the administrative aftermath of the Seven Years' War (1756–63), although the colonels were able to escape almost unscathed, the incidental income of the captains, an attraction of military life since the high Middle Ages, was sharply restricted.

The motive power behind this administrative reform was supplied by the Crown. The process was initiated by George I and was almost incidental to his immediate wish to take a firm grip on his newly acquired British regiments and fully understand their workings. But, as pragmatic responses were made to particular administrative problems, the succession of royal warrants had the cumulative effect of defining, fixing and regulating hitherto obscure customary arrangements and preparing the way for more radical intervention in the regimental economy, sponsored this time by the House of Commons, at the height of the War of American Independence.

For the purposes of this study the term 'standing army' embraces the household Troops of Horse and Horse Grenadier Guards, the regiments of Horse, Dragoon Guards, Dragoons and Light Dragoons, the three regiments of Foot Guards who spent much of their peacetime service on duty in London, the 'marching regiments', who moved from quarter to quarter in Great Britain, Ireland and the Empire, the independent companies of foot in the Scottish Highlands and the Plantations, and the regiments and companies of Invalids. Artillery and Engineers were administered by their respective Boards of

Preface and acknowledgements

Ordnance in Great Britain and Ireland and are excluded. Included, however, are ten regiments of Marines, raised for service in the war against Spain which broke out in 1739 and which broadened into the War of the Austrian Succession, 1740–48. The Marines were administered by the War Office until 1747 and disbanded in 1748, but their accounts were not cleared until 1764, and, as will be seen, were a cause of infinite trouble and embarrassment.

The regular army was divided between two 'Establishments': Great Britain and Ireland. A third, Scotland, had vanished in the Union of 1707. When these Establishments are referred to, the higher case is invariably used. In the lower case, 'establishment' indicates the paper strength of a regiment, troop or company or the command – staff of the army, the 'establishment of general and staff officers'.

The terms 'unit' and 'formation' are modern anachronisms but are sometimes made use of to avoid excessive repetition of 'regiment', 'battalion', 'troop' and 'company'.

Strictly speaking, colonels, lieutenant-colonels and majors are all 'field officers' but for the purposes of this study the description is only applied to the lieutenant-colonel and major.

During the research for the doctoral thesis on which this study is based and the writing of the book itself, it has been my good fortune to benefit from the advice and assistance of a large number of people and institutions.

My principal debt of gratitude is to the Department of Education and Science for funding my Major State Studentship during 1974–77 and to Dr Eric Stone and Mr Douglas Price at Keble College, Oxford, for encouraging me to apply for it. The guidance provided since that time by three supervisors, Professor Norman Gibbs, Mr Charles Stuart and Dr Peter Dickson, was essential to the completion and submission of the doctoral thesis at the end of 1982. I hope the present study is an adequate reflection of the value I place on the criticism and advice of my examiners on that occasion, Dr Piers Mackesy and Dr Ian Roy.

Since October 1977 I have gained immeasurably from the fraternal advice and encouragement of my colleagues in the National Army Museum, notably the Director, Mr William Reid, Mr Peter Hayes and Mr Michael Baldwin of the Department of Weapons and Mr Peter Boyden of the Department of Records, who supplied me with a number of important references. Dr Stephen Roberts of the Royal Commission on Historic Manuscripts has been an unfailing source of erudition and scholarly good cheer from the very outset of the project when we were both postgraduate students at Keble College. Mr DeWitt Bailey has selflessly shared with me material from his extensive research into the workings of the eighteenth-century Board of Ordnance. Major-General Rex Whitworth provided me with some illuminating insights into the career of William Augustus, Duke of Cumberland. Mr Glenn Steppler kindly read the manuscript of the doctoral thesis and offered some important criticisms and suggestions. Dr

Preface and acknowledgements

Kenneth Ferguson kindly made available some information from his recent research in Irish archives. Dr John Childs made a number of important suggestions and urged me, I hope successfully, to purge the text of the blemishes of 'thesis-speak'.

I acknowledge the gracious permission of Her Majesty the Queen to quote from the papers of William Augustus, Duke of Cumberland, in the Royal Library, Windsor Castle, recently published on microfilm. The Bryce and Read Funds of the University of Oxford provided financial assistance towards the cost of borrowing boxes of microfilm from the British Library Lending Division.

I am greatly in debt to the Archivists, Librarians and staff of the following institutions: the Bodleian Library, Oxford; the Department of Manuscripts and the Reading Room at the British Library, Bloomsbury; the Institute of Historical Research, University of London; the National Army Museum, London; the Royal Commision on Historic Manuscripts, London; the Public Record Office, Chancery Lane, London, and Kew; the Ministry of Defence; the Dorset Record Office, Dorchester; Gateshead Public Library; the Brynmor Jones Library, University of Hull, the John Rylands University Library of Manchester (in particular Dr Frank Taylor and Miss Glenise Matheson), and the Suffolk Record Office, Ipswich.

My dear wife Vivien and son Joseph saw all too little of me while this study was being prepared, only the all too frequent bursts of ill-temper at late hours and tatters of drafts and fragments of drafts. Between them, in distracted times, they provided an environment of the kind necessary to keep scholars sane, and it is to them that the final production is dedicated.

A.J.G.

Abbreviations

ARNAM.   *Annual Report of the National Army Museum*
BJRL.   *Bulletin of John Rylands University Library of Manchester*
BL. Add. MSS.   British Library, Additional Manuscripts
BIHR   *Bulletin of the Institute of Historical Research*
Cal. SP. Dom.   *Calendar of State Papers Domestic*
Cal. Treas. Paps.   *Calendar of Treasury Papers*
A Collection of Regulations   *A Collection of Regulations, Orders and Instructions formed and issued*
   for the Use of the Army (London, 1788)
Committee Report, (1746)   'Report of a Committee appointed to consider the State of His
   Majesty's Land Forces and Marines', 6 June 1746: *Reports from Committees of the House of*
   Commons ii. 74–211
DNB   *Dictionary of National Biography*
DRO.   Dorset Record Office, Dorchester
EHR   *English Historical Review*
GPL.   Gateshead Public Library
Gents. Mag.   *The Gentleman's Magazine*
House of Commons, 1714–54   R. Sedgwick ed., *The History of Parliament: The Commons 1714–54*
   (London, 1971)
House of Commons, 1754–90   L. B. Namier, J. Brooke eds., *The History of Parliament: The*
   Commons 1754–90 (London, 1964)
Hist. Mss. Comm.   Historical Manuscripts Commission
HUL.   Brynmor Jones Library, University of Hull
Journals, H.O.C.   *Journals of the House of Commons*
Journals, H.O.C. (Ireland)   *Journals of the House of Commons of Ireland*
JRL.   John Rylands University Library of Manchester
JSAHR   *Journal of the Society for Army Historical Research*
NAM.   National Army Museum, London
Parl. Hist.   W. Cobbett, *Parliamentary History of England*, VII–XV (London, 1811–13)
PRO. Adm   Public Record Office, Admiralty
PRO. AO   Public Record Office, Audit Office
PRO. CO   Public Record Office, Colonial Office
PRO. SP   Public Record Office, State Papers
PRO. WO   Public Record Office, War Office
R. A. Cumb.   Royal Archives, Windsor: Papers of HRH William Augustus, Duke of
   Cumberland
SRO.   Suffolk Record Office, Ipswich
Standing Orders (Ireland)   *Standing Orders to be observed by His Majesty's Forces in Ireland* (Cork,
   1764)

'He said his only account books were his right and left hand pockets; into one he put what he received, and from the other he paid out.' *Reminiscence of Francis Grose, military antiquary and adjutant and paymaster of the Surrey Militia*

'All that constitutes a good army may be comprehended under these two general heads; its oeconomy and discipline.' *Lieutenant-General Richard, Viscount Molesworth*

'... a soldier gets as little as any man can get.'
Samuel Johnson

1

The regimental economy

Administrative, constitutional and political developments

Attempts to simplify and explain the interior management and economy of the British army of the eighteenth century have often focused on the convenient metaphor of the regiment as a commercial enterprise. The officers, it is argued, made their initial investment by purchasing commissions or raising recruits. Their profits, obtained historically from the pillage of cities and the ransom of captives, came in this more civilised age from salaries and from dividends on the management of soldiers under their immediate command. At its simplest, the assumption is that soldiering was mercenary and speculative, that colonels 'owned' their regiments and captains their troops and companies, that their returns, like income from government stocks, were proportional to the investment and were sure and regular.[1]

This study offers a corrective description and analysis of proprietary command and administration in the standing army of the first two Georges. It attempts to show how the familiar metaphor is too simple a device for understanding the regimental economy and describes the way in which the Crown prosecuted its centuries-old campaign to assert the power of the purse over its military projectors and pay only for effective rank and file, properly fed, clothed, armed and equipped.

Georgian army officers looked on administrative arrangements and incidental bonuses established by long prescription and convenience as integral to property rights associated with their commissions. The first two Georges did not subscribe to this interpretation. They regarded the captains' access to dividend income as an act of grace, '... partly in aid of their extraordinary expenses and partly as a reward of their care and diligence in completing their companies'.[2] The Crown recognised few moral obstacles to regulating it, or, for that matter, most other sectors of the gothic regimental economy. Of greater practical concern were the obstacles of insufficient or inaccurate data, feeble administrative machinery, over-dependence on the co-operation of senior officers and the division of high command between the military Establishments of Great Britain and Ireland. From 1714, these obstructions were successfully overcome to to the extent that strictly limited allowances were substituted for hitherto flexible dividends enjoyed by the proprietary captains, without any compensating increase in their personal pay. This reform was achieved by a succession of royal warrants which gradually

1

restricted the operation of 'the custom of the army', by an alteration in the mechanics of muster and review and by arbitrary controls applied to the issue of regimental funds. By 1766, executive control over the semi-autonomous regimental concerns had been greatly extended and a transformation wrought in the venal character of officership, two developments which brought Britain into line with the continuing military-bureaucratic revolution in the standing armies of the European monarchies. Only the proprietary colonels of regiments got off with their most valuable perquisites still intact.

1 Military proprietorship

In England, soldiering as a proprietary venture probably began under the Angevin kings, who engaged bands or companies of mercenaries to supplement forces available through the forty-day feudal levy or the militia. These soldiers of fortune were themselves militarily unreliable, and successive monarchs attempted to secure their allegiance by entering into detailed indentures (specialised forms of personal contract) with each independent captain. In return for a promise of fixed and regular wages for himself and the men under his command, out of which he would feed, clothe and otherwise support them, the captain undertook to provide a stipulated number of soldiers for a certain period, and agreed to make periodic musters of them in front of commissaries appointed by the King. The exact amount payable to the captain at any time, including his personal pay and legitimate profits, depended on the evidence of the muster rolls.

The efficiency of monitoring systems of this sort was of critical concern throughout early modern Europe. The extent to which each government was able to establish control over its mercenary officers to a large measure determined its effectiveness as a military power. 'All that constitutes a good army,' summed up Lieutenant-General Richard, Viscount Molesworth in 1744, 'may be comprehended under two general heads, its oeconomy and discipline.'[3] More was at stake here than mere pecuniary honesty, for the word 'oeconomy' embraced the twin notions of clear-cut administration and frugality, linked by the word 'discipline' to the modern military virtues of uniformity and subordination. Even by the beginning of the fifteenth century, exact performance of the terms of an indenture was looked upon as a public duty and any evasion of that duty as a crime against the King. This attitude of mind and the parallel development of agencies of supervision were steps of fundamental importance towards the modern idea of an army.[4]

Under this novel regime, units were mustered quarterly, not by their officers, but by civilian officials reporting direct to the Crown. The muster rolls itemised each officer and man and were subscribed to under oath. Exact comparisons were made with previous rolls, irregularities were reported in detail and drawbacks or 'respites' of wages were imposed for missing men and damaged equipment.

For their part, the captains attempted to keep the agents of central authority at a safe distance. It proved relatively easy to do this once a unit took the field and this factor contributed greatly to the appalling moral reputation of the Tudor and early Stuart captain. It was avowed that whole formations in Ireland and Flanders, and even in some of the more isolated garrisons at home, had been robbed of their pay, embezzled of their weapons and clothing and either kept way below establishment or padded out with '... boys, aged or impotent persons, rogues, thieves, notorious rioters and bankrupts', rather that honest, able-bodied men-at-arms. The aim of these captains, complained Sir Henry Knyvet in 1596, was to make '... merchandise of their places ... without regarde of their duty or respect of their conscience'.[5] Even in the New Model Army of the Commonwealth and Protectorate, a force with an enviable reputation for honesty and equity, any relaxation of control resulted in false mustering, '... aggravated by every circumstance that could encourage fraud or injure good discipline'.[6]

Sir John Fortescue attributed this lapse to the fickleness of puritan morality, but a likelier cause was the chronic inability of the Tudor and Stuart state to defray its military expenditure. Units were often entirely without funds. For example, in 1626 the garrison of Pendennis Castle, Falmouth, was reported to be two years in arrears of pay and reduced to dining on limpets, while a year later news came that the garrisons of West Tilbury and Milton bulwarks had been driven to such an extremity by their lack of cash that they had pawned their beds and clothes.[7] In some places the only method of subsisting the common soldiers was by allowing them to ply a trade in addition to their military calling,[8] while in others the officers ruined themselves supporting their commands.[9]

This failure to provide adequate public funding effectively undermined any attempt to transform the officers into pillars of financial rectitude. Instead, it became necessary for the companies and regiments in which they were grouped for tactical pruposes to 'live of their own', a method of self-financing commonly referred to under its German name of *Kompanie-Wirtschaft*, 'company management'. The captains were permitted to convert a proportion of the illegal vacancies in their muster rolls into officially sanctioned 'dead pays', often dignified with fictitious names, which then furnished the company with funds for routine contingencies (notably recruiting), compensated them for any money they had laid out and augmented their irregular paid personal salaries. In the armies of King Charles II and Queen Anne these 'dead pays' accounted for up to ten per cent of peacetime establishments and in time of war their number proliferated. It was cynically assumed by all parties that if on some occasions the officers would be obliged to dip into their pockets to service their commands, then on others they would cream off the public money entrusted to them. The narrow line between legitimate emolument and fraud was easily crossed.[10]

2. Anti-army feeling and parliamentary hostility

That the rackety regimental economy was allowed to linger into the eighteenth century had much to do with the troubled history of regular land forces in

3

England. Ten years before the Armada it had already been noted that English-men '... hath alwayes had that faute ... of being unnatural and unthankful' to their soldiers.[11] Girdled by water and protected by a powerful navy, the nation enjoyed a large measure of psychological security, buttressed by a large reserve of semi-efficient manpower in the militia trained bands. When soldiers were required other than court bodyguards or district establishments of coast gunners they were obtained by a press of the sturdy poor, a measure which did nothing to endear the military to the citizen at large, for these levies were usually bereft of pay and conspicuously disorderly.

The Civil War converted this vague antipathy into lasting distrust. Before the war there were only about 1,000 persons in the regular military employ of Charles I, hardly a standing army. But before the end of the first year of hostilites there were perhaps more than 100,000 men under arms. They were taken from the plough at the height of the farming season. Their draught animals were requisi-tioned to haul supply wagons and artillery. Communications and trade were disrupted, towns crowded out with sickly and unruly garrisons, and harsh demands made for money and provisions. [12] In the wake of Parliament's victory, traditional hierarchies and jurisdictions were trampled on by a socially disrup-tive regular army, led by men who parleyed with their rank and file, executed their consecrated monarch and made and unmade parliaments.[13] Worst of all, after Colonel Penruddock's abortive royalist rising of 1655, the English provinces were subjected to the rule of ten, later twelve, major-generals, supported by squadrons of horse from the local militia, paid for by a decimation tax, but backed in the last resort by regulars. The major-generals combined the military functions of suppressing tumults and hunting down enemies of the state with a range of petty civil duties such as crime-fighting, licensing alehouses, closing down brothels and gaming houses and promoting godly behaviour. They closely resembled the contemporary French *commissaires* or intendants and prefigured the imposition of some form of direct rule in which supervision of a locality would be combined with an element of military administration. Fortescue maintained that even though the forces at the immediate disposal of the major-generals were little more than mounted constabulary, '... yet it is probable that no measure brought such hatred of the army as this'.[14]

The regime of the major-generals proved to be too short-lived to act as a proving ground for wider operations of government and marked the high point of the penetration of military institutions into English sociey. The Restoration of 1660 and the return to power of the natural rulers of the counties saw England turn decisively away from the militarisation of government that was becoming commonplace elsewhere in Europe. This had important implications for the humble proprietary officer, for it was now inconceivable that there could be any British parallel to the contemporary Swedish system of *Indelningsverket*, by which groups of properties were designated for the support of regular officers and soldiers, or the later, but essentially similar, Prussian *Kantonsystem*, which was to make the peasant regiments of Frederick the Great virtually immortal.[15] In Great Britain the autonomous, semi-self-financing regimental machine recruited the country's idle mouths by beat of drum, at minimum cost to the state and with minimum disruption to the economy or social structure.

In 1660 the Convention Parliament prudently disregarded recent experience and declared that '... sole command of the militia and all forces by land and sea is and by the laws of England ever was the undoubted right of the King and his predecessors and that neither House could pretend to the same'. Charles II was allowed to retain an unspecified number of 'Guards and Garrisons' out of his personal revenue.[16] Parliament winked at their extra-legal status,[17] knowing that the levers of government, and control of the militia as a counterpoise to the regular establishment, were safely in the hands of the gentlemen of England. But, tiny as it was, the standing army did not fail to make itself unpopular. The crime of soldiers living at free quarter on the citizen was widely reported. They were notoriously unruly; many of the officers openly swindled their men and were rumoured to be contemptuous of the authority of Parliament and the common law.[18] Moreover, it was evident that the real purpose of this army was to provide the King with an instrument of political control, and the excellent results achieved by even a small show of force, no more than 500 men, at the Oxford Parliament in 1681 emphasised this point. It was not surprising therefore that the much higher profile of the army under James II revived the latent nightmare of military despotism. The King's long-term objectives were (and remain) obscure, but there is no doubt that he wished to have under command in Great Britain and Ireland a large and politically subservient regular establishment, officered wherever possible by his Roman Catholic co-religionists and, failing that, by led-captains who had served in the bracingly arbitrary garrison of Tangier or in some foreign army. The greatly increased size of the army under James, the priority given to quartering and subsisting it over the liberties of the subject, its use as an instrument of coercion and its habitually brutal behaviour whether on a political mission or not, blackened the reputation of professional soldiers for generations and, in the aftermath of the Glorious Revolution of 1688, induced Parliament to take steps toward controlling it.[19]

Although the House of Commons was not prepared to revive old disputes by denying to the incoming William of Orange a position of constitutional supremacy over the land forces (this survived unharmed to provide the basis of the military authority of George I), it took the revolutionary step of asserting in the Bill of Rights and the first Mutiny Act (28 March 1689) that a standing army in time of peace without the consent of Parliament was illegal.[20] In the session of 1690–91 it assumed responsibility for financing the army by votes of supply. By 1697 the practice had evolved of stating the number and exact composition of the land forces annually to the House before any supply was voted. Details of the request were sometimes given a very rough passage and it was exceptional for the full sum to be granted.

Oeconomy and discipline

Between the Peace of Ryswick (1697) and the 1699 session, the army was reduced from King William's minimum acceptable figure of 30,000 officers and men to a mere 7,000 on the English Establishment and 12,000 in Ireland, paid for out of the revenues of that kingdom. This was regarded by the House of Commons as a permanent settlement and each year, until 1702, £300,000 was voted to support the 7,000 men. Thereafter, any augmentations were debated and voted separately, subjecting the policies the reinforcements were intended to carry out and, by extension, the troops themselves, to an annual Parliamentary scrutiny. The rigid distinction between permanent and additional forces broke down in 1713 when the Mutiny Act was transformed into a rudimentary army Act authorising a given number of soldiers *per annum* as well as providing for the punishment of mutiny and the desertion, but the annual feature of a trial of strength with the opposition over the army vote survived to disturb the ministers of George I.[21]

Any enthusiasm for the great victories of the Duke of Marlborough quickly evaporated after 1714. All that remained was the memory of their great human and financial cost. The army as an institution was almost universally unpopular. As Lord Hervey explained to King George II and Queen Caroline, '... there was nothing so odious to men of all ranks and classes in this country as troops; that people who had not sense enough to count up to twenty, or to articulate ten words together on other subjects had their lessons so well to heart that they could talk like Ciceros on this topic, and never to an audience that did not chime in with their arguments'.[22]

The reasons for this dislike are not hard to find. In the first place the alien and unpopular Hanoverian dynasty openly relied on armed force at a critical period. The Jacobite rebellions of 1715 in England and Scotland came perilously close to a national uprising[23] and government margins of victory on the battlefield were narrow.[24] In the wake of the revolt, the three regiments of Foot Guards and all six Troops of Horse and Horse Grenadier Guards were needed on the streets of London to overawe the militant Tory mob.[25] Genuine fears of insurrection were juxtaposed with elements of fantasy and political calculation which, in the absence of any alternative *gendarmerie*, continued to provide the army with a damagingly high profile. A belief in 1715 that the scholars of Jacobite Oxford were about to rise resulted in the city being blockaded by a regiment of dragoons.[26] The detection of the Atterbury plot in 1723 was followed by a government show of strength, with thousands of troops being marched through London to an encampment in Hyde Park.[27] Almost any civil tumult (and there were many such in Georgian England) was seen as containing the germ of rebellion,[28] and even the smugglers of Kent and Sussex were regarded as the vanguard of Jacobitism.[29] Thus, with one eye on the uneasy diplomatic climate of Europe and the other on his personal security, Sir Robert Walpole argued that '... whatever other impracticable notions some gentlemen may entertain, I believe that there is no maxim more true than that force is necessary for the support of government.'[30]

This view was opposed by influential sections of Commons opinion. The Tories, resentful at their post-1714 exclusion from the political heights and critical of what they saw as a gimcrack Whig junto, propped up by mercenary bayonets, reminded George I that it had been a professional army, the tool of an upstart faction, that had martyred Charles I. This interpretation of recent history merged with a 'country' ideology common to both sides of the Whig–Tory divide which was alarmed at the relentless growth of the military machine during the wars of King William and Queen Anne and the opportunities this had afforded to ministers and courtiers of manipulating politics by the gift of lucrative military commissions and government contracts.[31] At the outset of every session, the Tories and their time-serving Whig allies assailed the Mutiny Bill, '. . . a constant day for young and callow orators to soar.'[32] Beneath the rhetorical froth about the fate of the Roman Republic, the vanished liberties of Europe and '. . . an English army, raised and maintained by the House of Commons . . . [which had] imbrued their hands in the blood of their Sovereign' were economic arguments shrewdly calculated to appeal to the country vote. When he returned home, avowed Joseph Danvers, MP, '. . . he should be glad to have something to tell his country neighbours that would please them: they did not understand treaties, nor did they trouble their heads much about distant prospects of wealth and happiness, but he wished he could tell them that some part of our debts were paid off, or that some of our taxes were abolished or the standing army disbanded. These were effects they would immediately feel.'[33]

Added weight was given to this text by the fact that the Commons had already bestowed their chief emotional commitment on a world-class, constitutionally pure naval armament. Ships posed no threat to the liberties of the freeholder, the corporation or the legislature. At the end of a war they were mothballed 'in ordinary', with only a few officers on half pay, and their seamen were dismissed to the productive merchant service.[34] Soldiers, by contrast, were synonymous with onerous continental obligations, now including, for the first time, the prospect of waging war in the interest of the Electorate of Hanover. In addition they could be seen under arms throughout the year, quartered in the insalubrious environment of '. . . inns, livery stables, alehouses, victualling houses and all houses selling brandy, strong waters, cyder or metheglin',[35] 'wantoning in lewdness and luxury 'till they have quite lost the spirit of Englishmen and become fit to be made slaves themselves, nay, easily persuaded to make slaves of their fellow subjects'.[36]

The King's ministers were never able to determine the extent of the parliamentary threat in advance of the session.[37] It was axiomatic therefore that the military estimates should be presented with discretion. There was no army equivalent of the long-standing system of credit developed in the Navy Debt where awkward bills could be sunk.[38] Instead, the bulk of military expenditure, trimmed as it was to the lowest farthing, had perforce to be submitted to the

House as estimates of gross pay for individual formations. Almost the only thing capable of being screened was the precise method of dividing that gross pay to provide essential regimental services, plus an augmentation to the pay of the officers. It was here that the traditional regimental economy was still so useful.

Even this degree of camouflage had not always seemed viable, for the House of Commons had long since asserted a right to audit the military expenditure it had grudgingly voted. In an attempt to stave off the kind of personal attacks that had destroyed the reputation of the Paymaster General, Richard Earl of Ranelagh in 1703, Queen Anne's ministers had instituted a department of Comptrollers of the Accounts of the Army. The Comptrollers had been intended to operate as roving auditors of army accounts.[39] Their brief, issued on 26 June 1703, less than six months after Ranelagh's disgrace, was extensive. It included authority to record issues of arms, equipment and supplies from the Queen's stores, power to ensure that colonels contracted properly for regimental clothing, power to review the muster rolls and regimental accounts, instructions to keep account of deductions from gross pay, to keep records of payments made to colonels, their agents and clothiers, to make sure that cash was not held up in the accounting system and to report '. . . all frauds, neglects, abuses and defaults which shall occur to them'.[40]

This measure suggested that the whole penetralia of regimental administration would henceforth be open to scrutiny, and so it might have been, were it not for the minuscule staffing levels of the department and the multiplicity of duties which led, by 1746, to a total preoccupation with the victualling accounts.[41] But, paradoxically, the appointment of the Comptrollers was important for another reason, for by appearing to act as a check on maladministration and corruption, they lifted the workings of the regimental economy right out of the arena of public debate.

For its part, the Crown had demonstrated by making the appointment that it was responsive to parliamentary criticism and was ready to initiate reforms of its own. This policy was continued under George I, and an obvious example of it was the reform of the half-pay list. A number of half-pay officers had been out in the 'Fifteen' on the rebel side and after the rising the list was examined by the Board of General Officers, assisted by the Paymaster General, the Secretary at War, the First Lord of the Treasury and the Comptrollers of the Accounts of the Army. The scope of the investigation was broadened in order to detect unreported deaths, impostures, the introduction of juveniles, unwarranted claims, omissions and other 'inadvertencies'.[42] The purge which resulted from this 'particular and strict examination' was insufficiently searching to satisfy Archibald Hutcheson, MP for Hastings, who on 22 January 1718 submitted to the House his own list of half-pay officers, many of whom, he alleged, had no right to the bounty. He was ably supported in his attack by Robert Walpole, who in his late capacity as First Lord of the Treasury was armed with telling data from the recent investigation.[43] The ministry was roughly handled in the debate that followed, and it was thought necessary to proceed at once to a fresh inquisition. As well as convoking a Board in 1718, it conducted additional investigations in 1722 and 1726 without any prompting from the House.[44]

This sequence of events was highly revealing of the delicate balance of power between Crown and Commons on the military question. A legislature that was prepared to lay out hundreds of thousands of pounds on the land forces in time of war was capable of gagging on a few score in time of peace. Accordingly, the Crown was scrupulous to limit its demands to what it thought a potentially hostile House would stomach. This meant shelving indefinitely any plan to increase the pay of even the most deserving grade of regimental officer, the subalterns of infantry,[45] and leaving the familiar external features of the regimental economy well alone. This did not mean, however, that old ways of sharing out money within the regiment would always be allowed to remain the same. The Georges had interests of their own in army reform. They wanted a loyal and disciplined corps of officers, cleansed of the taint of corruption, deprived of the ability to merchandise their commands and operating an economical and uniform system of regimental administration. If this objective was to be achieved without approaching Parliament for additional supply, then it was inevitable that some of the officers who relied on customary emoluments would have them clipped. Implicit personal and institutional shortcomings of Georgian government ensured that it would be the less influential stratum of proprietors, the captains, who bore the brunt of reform rather than the privileged minority of regimental colonels. To those that had, more would be given: from those that had not, even that which they had would be taken away.

3. The British army 1714–63

Between the accession of George I and the Peace of Paris the established strength of the army on the British Establishment fluctuated dramatically in response to the pressures of war, diplomatic uncertainty and the economic tyranny of peace. Parliamentary estimates of 1715 allowed for 15,851 officers and men in Great Britain, the Mediterranean garrisons of Gibraltar and Minorca, New York, Annapolis Royal (Nova Scotia), Placentia (Newfoundland), and the 'Plantations', Bermuda, Jamaica and the Leeward Isles. By the late 1720s the customary peacetime Establishment had grown to around 18,226 and in the 1730s it rose inexorably to 26,314. After the outbreak of war with Spain in 1739 numbers proliferated: 45,349 in 1740, 68,161 in 1745 and 76,516 in 1748, including 11,550 Marines under War Office administration. In the early 1750s the peacetime Establishment of 29,132 was significantly higher than before the war, to be followed by massive augmentations during the Seven Years' War. At the height of that conflict in 1762, the exchequer was supporting a military Establishment of 111,553 officers and men.[46]

These figures were exclusive of regiments quartered on the Irish Establishment. The political settlement of 1699, '... for granting an aid to His Majesty for disbanding the Army and other necessary occasions', usually referred to as the

'Disbanding Act' (10 William III, cap 1), which had reduced the English army to a puny 7,000, had pegged the number of the King's '... natural born subjects, commission and non-commission officers' in Ireland to 12,000. This act operated in Ireland by authority of royal proclamation under the great seal; there was no Irish Mutiny Act, and the Irish Parliament in Dublin could not reduce the quota. Although they were supported by Irish revenues, the regiments in Ireland were not an 'Irish Army' as such, only a strategic or imperial reserve, drawn on by the British Crown almost at will. In time of war the figure of 12,000 was sometimes broken through, but only with circumspection, for there was a widespread fear, even among the Protestant ruling caste, that a standing army was inimical to liberty. For some months during 1756–57 Ireland maintained an army of 17,000 and after a vote of credit in 1761 the Establishment funded 24,000 officers and men for two years, 8,000 of them serving abroad. The Duke of Cumberland, anxious to preserve as many seasoned battalions as possible after the Peace of Aix-la-Chapelle (1748), would have liked to augment the peacetime Irish Establishment, and growing imperial obligations post-1763 added weight to this requirement, but it was only put into effect in 1769 when the total was raised to 15,325 of all ranks on an assurance that 12,000 officers and men would always be reserved for the defence of the kingdom.[47]

The effective strength of units in Great Britain, Ireland or elsewhere was always significantly below these paper establishments. Parliamentary estimates of numbers were essentially spurious, for they concealed a substantial contingent of 'ideal non-effectives', initially fictitious names and later 'warrant' or 'contingent' men, income from whom was used to generate regimental funds and augment the personal pay of the proprietary officers. Warrant men accounted for up to six men per troop or company in peace or war (sixty men in a regiment of foot of ten companies) and contingent men for up to four more (forty men in a regiment of foot of ten companies). The futher subtraction of 'real non-effectives' – dead, drafted, deserted, missing or reduced men (some of whose income was also utilised for regimental funds and personal bonuses), cut deep into effective strengths. On 10 April 1755 ten battalions of foot in England wanted 1,629 men between them. Four of the battalions, each with an establishment of 785 officers and men, were between 200 and 300 men short.[48] Moreover, many of the men deemed 'effective' in monthly returns might in reality have been incapable of any strenuous duty. In 1750 the Commander-in-Chief in Ireland, Lieutenant-General Gervais Parker, calculated that the high proportion of sick and semi-disabled veterans on that Establishment was resulting in a chronic wastage of 1,000 rank and file, the equivalent of three Irish battalions.[49] One important consideration, however, was that any 'effective' men served with the colours all year. They were not dismissed to help with the harvest like the cantonal recruits of the Prussian army, or allowed lengthy periods of peacetime furlough like the men of King George's other army in Hanover. The opportunities this gave of fingering large amounts of company pay were thus permanently denied to the British captain.[50]

The regimental economy

The standard administrative formation of the army was the regiment, sub-divided into troops of horse or dragoons and companies of foot. In the absence of almost any form of conscription, augmentations were based on the regimetal structure, either by adding men to existing troops and companies, increasing the number of troops and companies in each unit, or by raising new regiments by beat of drum. Accordingly, as votes of men fluctuated, so did the number of regiments.

At the end of the War of the Spanish Succession in 1714 the army was reduced to four troops of Horse Guards, two troops of Horse Grenadier Guards, eight regiments of horse, six of dragoons, three of Foot Guards, and thirty-one marching regiments. During the 1720s and 1730s there was a permanent addition of eight regiments of dragoons and ten marching regiments. By 1748 there were under arms two troops of Horse Guards (the third and fourth troops having been disbanded at the end of 1746), two troops of Horse Grenadier Guards, the Royal Regiment of Horse Guards, four regiments of horse, three of 'dragoon guards' (formerly three senior horse regiments), fifteen regiments of dragoons, three regiments of Foot Guards, fifty-six marching regiments and ten regiments of Marines. All the latter, seven marching regiments and the youngest regiment of dragoons were broken that year, but forty-eight cadres of marching regiments were preserved, more than before the war, and more than the Duke of Cumberland, Captain General, had once dared to hope.

No additional regiments were recruited until 1755, but drastic augmentations quickly followed, notably in the spring of 1758, when several second battalions of marching regiments were themselves regimented, and during 1759–62, when a large number of ambitious officers were allowed to raise men for rank. By the Peace of Paris the army comprised two troops of Horse Guards, two troops of Horse Grenadier Guards, the Royal Regiment of Horse Guards, four regiments of horse, three of dragoon guards, fourteen of dragoons and seven of light dragoons, three of Foot Guards, 126 marching regiments, independent companies of foot, rangers and pioneers and even the 'Britannic Legion', a force of 3,110 deserters and other renegades serving in Germany under Prince Ferdinand of Brunswick and commanded by British officers.

In terms of career and investment opportunities in military command, it is clear that the great wars of mid-century, like the wars of William and Anne, offered considerable expansion. The number of regular commissions climbed from around 2,000 during the 1730s to 3,000 during the War of the Austrian Succession and over 4,500 at the height of the Seven Years' War. Many of them, though, were only valuable in that they offered an immediate step in rank and an encouragement to further preferment in an old regiment, for even though, as we have seen, the number of men and regiments kept standing in time of peace steadily rose, most young corps were broken at the end of a war and the additional troops and companies of old regiments were reduced.[51]

The wartime establishment of a battalion of foot consisted of between nine, ten and twelve companies each of between seventy and 100 private men, two or three drummers, three or four corporals, three or four sergeants, two or three subalterns and a captain. Troops of horse and dragoons, of which there were between six and nine per regiment in time of war, had smaller establishments of up to sixty private men. In peacetime the establishments of rank and file were much reduced, but the regiments were kept 'thickly officered' to ensure that they could be quickly augmented by beat of drum. The regimental structure was completed by topping and tailing the troops and companies with a cadre of field and staff officers.[52]

A regimental proprietor was usually a colonel. Some young regiments raised for rank during the Seven Years' War were commanded by lieutenant-colonel and major commandants, but this only affected their rates of personal pay, not their perquisites. Commandants of the young cavalry regiments kept up after the war were given full colonelcies.

It was customary for only the junior colonels to appear regularly at regimental headquarters. Most senior colonels, who were usually general officers and sometimes of advanced age, were absentee. The affairs of their proprietary troops or companies were managed by a captain-lieutenant, and effective command of the corps was devolved to the two field officers, the lieutenant-colonel and the major. Absentee or not, however, the colonel obtained considerable advantage from perquisites associated with his command and it was the aim of government to make him responsible not just for its battle worthiness, but also for its financial well-being.

In public and private correspondence it was usual to refer to the lieutenant-colonel as 'colonel', which is sometimes confusing, but serves to reflect his status in the corps, of which he was usually the effective commander. Major Samuel Bever (46th Foot) observed that if a man made good use of this authority he was virtually 'uncontrollable' in his office; he hoped nevertheless that the lieutenant-colonel would be regarded as a brother by his fellow officers and as a father by the private men, '... to be obeyed by both with pleasure and resignation'.[53]

The lieutenant-colonel shared the daily burden of command with the major. If both officers were at their posts it was understood that the enforcement of discipline and the maintenance of a good regimental appearance was the particular responsibility of the major. He drilled the corps, corrected errors on parade, inspected the men's quarters and viewed the regimental books.[54]

Attendance regulations insisted that one of the field officers should always be in residence.[55] To have both was the ideal, for one of them would then be free to make the circuit of outlying quarters, a task of great importance when troops, companies and smaller detachments were away from the main body for months at a time. In the best of worlds, a field officer would have made his circuit once a quarter, and certainly once a year when new clothing was delivered, but as long as there was only one field officer at regimental HQ, such exact requirements could not be observed.[56] The temptation to stay at home would in any case be strengthened by inclement weather, and the need to nurse the field officer's own proprietary troop or company. Colonel Henry Hawley suggested that the service would benefit greatly by field officers being deprived of their proprietary commands in return for an increase in their personal pay. He hoped that this would encourage them to ride out and find fault boldly, but the idea was inimical to military budgets which absorbed pluralism more easily then bigger salaries.[57]

The field officers were such important figures in the life of the regiment (if one of them failed to pull his weight there was little even the colonel could do about it) that the first two Georges attached great importance to their being men of distinction and service. A good record in one of these demanding commands was a prerequisite for a regimental proprietorship in later life.[58] The officer corps was still small enough for men of command potential to be spotted by the King or the Duke of Cumberland; the young James Wolfe, destined by Cumberland for the majority in Bragg's 28th Foot, actually took effective command of Bury's 20th 'at the turbulent age of twenty-three'[59] and Major John Severn attracted notice at court after his prudent care of the young 47th.[60] Ironically, one field officer became so useful in that role that the King himself was loath to promote him,[61] and Wolfe was so indispensable to the 20th Foot that Cumberland was reluctant to grant him leave.[62]

Proprietary captains provided the backbone of regimental command and administration. A captaincy was the first commissioned grade which afforded a decent return on the occupier's time and money. The captain-lieutenant was excluded from this humble felicity, for although he ranked as a junior captain, he only drew a lieutenant's pay and was denied any of the profits of company command unless the colonel opted to share them.[63]

The captain was in immediate command of up to 100 private men and non-commissioned officers. If he kept them up to strength and managed their affairs efficiently he could look forward to a legitimate dividend, partly obtained from their pay. A careful captain would know all his men by name, have an exact idea of the state of their weapons, ammunition, clothing, accoutrements and necessaries (all potential loss-makers), inspect their quarters regularly and visit sick men in the regimental infirmary. To do justice to his own interest it was expedient for him to cultivate a sound knowledge of regimental accounts.[64] A captain of horse or dragoons required a knowledge of horseflesh equal to his understanding of men.[65]

With the exception of routine usages such as 'colonel's company', 'major's company' or 'grenadier company', individual troops or companies were distinguished by their captain's name. Musters were carried out on the basis of individual troop and company rolls and the accounts drawn up likewise. This emphasised the mercenary origin of the regimental economy and the devolution of administrative responsibility within each corps.

The captain buttressed his financial security by schooling his subalterns. If they were able to manage the company in his absence, this reflected credit on him and ensured his peace of mind, for a wide spread of quarters, generous leaves of absence, sickness and wartime casualties frequently resulted in subalterns exercising control with minimal supervision.[66] As attendance regulations permitted between half and one-third of the captains to be absent in time of peace, it was particularly important for the lieutenant to be a complete understudy. He was assisted by a second-lieutenant or ensign (cornet in the cavalry) who, as a young gentleman just embarking on service, was expected to exhibit ardour and intrepidity rather than any profound understanding of military economics and the tricks of soldiers. This was unfortunate in the light of many important duties which might fall to him by lot, of which recruiting was potentially the most financially hazardous.

In addition to the administrative and financial chores shouldered by field officers and captains, a number of more precisely defined tasks were carried out by the staff officers of each regiment. Three of these gentlemen, the chaplain, surgeon and surgeon's mate, had specialist functions which are not our concern. The remaining staff appointments—adjutant, quartermaster and paymaster— were usually, but not invariably, held by subalterns in addition to their commissions in the line. Adjutancies and quartermasterships appeared on the regimental establishments and had personal pay attached to them. This was not the case with the paymastership, and the duties and remuneration associated with that office are dealt with in a later chapter.

The principal duty of the adjutant was to act as assistant to the major, superintending the drilling of recruits, issuing orders to the sergeants, supervising the carrying out of punishments imposed by regimental courts-martial, compiling the monthly returns and taking custody of the regimental books.[67] This last was a more risky obligation than appeared at first sight; on 9 July 1755 the wounded adjutant of the 44th Foot, Lieutenant Daniel Disney, was hotly pursued by Indians as he rescued the vellum-bound regimental folio from the disastrous battle of the Monongahela.[68] Adjutancies were in the disposal of the colonels until 1760, when, at the King's command, Viscount Barrington declared an end to the traffic.[69] Later evidence suggests that he was not entirely successful.[70] It was clearly in the interest of colonels to appoint an experienced subaltern, someone '... of abilities and integrity with many more accomplishments ... for he cannot have too many virtues, too much knowledge or experience'.[71] It is surprising to find that the place was sometimes bestowed on the youngest ensign, or to individuals plainly lacking the capacity for it.[72]

The battalion quartermaster took charge of the regimental equipage, forage and rations. When a unit was in quarters or garrison it was his responsibility to make sure that the men's billets were properly organised.[73] He should always have been '... an honest, careful officer, exact of his pen and a steady accomptant, very well skilled in the detail of the battalion and perfectly well acquainted with every individual circumstance of its duty and finances'.[74] Regiments of cavalry had a quartermaster attached to each troop. Outside the troops of Horse Guards the rank was looked on as menial, and unless they already held some other regimental commission troop quartermasters were treated only as slightly superior warrant officers. As the century progressed, troop and battalion quartermasterships were increasingly regarded as fitting rewards for senior sergeants, not least as this would entitle them to modest half pay on disbandment.[75] Despite the limited attractions of the grade, some impecunious young gentlemen continued to apply for it, in the hope of rising thereby to a subaltern's commission without purchase.[76]

Notes

1 The classic exposition is offered by J. W. Fortescue in *The British Army 1783–1802*, London, 1905, p. 8, and in an important essay, 'The Army' in A. S. Turbeville ed., *Johnson's England*, Oxford, 1933, II, p. 66.

2 A principle enunciated restrospectively and at the moment of its practical violation; PRO.WO 26/24 f. 387 Warrant for Applying the Non-effective Balances of the Regiments of Infantry, 17 March 1761.

3 *A Short Course of Standing Rules for the Government and Conduct of an Army*, 'by a Lieutenant-General in His Majesty's Service', attributed to Richard, Viscount Molesworth, London, 1744, p. 1.

4 R A. Newhall, *Muster and Review: A Problem of English Military Administration 1420–1440*, Cambridge, Mass., 1940, *passim*; A Corvisier, *Armies and Societies in Europe, 1494–1789*, Bloomington, Ind. and London, 1979, pp. 64–82; A. P. C. Bruce, *The Purchase System in the British Army, 1660–1871*, London, 1980, pp. 7–10.

5 C Falls, *Elizabeth's Irish Wars*, London, 1960, *passim*; C. G. Cruickshank, *Elizabeth's Army*, second edn., Oxford, 1966, *passim*; H. J. Webb, *Elizabethan Military Science*, London, 1966, pp. 58–69; PRO. SP 16/13 f. 85, Ordinances propounded by the Council of War to be considered by the Council of State, *c.* 1625.

6 Sir J. Fortescue, *The History of the British Army*, London, 1935, I, pp. 285–6.

7 A. D. Saunders, *Pendennis and St. Mawes Castles*, London, 1975, p. 10; *Cal. S. P. Dom. 1627–28* pp. 23, 54.

8 In early seventeenth-century Portsmouth, for example, some soldiers kept taverns while others laboured in the royal dockyard. This custom was highly injurious to discipline and caused a great deal of ill-feeling in the community. Attempts to put a stop to it broke down, however, as the Crown was unable to provide the men with regular subsistence; R. East ed., *Extracts from Records in the Possession of the Municipal Corporation of Portsmouth*, Portsmouth, 1891, pp. 686–9; *Cal. S. P. Dom. 1629–31*, pp. 288, 304; *Addendum 1625–49*, p. 375.

9 R. A. Preston, *Gorges of Plymouth Fort: A Life of Sir Ferdinando Gorges*, Toronto, 1953, pp. 63–4, 90–102.

10 Some penetrating observations on this cynical balance of interests are made by J. Childs, *Armies and Warfare in Europe 1648–1789*, Manchester, 1982, pp. 63–4.

11 Barnaby Googe, quoted by L. G. Schwoerer, *No Standing Armies! The Anti-Army Ideology in Seventeenth Century England*, Baltimore and London, 1974, p. 9.

12 I. Roy, 'The English Civil War and English Society' in I. Roy, B. Bond eds., *War and Society*, London, 1975, pp. 24–43.

13 C. Hill, *The World Turned Upside Down: Radical Ideas during the English Revolution*, Penguin edn., Harmondsworth, 1975, pp. 57–61.

14 Fortescur, *History*, I, p. 238; I. Roots, 'Swordsmen and Decimators: Cromwell's Major Generals' in R. H. Parry ed., *The English Civil War and After*, London, 1970, pp. 78–92.

15 For these developments see O. Hintze, 'The Commissary and his Significance in General Administrative History' in F. Gilbert ed., *The Historical Essays of Otto Hintze*, New York, 1975, pp. 268–301; C. Jones, 'The Military Revolution and the Professionalization of the French Army under the Ancien Regime' in M. Duffy ed., *The Military Revolution and the State, 1500–1800*, Exeter, 1980, pp. 29–48; Corvisier. *op. cit.*, pp. 51–60; C. Duffy, *The Army of Frederick the Great*, Newton Abbot, 1974, pp. 54–7.

16 F. W. Maitland, *The Constitutional History of England*, Cambridge, 1908, p. 326.

17 J. Childs, *The Army of Charles II*, London, 1976, p. 220.

18 *Ibid., passim.*

19 Childs, *The Army, James II and the Glorious Revolution*, Manchester, 1980, *passim.*

20 Schwoerer, *op. cit.*, pp. 151–2.

21 These developments are exhaustively described by I. F. Burton, 'The Secretary at War and the Administration of the Army during the War of the Spanish Succession', unpublished Ph. D. thesis, University of London, 1960, pp. 47–91. In 1700, in a frame of mind similar to that of the English Parliament during 1697–99, the Scottish Parliament resolved that forces there should be limited to 3,000. Three regiments of foot had to be transferred to the Dutch service to accomplish this. In 1708 the Scottish and English Establishments merged to form a single British Establishment.

22 R. Sedgwick ed., John, Lord Hervey, *Some Materials towards Memoirs of the Reign of King George II*, London, 1931, III, p. 525.

23 Here I follow the argument of B. Lenman, *The Jacobite Risings in Great Britain 1689–1746*, London, 1980, p. 107–54.

24 J. Baynes, *The Jacobite Rising of 1715*, London, 1970, *passim.*

25 N. Rogers, 'Popular Protest in Early Hanoverian London,' *Past and Present*, No. 79, 1978, pp. 70–100.

26 W. R. Ward, *Georgian Oxford: University Politics in the Eighteenth Century*, Oxford, 1958, pp. 59–60.

27 J. H. Plumb, *Sir Robert Walpole*, II, *The King's Minister*, London, 1972, p. 43.

28 T. Hayter, *The Army and the Crowd in Mid-Georgian England*, London, 1978, pp. 20–1.

29 P. Muskett, 'Military Operations against Smuggling in Kent and Sussex, 1698–1750'. *JSAHR*, LII, 1974, pp. 89–110.

30 *Parl, Hist.* IX, p. 1311, 18 Feb. 1737.

31 L. Colley, *In Defiance of Oligarchy: The Tory Party 1714–60*, Cambridge, 1982, pp. 87–91; H. T. Dickinson, *Liberty and Property: Political Ideology in Eighteenth Century Britain*, London, 1979, pp. 104–11.

32 Lord Holland, ed. Horace Walpole, *Memoirs of the Reign of George II*, London 1846, I, p. 410.

33 *Parl. Hist.* VIII, p. 874, 13 Jan. 1732.

34 M. Duffy, 'The Foundation of British Naval Power' in M. Duffy ed., *Military Revolution*, pp. 49–83.

35 The wording of the 1703 and successive Mutiny Acts, quoted by R. E. Scouller, *The Armies of Queen Anne*, Oxford, 1966, pp. 164–5.

36 *Parl. Hist.* IX, p. 281, 6 Feb. 1734.

37 A. S. Foord, *His Majesty's Opposition*, Oxford, 1964, pp. 176–7.

38 D. A. Baugh, *Naval Administration in the Age of Walpole*, Princeton, 1965, pp. 467–72.

39 C. M. Clode, *The Military Forces of the Crown: Their Administration and Government*, London, 1869, I, pp. 112–18, Scouller, *op. cit.*, pp. 9, 29–32.

40 Instructions to the Comptrollers of the Accounts of the Army, 26 June 1703, reprinted in *Report of a Committee appointed to consider the State of His Majesty's Land Forces and Marines*, 6 June 1746, *Reports from Committees of the House of Commons*, II, p. 198 (hereafter *Committee Report* (1746).

41 *Ibid.*, pp. 119–20.

42 PRO. WO 26/14 f. 263, Order convoking a Board of General Officers, 16 Nov. 1716.

43 *Parl. Hist.*, VIII, pp. 534–5, 22–25 Jan. 1718.

44 PRO. WO 26/15 f. 127, Order convoking a Board of General Officers, 15 April 1718; WO 26/16 f. 198, Order convoking a Board, 6 Aug. 1722; WO 26/17 f. 128, Order regulating the conduct of half-pay officers, 14 Dec. 1726.

45 J. L. Pimlott, 'The Administration of the British Army, 1783–1793', unpublished Ph.D. thesis, University of Leicester, 1975, p. 205.

46 *Journals of the House of Commons* (various); Sir Charles Whitworth, *Public Accounts of Services and Grants, 1720–1770*, London, 1771, *passim*.

47 PRO. SP 63/420 f. 26, Memorandum by Charles Yorke, Attorney General, 27 Dec, 1762; A. J. Guy, 'A Whole Army Absolutely Ruined in Ireland', *ARNAM*, 1978–99, pp. 30–43; K. P. Ferguson, 'The Army in Ireland from the Restoration to the Act of Union', unpublished Ph.D. thesis, Trinity College, Dublin, 1980 pp. 60–4; T. Bartlett, 'The Augmentation of the Army in Ireland, 1767–69', *EHR*, 96, 1981, pp. 540–59. The Irish Parliament's fears were not entirely unfounded. In the early part of the century, the army could almost have been paid for out of the Crown's hereditary revenues in the kingdom, and in 1720 a scheme to that effect was drawn up for Charles Duke of Bolton (Lord Lieutenant, 1717–20), who hoped by this means to avoid the obligation of summoning Parliament; Ferguson, *op. cit.*, p. 63.

48 R. A. Cumb. C46/6, 'Abstract of the Foot in England', 10 April 1755.

49 R. A. Cumb. C44/145, Analysis of the military situation in Ireland, *c.* 1750. In his survey Parker discovered 2,094 men in the Irish army who had served between fifteen and thirty-five years in the ranks.

50 C. Duffy, *Army of Frederick the Great*, p. 32; J. Niemeyer, G. Ortenburg, *The Hanoverian Army during the Seven Years' War*, Copenhagen, 1977, p. 15.

51 *Journals, H.O.C.* (various); Manuscript Army Lists compiled by A. S. White and now at the National Army Museum, London; *Army Lists* (various), *Court and City Registers* (various); J. B. M. Frederick, *Lineage Book of the British Army*, Cornwallville, N.Y, 1969; J. A. Houlding, *Fit For Service: The Training of the British Army 1715–1795*, Oxford 1981, pp. 8–12, 99.

52 Houlding, *op. cit.*, pp. 415–22, has a valuable 'Table of Regimental Establishments during Selected Years'.

53 Major Samuel Bever, *The Cadet, A Military Treatise*, Dublin, 1756, p. 163; Capt. Bennett Cuthbertson, *A System for the Complete Interior Management and Oeconomy of a Battalion of Infantry*, Dublin, 1768, p. xxxviii.

54 Capt. Thomas Simes, *The Military Guide for Young Officers* London, 1772, p. 168; Simes, *The Regulator, or Instructions to Form the Officer, and Complete the Soldier*, London, 1780, pp. 120–1; Cuthbertson, *System*, pp. 178–9.

55 PRO. WO 26/17 f. 4, Regulations for the Attendance of Officers at Quarters, 4 May 1724; HUL. DDHO4.285 *Standing Orders* (Ireland), Section VIII, 18 Oct. 1751; WO 26/26 f. 460, Regulations for the Attendance of Officers, 27 July 1764.

56 Molesworth, *Short Course*, p. 160.

57 NAM. 7411–24–16. Hawley's criticism of field officers was '... not meant in general, but there are many who do this'; 'Some thoughts', *c.* 1725.

58 BL. Add. MSS 32,707 f. 223, William, Viscount Barrington, Secretary at War, to the Duke of Newcastle, 14 June 1760.

59 James Wolfe to his mother, Mrs Henrietta Wolfe, 13 Aug. 1749, R. Wright, *The Life of Major General James Wolfe, illustrated by his Correspondence*, London, 1864, pp. 134–5. Wolfe was gazetted major of the 20th in January 1749 and lieutenant-colonel in March 1750.

60 BL. Add. MSS. 35, 354 f. 14, The Earl of Hardwicke to his son, Ensign Joseph Yorke, 2nd Foot Guards, 10 Oct. 1742.

61 P. C. Yorke, *The Life of Lord Chancellor Hardwicke* London, 1913, II, p. 174.

62 Wolfe to Capt. William Rickson, 9 June 1751, Wright, *Wolfe*, p. 172.

63 The rank was considered to be '. . . the worst in the service' and was only worth having because it was cheaper than a captaincy and gave a step over the other subalterns if a captaincy became vacant without purchase; Simes, *Military Guide*, 'Captain-Lieutenant'; NAM. 7411–24–16, 'Some thoughts', by Col. Henry Hawley, *c.* 1725.

64 A summary of the attributes of the ideal captain is provided by Simes, *Military Guide*, p. 168.

65 Henry Earl of Pembroke, *Military Equitation*, London 1761, *passim.*

66 *General Wolfe's Instructions to Young Officers*, London, 1768, p. 57; Simes, *Military Guide*, p. 168.

67 Francis Grose, *Military Antiquities respecting a History of the English Army from the Conquest to the Present Time*, London 1786, I, pp. 316–17; Molesworth, *Short Course*, pp. 16–17; Cuthbertson, *System*, pp. 178–79; R. Hamilton, *The Duties of a Regimental Surgeon*, London, 1794, II, note, p. 49.

68 C. Hamilton ed., *Braddock's Defeat*, Norman, Oklahoma, 1959, p. 61.

69 PRO. WO 4/59 f. 578, Barrington to John Calcraft, regimental agent, 24 Jan 1760.

70 Bruce, *Purchase System*, pp. 28–9.

71 Simes, *A Military Course for the Government and Conduct of a Battalion*, London, 1777, p. 228.

72 *Loc. cit.*; Grose, *op. cit.*, I, p. 317 and note.

73 *General Wolfe's Instructions*, pp. vi–vii; Cuthbertson, *System*, p. 39.

74 Simes, *Military Course*, p. 222.

75 PRO. WO 34/87, Col. Francis Grant to Maj-Gen. Jeffery Amherst, n.d. (Oct. 1761?).

76 In 1732 John Mackenzie, heir to the impecunous laird of Suddie, was looking for a cheap troop quartermastership as a means of escape from the ranks of the 5th Dragoons, but at £300 he thought that prices were very inflated. BL. Add. MSS. 39,189 f. 25, John to his brother Kenneth, 13 June 1732. King George II was reputedly averse to granting higher commissions to troop quartermasters; J. Hayes, 'The Social and Professional Background of the Officers of the British Army, 1714–1763', unpublished M.A. thesis, University of London, 1956, p. 207.

2

The army and the Crown

Authority and resistance

In the decades after the accession of George I the effective authority of the Crown over the army waxed considerably but a number of counteracting influences combined to ensure that the full potential for administrative reform was not realised. First among them was the capricious character of the royal will itself; second was the inherent weakness of the administrative machine through which royal wishes were to be put into effect, and third was the pugnacious and individualistic spirit of the British officer, upon whose goodwill discipline and effective administration ultimately depended

1. The personal character of royal authority

The constitutional struggles of the seventeenth century had resulted in Parliament winning control of the military purse but the personal elements of honour, preferment and command were still seen as flowing direct from the Crown. In Britain, as in France, Prussia and other aristocratic societies of the *ancien régime* it was thought especially appropriate for young gentlemen to put on the king's coat. All their 'streams of honour', it was maintained, derived from the 'original fountain' of the throne.[1] By taking His Majesty's commissions they at once became the immediate servants of the King, with an infinitely nobler status than churchmen, lawyers, doctors or members of the liberal professions.[2] Moreover, such devotion to the service of the sovereign was not to be corrupted by any intermediate obligation. Thus the penurious Lieutenant-Colonel James Wolfe declined a lucrative season bear-leading the young third Duke of Richmond round the military capitals of Europe, 'on account of the pension that might follow ... it is very certain it would not become me to accept it. I can't take money from anyone but the King my master or one of his blood.'[3]

The first two Georges had a much better chance of appealing to these lofty sentiments than poor moribund Queen Anne. George I's military career, although unspectacular, had included service under William III and a worthy tour in high command on the upper Rhine. The Prince of Wales, later George II, had served under Marlborough and although lacking experience of independent command had greatly distinguished himself in a cavalry charge at the battle of Oudenarde (1708). His own horse had been killed in the melée and the squadron commander with whom he rode was killed as he helped him remount.[4] He was, as is well known, the last king of Great Britain to lead his troops into combat, at Dettingen on 27 June 1743.

It was in the character of George II that the martial pretensions of the Hanoverian dynasty were most obvious (and, thought some, most ridiculous).[5] The King saw himself, not unlike his cousin the extraordinary Frederick-William I of Prussia, as a kind of *primus inter pares* in his corps of officers. He prided himself on a close personal acquaintance with their characters and attainments, perfectly possible in an army which in time of peace had only about 2,000 officers, and he kept this information in a book close at hand when discussing preferments.[6] These he guarded almost as jealously as appointments to his bedchamber, and though in reality most commissions were distributed to members of governing class or their nominees, he resented overt interference with promotions by politicians. On one occasion when Sir Robert Walpole mentioned an officer's name he was curtly told, 'I won't do that; you always want to have me disoblige all my old soldiers, you understand nothing of troops. I will order my army as I think fit.'[7] Horatio Walpole thought that in general his brother '. . . has very little to do with the military promotions. He recommends friends and relations of Members of Parliament to be ensigns and cornets, but His Majesty himself keeps an account of all the officers, knows their character and long services and generally nominates at his own time to vacant regiments. He frequently mentions these promotions to my brother who, when he lets fall a word or two in favour of some officer is told . . . that he does not understand anything of military matters.'[8]

Similar rebuffs were sustained by the Duke of Newcastle later in the reign. 'The affairs of the army, are totally out of my department,' he whined, 'and if I mention them to the King, I must own His Majesty is not pleased with it.'[9] Even the Duke of Cumberland, Captain General and favourite son, whose advice carried great weight with his father, was sometimes disappointed in the matter of promotions when he thought every obstacle had been overcome.[10] To the very end of his life, and in the middle of a world war, the King insisted on going his own way, deferring appointments to colonelcies until the close of the campaigning season to judge which of the field officers was most worthy.[11]

If an officer found favour with the King, the expression of that favour was characteristically blunt. 'As for you, sir,' he told the Earl of Cathcart, 'you saw when a regiment of horse fell vacant I gave it to you . . . I know you to be a man of honour and if you continue to behave yourself to me, I'll take care of you.'[12] Conversely, if he took exception to a man, he was implacable. James, Earl of Balcarres, had erred in his youth by joining the rebellion of the Earl of Mar in 1715. Notwithstanding his return to allegiance, his distinguished behaviour at Dettingen and the repeated intercession of two distinguished military uncles, John Earl of Stair, and Sir James Campbell of Lawers, he never got beyond junior rank in the army.[13] The career of Henry Seymour Conway, later secretary of state and Commander-in-Chief, languished until the old King's death once George had concluded he had not done his all to promote Sir John Mordaunt's amphibious raid on Rochefort (September 1757), to which he had been appointed second-in-command.[14] The wording of the public disgrace meted out to Lord George Sackville after his failure at the battle of Minden (1 August 1759) was thought to be worse than death,[15] while the King's brutal reception of Cumberland after the latter's return, ill and defeated, from Germany in 1757 moved even the adamantine Horace Walpole to pity.[16]

This arbitrary or whimsical behaviour was all the more significant since it was based on undoubted prerogative. If he chose, the King could promote an officer over the heads of many equally worthy candidates; [17] likewise, he could cashier him regardless of any property right he might rashly have assumed to belong to his expensive commission. The broken officer had no claim against the Crown for the cash value of the commission; such compensation as was allowed to suspected Jacobites superseded in 1715 was an act of grace.[18]

Having agreed willingly to an anti-Jacobite purge on the assumption that the King was the person best fitted to assess the loyalty of officers, MPs who objected to the subsequent removal of Whig dissidents found themselves on weak ground. In 1733 George II dismissed two senior regimental proprietors, Charles, Duke of Bolton, and Richard, Viscount Cobham. There were some doubts about Bolton's record as colonel of the Royal Regiment of Horse Guards: 'The dirty tricks he played,' claimed Lord Hervey, '. . . to cheat the government of men, or his men of half-a-crown, were things unknown to any colonel but his grace, no griping Scotchman excepted,'[19] but Cobham was a veteran of tried merit, and it was obvious that his real crime was his sponsorship of a noisy group of patriot Whigs nicknamed 'Cobham's Cubs'.[20]

Sir Robert Walpole's many enemies in both Houses of Parliament tried to unmask him as instigator of these cashierings and attempted to push through Bills that would have prevented any officer under the rank of general officer from being dismissed except by the verdict of a general court-martial or an address by both Houses, but although a large number of MPs did not approve of the King's action in this instance, they could not think of anyone more suitable to whom to entrust the governance of the army, least of all the army officers. This point struck home to the Tories, who, much as they loathed Walpole and the Whig oligarchs, had a due regard for the sanctity of the royal prerogative.[21] The attack faltered. 'Lopping off so great a branch of the prerogative,' maintained the Whig Thomas Robinson, '. . . will disarm the Crown of a power necessary to keep the army firm and steady to the present establishment and . . . by trusting it in the hands of soldiers may throw a great deal of independent strength into the army itself.' General George Wade supported this argument with the alarming claim that officers were already so negligent in attending courts-martial that they were quite unfit to be trusted with any greater responsibility. It was already hard enough to keep them at their business, he claimed, without loosening royal authority over them.[22] By such means were the old arguments that an army subject to the whims of Princes was a threat to the constitution turned on their heads, and the King continued to use his power of dismissal against officers whose political conduct displeased him. The following year John, Earl of Stair, was dismissed from the colonelcy of the Inniskilling Dragoons for supporting the cause of Bolton and Cobham;[23] in 1736, William Pitt, one of 'Cobham's Cubs', was deprived of his humble cornetcy in Cobham's regiment of horse after a facetious speech on the projected marriage of Frederick Prince of Wales[24] and in 1737 John Fane, Earl of Westmorland, a veteran of Malplaquet, was dismissed from command of the First Troop of Horse Guards, after a vote in favour of augmenting Frederick's allowance. It is indicative of the King's very personal view of military obligation that Fane, an officer of his household troops, was treated particularly harshly. He was not allowed to sell his commission and as a result was believed to have lost £6,500. He took his revenge by burning Sir Robert Walpole in effigy, but this cannot have been much compensation for his financial loss. Moreover, although he was later reinstated in the army with retrospective promotion, he was never given command of a regiment or reimbursed.[25]

The granting or withholding of grace and favour may have gone a long way towards reminding officers where their loyalties lay (as we shall see, it had somewhat the reverse effect on some more sensitive souls), but the paramount virtue of the incoming dynasty was its regard for military efficiency, clarity of adminstration, frugality and discipline. George I's Electoral regiments were organised on generally the same lines as his newly acquired British units,[26] and although they were not up to the most exalted European standards,[27] they were believed to be generally well run. The King's long experience of managing them was a useful preparation for filling a power vacuum at the summit of the British army greater than would normally have been the case at a change of monarch. The Duke of Marlborough had succeeded in engrossing by force of personality and achievement much of the military authority rightly belonging to the Crown, but his growing number of enemies had not been prepared to let him keep it. In 1711 they had tried to circumscribe his influence by establishing a committee of cabinet ministers and general officers who were also privy councillors to advise Queen Anne independently on military business. This measure had had the useful effect of reclaiming to the Crown such important matters as the regulation of regimental seniority and brevet promotions, but the rapid decline of the committee (by-passed by the Secretary of State, Henry St John, who preferred to deal with Marlborough direct), the Duke's subsequent disgrace and the winding up of the War of the Spanish Succession meant that the King was suddenly obliged to provide for the urgent and impartial resolution of a flood of controversial business with almost nobody but the Board of General Officers to assist.[28]

His first step, however, was to acquaint himself with the internal condition of the army. This he did by applying to the monthly returns of effectives. From his brusque reaction, it is clear that he found them thoroughly unsatisfactory. Many of the battalions were weak; at least one officer was suspected of sabotage in this area and the King, *via* his Secretary at War, threatened that commanders who failed to keep their units up to strength would either be superseded or have their customary perquisites witheld.[29] Though it could scarcely have seemed so at the time, the King's response to this fistful of returns marked the first step in a long and irregular sequence of administrative reforms that would end in the transformation of the traditional character of military management in Britain. But in order to understand how this took shape, it is first necessary to look at the organisation and personnel of the civil and military agencies which stood ready to put the royal will into effect.

2. Lineaments of control: civilians

The constitutional upheavals of the seventeenth century had left the King of Great Britain without any organisation that could be properly described as a Ministry of War. Instead, a number of civil and military officers held overlapping administrative briefs, their respective influences depending largely on their characters, their political weight and whether the King actually chose to fill every office. For example, during many years of their reigns the first two Georges chose to do without the services of a Captain General or Commander-in-Chief.

This was not the sort of arrangement out of which any strikingly coherent programme of military reform could be expected to emerge, and indeed the scene becomes even more murky when we consider that one powerful officer of state, the Lord Lieutenant of Ireland, had vice-regal authority over a separate military Establishment of 12,000 officers and men. The implications of this division of authority are explored later in the chapter.

Below the commanding heights of military administration, the Crown entirely lacked any powerful administrative framework capable of bringing the semi-autonomous regimental concerns under firm control, having only the amateur gentlemen deputy commissaries reporting to the tiny office in Whitehall of the Commissary General of the Musters and the army officers themselves who were always to some extent judges in their own cause.

In this section we are concerned only with the roles of the Secretary of State, the Secretary at War and the Commissaries of the Musters. A general guide to the interrelationship of the Crown's civil and military officers can be found in Fig. 2.1. Changes in the operation of the office of the Comptrollers of the Accounts of the Army are explored in Chapter Four in the paragraphs dealing with regimental musters.

(i) Secretaries of State

All warlike preparations required an instruction from a secretary of state. He framed the orders directed to field commanders and received their despatches; he countersigned military commissions, warrants to government departments and conveyed military instructions to the Lord Lieutenant of Ireland. Great burdens of office usually prevented him applying himself to military minutiae (though William Pitt for one was a sometime exception to this rule), but he would still be expected to interest himself in the patronage area of preferment, in the selection of

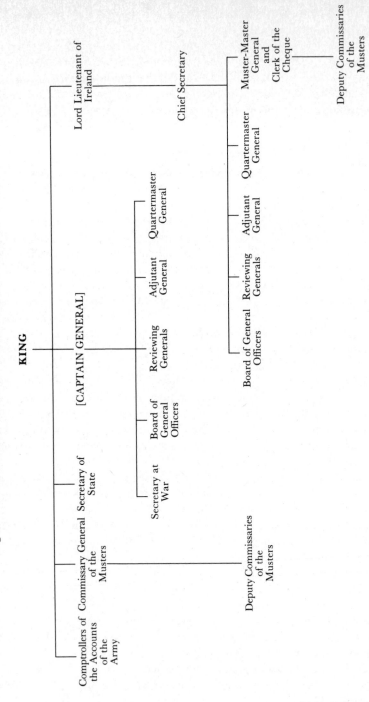

Fig. 2.1 *Elements of military administration (command and regimental finance)*

regiments for foreign service and their distribution between the British and Irish Establishments. Most of the administrative drudgery associated with the army was delegated to a junior minister, the Secretary at War.[30]

(ii) The Secretary at War

The Secretary at War was the nearest approximation to a war or army minister available to the first two Georges. He appeared on the establishment of general and staff officers, had a commission worded similarly to that of a combatant officer and was thus technically part of the army. However, from his origins in the seventeenth century as a clerk to a commander-in-chief or the monarch, he had almost always been a civilian, first a lawyer-administrator like William III's Secretary at War, William Blathwayt, and then from 1704, when Henry St John acquired the office, a politician and member of the government.[31] Among the Secretaries at War of the first two Georges only Henry Pelham, (April 1724–May 1730), had any military experience, having served as a volunteer captain in Brigadier-General Dormer's regiment during the Jacobite rebellion of 1715.[32]

The War Office was a small department headed by the Secretary, plus a Deputy Secretary at War, a First Clerk, up to twelve other clerks of various grades, the Paymaster of the Widows' Pensions, his deputy, a messenger and an office keeper.[33] In time of peace, when it took several years to fill a folio volume with out-letters, it was a pleasant enough retreat for gouty, superannuated cronies of Sir Robert Walpole like Sir William Strickland or Sir William Yonge, but in wartime, when identical volumes bulged in a mater of weeks, it was 'a laborious employment' with business 'from morning to night'.[34]

Much of this business was truly secretarial, involving detailed logistical arrangements for troop movements and foreign expeditions, the deployment of soldiers in support of the civil magistrate or the revenue service and extensive correspondence with military officers, regimental business agents, and with gentlemen and corporations who were either begging for the assistance of troops or begging to have them withdrawn. Many of the letters, papers and memorials generated by this bureaucratic endeavour, including those relating to the sensitive patronage areas of appointment and promotion, were submitted direct to the King. The Secretary also had important financial responsibilities, including regulating the issue of funds to the regiments according to their current manpower ceilings or the state of their credit. This involved him in framing detailed notifications to the Paymaster General and Commissary General of the Musters and inspecting the accounts of the regimental agents. He was also consulted in the framing of financial regulations (which brought renewed contact with the King) and the determination of specific financial disputes, which made it necessary for him to work closely with the Board of General Officers, individual officers and the firms of regimental agents.

Such a combination of secretarial and financial duties meant that, of all the King's ministers, the Secretary at War had the fullest appreciation of the current strength, disposition, management and interior economy of the army. During the

War of the Spanish Succession that knowledge had given the thrusting Henry St John an important Parliamentary role as manager of the complex army estimates, principal mouthpiece of the policy of committing large land forces to Spain and chief provider of men to carry that policy out. Even after the disastrous battle of Almanza in 1707, St John's resignation and the painful contraction of the Spanish theatre, the Secretary's Parliamentary functions remained important and they would remain so as long as the state required its unpopular standing army.[35] He piloted the annual Mutiny Act and estimates through the sceptical House of Commons and, in an important public relations exercise, responded to MPs' criticisms of the behaviour of soldiers in their quarters.[36] Successive Secretaries attempted to evade a precise definition of their responsibility to the House but during the 1734 session the War Office was made liable for ensuring that no troops were quartered at the scene of an election.[37]

In general, a Secretary's latitude in office depended on his standing with the King, his personal energy and whether or not there was a Captain General or Commander-in-Chief in being. The appointment of a military chief, working in close concert with his Adjutant General and private secretary, could not help but diminish the status of the Secretary at War, who was technically his subordinate. Even the ambitious Henry Fox, the most competent and adroit Secretary of the period, dreaded being put into harness with the powerful Duke of Cumberland, and even though he and the great man developed a very harmonious working relationship, Fox was always the junior partner in their military and political alliance.[38] His successor, William, Viscount Barrington, although sometimes churlish to subordinates and preaching to his correspondents, was scarcely the man to impose himself on the Duke; indeed, he was frightened of him and willing to hide behind his coat-tails on a controversial point, but with Cumberland's disgrace in 1757 and the onset of the King's dotage he became noticeably less inclined to hide his light. Lord Ligonier, who was elevated to the chief command but denied the resounding title of Captain General, could not overawe Barrington as Cumberland had done, but the Secretary was equally unable to master the wily old general. As neither of the contenders was fully able to assert himself, observers detected perplexing, sometimes amusing, signs of dysfunction in the military hierarchy.[39] Barrington's successor, the unsteady Charles Townshend, converted this polite contest into something more like a public feud, which he generously extended to include the young George III's favourite, the Earl of Bute, whose attempts to interfere in promotions he fiercely resented. Townshend pictured himself as struggling against '... jealousy, prejudice, combinations, precedents, ill-will and party', his only reward '... injustice, ingratitude and unmerited reproach'.[40] The subordinate clerks struggled to maintain the flow of wartime business against this counterpoint of strife, but they were rarely able to probe beneath the surface of the ocean of financial claims pouring into the War Office.[41]

(iii) The Commissary General of the Musters and his deputies

The importance of mustering machinery in the development of British and European military institutions has already been discussed.[42] Unfortunately, the Commissary General's department under the first two Georges was still too weak and inadequately staffed to overcome problems which had vexed military administrators since the high Middle Ages.

The department consisted of the Commissary General himself, a Deputy Commissary General, six deputy commissaries for England and Wales, a deputy for Scotland (or 'North Britain' as it was commonly referred to), a deputy for Jersey and Guernsey, a deputy for the Scillies and two clerks. The number of field deputies remained the same throughout our period despite the increase in the number of regiments and large-scale wartime augmentations of men.[43] On the Irish Establishment there was a small department of six deputy commissaries headed by the Muster Master and Clerk of the Cheque.[44]

From time to time additional deputies were appointed, usually to foreign garrisons or to expeditionary forces. In 1746 there were deputies in Minorca, Gibraltar, Annapolis Royal and Canseau (Nova Scotia).[45] After 1747 the large-scale military occupation of the Scottish Highlands made the appointment of two assistants to the deputy in North Britain necessary,[46] and in 1754 a retired officer, Thomas Pitcher, was sent with General Braddock's expedition to Virginia with authority to appoint an assistant if required. The assistant, John Billings, was obliged to take over the whole duty when the indefatigable Pitcher stepped into grand history by mustering the garrison of Oswego when the men would have been better employed strengthening their wretched defences. On 18 July 1756 the fort fell, and Pitcher was led into captivity.[47]

Deputies made occasional sorties into other theatres of war. Thomas Watson, MP for Berwick upon Tweed and one of the deputy commissaries for South Britain, was sent to Europe in 1741 and served there until at least 1747.[48] Unlike Pitcher, however, Watson's musters were essentially spurious: he began by calling the men out but he was then instructed by successive British commanders, including the Duke of Cumberland, that this was inconvenient, and that he could sign the muster rolls just as they came to him from the company officers.[49] The large British forces sent to Germany from 1758 lacked deputy commissaries until Richard Veal was sent out to take retrospective (and hence essentially bogus) musters at the end of the war.[50]

The deputy commissaries can scarcely be described as powerful agents of central government. As civilians they were not always received by the officers in a manner appropriate to their self-esteem and attempts were sometimes made to intimidate them.[51] Their weakness was rooted in their essentially amateur status. They were private gentlemen who had purchased their places (which lay in the nomination of the Secretary at War) for between 800 and 2,000 guineas.[52] Salaries of 10s per diem (8s in Ireland, raised to 10s 6d in April 1746)[53] made the posts attractive to gentlemen who could combine the work with other business interests or pay a substitute to carry it out.[54] Far from exposing the sins of military proprietors with ruthless zeal, many of these gentlemen, as we shall see, acted with a persistent disregard for method, detail and even honesty. The crucial mustering exercise was almost reduced to the level of farce.[55]

3. Lineaments of control: officers

(i) Captain General and Commander-in-Chief
When a Captain General or Commander-in-Chief was appointed he enjoyed great if rather ill-defined power over the administrative machine. In the hands of a military genius like John Duke of Marlborough or a prince of the blood endowed with such a commanding presence and powerful intellect as the Duke of Cumberland, the chief command was equal in weight to a secretaryship of state.

The honorific title of 'Captain General' bestowed on Marlborough and Cumberland emphasised their particular distinction in the state. The title 'Commander-in-Chief' implied a lesser dignity and if like Lord Ligonier the chief officer lacked political weight independent of his office, a forward secretary at war might dispute the governance of the army with him. Not surprisingly, Ligonier thought that such affronts to his authority opened the door to political interference in the army and indiscipline among the officers.[56]

For their part, politicians tried to set limits on the pretensions of the chief officer. A good example of this tendency is the campaign waged by the brothers-in-law Walpole and Charles, Viscount Townshend against William, Earl Cadogan from 1717 to 1725. Cadogan, Marlborough's former Quartermaster General and a brilliant staff officer, was not *de jure* commander-in-chief; the Captain Generalship was held by Marlborough himself, but as George I had denied him any effective power and as he had since fallen victim to a series of strokes, effective power had passed to Cadogan, a royal favourite. Cadogan, who had an inflated notion of his own importance, was an ally of the Stanhope–Sunderland Whig faction and an enemy of the brothers-in-law who led a ferocious attack on him in Parliament in 1717, accusing him of financial corruption. Cadogan survived this assault, but on their safe return to political power Walpole and Townshend used all their energy to prevent him becoming anything greater than eldest lieutenant-general on the British Establishment. In 1723 their patience was rewarded when Cadogan's *hubris* got the better of him and he styled himself Commander-in-Chief during the King's sojourn in Hanover. Cadogan hastened to excuse himself for this act of folly, but coming on top of a reputation for arbitrary behaviour and growing unpopularity among his officers, who resented his great wealth and rapid promotion, 'in a country of liberty it must be owned it was carrying his authority too far'.[57]

This verdict on Cadogan served equally well as an epitaph on the career of Britain's next *bona fide* Captain General, William Augustus, Duke of Cumberland, second and favourite son of George II.[58] At the time of his appointment to the Captain Generalship in 1745 he was only twenty-three years old and a junior major-general.[59] He had not yet exhibited any signs of military genius (it is arguable he never did, for in all his battles except his single victory at Culloden, 16 April 1746, he allowed his heart to prevail over his head), but he was formidably brave. At the battle of Dettingen he had received a ball in the calf of the leg, a dangerous wound at the time and one which, as age and corpulence increased, continued to trouble him. As Captain General he exposed his person so recklessly to enemy fire that even his father, not backward himself in this respect, begged him to take more care. His appointment was a consequence of the need to find a British commander of higher status than the venerable Austrian marshals serving with the allied forces in Flanders, but luckily the young Duke soon revealed more ample qualities than animal courage or a concern for the nicer points of military uniform. He was a student of administrative method[60] and soon achieved a formidable understanding of the character and deficiencies of his army and its leaders. He was successfully launched on an ocean of diplomatic and military correspondence by a veteran diplomat and *cognoscento*, Sir Everard Fawkener who was summoned from the Constantinople embassy to act as his private secretary[61] and his team was shortly strengthened by the appointment of the methodical and self-effacing Adjutant General, Robert Napier, who had first distinguished himself as the Duke's principal *aide-de-camp* at the battle of Fontenoy (11–12 May 1745).[62]

By the end of the War of the Austrian Succession in 1748 Cumberland's knowledge of the army rivalled that of the King himself. Nobody, lamented George in the aftermath of his son's disgrace in 1757, had ever kept the army in better order,[63] and as it grew in size after 1755 the Duke became an even more important factor in its management, '... the Captain General looking into military affairs with greater observation than our good monarch'.[64] But, despite his exalted rank, great intelligence and considerable personal influence, Cumberland's position at the apex of the military hierarchy was decidedly insecure. His well-intentioned projects to reform and discipline the army during the few years of uneasy peace between the Treaty of Aix-la-Chapelle and the despatch of Braddock's expedition against Fort Duquesne were frustrated by the corrosive political hostility of his elder brother, Frederick Prince of Wales, lukewarm support from his father's ministers, who resented his power and were fearful of his ambition, and, it must be said, personal failings of arbitrariness and vindictiveness which undermined his moral authority and perverted his good intentions.

(ii) The Adjutant-General

In a field army, the Adjutant-General bore the same relationship to his chief as a regimental adjutant did to his commanding officer, namely, keeping account of everything that passed in the army, relieving his superior of the more laborious routines, drafting orders and providing a channel of communication for administrative and disciplinary proceedings. In time of peace '... his branch of business has a natural connection with the War Office ... he receives the King's pleasure from the Secretary at War and the Commander-in-Chief when there is one and communicates the same to the troops with respect to all points of disposition, discipline, alteration in the manoeuvre, arms or uniforms of the several corps, the most suitable method for completing corps on service, whether by drafts from other regiments or by recruits, the method of conveying those recruits or drafts to the regiment, for which purpose he ought to enquire into the non-effective account to know the expense it will bear, he himself being supposed to have considered and recommended the expediency of all such alterations and methods. It is properly his business to collect the monthly returns of the forces and from them form a general one from time to time for His Majesty's information ... The instructions for recruiting or reviewing the forces, for their conduct in the field or on board ship fall within his inspection; he ought also to consider and recommend to the Secretary at War whatsoever allowances of camp necessaries, bat, baggage and forage he may judge needful for a regiment going on foreign service and the climate for which it may be destined. And in general I presume it is his duty to acquaint the Secretary at War of ev'ry rule and regulation which may appear to him useful, and expedient to be observed by the army.'[65]

Obviously, an Adjutant-General functioning at this level of effectiveness introduced yet another potentially powerful element into the central administration of the army and depending on the closeness of his relationship with the Captain General or the King, to whom he had right of access as principal staff officer, he was a threat to the pretensions of the Secretary at War. Certainly, as long as Robert Napier, 'the Duke's officer',[66] occupied the post it was a very influential one, though Napier was not the man to trumpet the fact. His diligent hand was at work in numerous draft regulations that survive in the Cumberland papers, as well as in the Duke's correspondence, some of which was of a highly sensitive nature.[67] One of Napier's most important tasks was to make the digest of his master's orders given in Flanders during the late war which, when promulgated to the regiments in May 1755, provided the basis for subsequent 'King's Regulations'.[68]

Fortunately for the Secretary at War, during much of the century the Adjutant-General's weight in the military hierarchy was affected by the relatively diminished status of the chief command after Cumberland's departure. King George III, notwithstanding an interest in army affairs which rivalled that of his grandfather and great-grandfather, made relatively little use of his Adjutant-General, a frustrating experience for some of the highly competent occupiers of that post.[69]

(iii) *The Board of General Officers*

Although by the last quarter of the eighteenth century the Board of General Officers seems to have degenerated into a forum for the discussion of military trivia,[70] this was far from being the case during the early and middle years of the Hanoverian dynasty. The first two Georges relied heavily on its accumulated wisdom.

Summoned on an *ad hoc* basis under Queen Anne in 1705, and established as a permanent military council in the following year, the Board's first task had been to investigate recruiting problems. In 1708 it had assumed responsibility for supervising the provision of regimental clothing, an important but dreary function which might have throttled it, had not the generals wisely delegated this aspect of their business to an annually constituted sub-committee, the Clothing Board. This left the main Board at liberty to concentrate on sorting out the administrative confusion which characterised the army after the decline of the 'committee of council at the War Office', the disgrace of Marlborough, the termination of the War of the Spanish Succession and the change of monarch. So great was the rush of business that the Board was all but swamped.

In fact, the King's urgent desire to establish '. . . a just oeconomy and due regulation' in the forces put the Board in a strong position.[71] In November 1714 he instructed the generals to sit for three months in order to clear up outstanding wartime business. Their decisions, once confirmed by him were to become '. . . an unalterable rule and regulation'. In March 1715 the Board's life was extended by another three months and thereafter by periods of up to six months at a time until December 1720, after which it was constituted annually but only met when specific issues were put to it.

Strict procedural rules were established as early as December 1714 and entered in a minute book for the information of successive Boards. General officers on the British Establishment took it in turn to serve; on the annual change of personnel it was customary to retain the services of one member from the previous year to ensure continuity of approach. The Board met in the Great Room at Horse Guards, though by 1734 its deliberations were being disrupted from time to time by showers of dirt from the decaying ceiling.[72] Thereafter for much of their business the generals switched to cosier quarters in the Judge Advocate General's residence in Privy Garden. The Judge Advocate General was a legal officer appointed to ensure the proper execution of the Crown's powers under the Mutiny Act and he attended the Board's meetings to advise it on military-legal issues.[73]

Despite occasional problems caused by the generals' inability to muster a quorum of five, overcome by the King's insistence on seeing a record of each meeting, signed by those present,[74] the Board settled quickly down to business and its opinion was sought on most draft regulations subsequently promulgated as royal warrants as well as on specific administrative questions or disputes between individuals which had some bearing on general matters of adminis-tration. Other officials, including the Secretary at War, Paymaster General and Comptrollers of the Accounts of the Army attended as required.

By bringing the generals together in this way, George I hoped to obtain '. . . great services and advantages from their impartial deliberations on all such matters as shall be laid before them . . . in which he is persuaded they will strictly report in all cases according to the rules of justice and general regulations of the army without any regard to persons for though HM can always act as he pleases ... he would have everyone else see that he is willing those who ought to know best the business and pretensions of the army should give their opinion on it'.[75]

This was an attractive-looking concession, appearing to offer the generals co-partnership in the governance of the army, and it can be argued that in the opening years of the reign the King had little option but to appeal to the accumulated wisdom of his senior officers. But, by exploiting the Board's knowledge, the Crown slowly forged its own instrument of control whose decisions, once they had been ratified by royal warrant, altered the hitherto nebulous 'custom of the army' into 'an unalterable rule and regulation', suscept-ible of inspection, review and, the King having reserved his prerogative of doing ultimately as he chose, arbitrary amendment. A significant instance of this took place over the wording of the Warrant for Regulating the Necessary Stoppages from the Regiments of Dragoon Guards and Dragoons of 19 June 1749, which, by virtually suppressing the captains' dividends, overrode the wishes of the generals who advised George II on what the warrant should contain.[76] On other occa-sions, however, the Crown was prepared to defer to the Board's opinion even when it easily could have been set aside. For example, the War Office's reluctance to press forward with a review of regimental agents' securities in 1760, an area in which regimental proprietors had a considerable personal stake, suggested that although the power of the executive was growing, it was not willing to confront the senior officers' interests head-on.[77]

(iv) Reviewing generals

George I was an active personal reviewer of regiments,[78] as was his son.[79] The Duke of Cumberland was equally strict, an unnerving prospect for officers who feared, for some reason or another, that their units were not in a fit state to be seen.[80]

Employing general officers to carry out reviews in the provinces was a direct extension of the royal commitment to personal inspections. The practice was instituted in July 1716.[81] The early sequence of reviews is tentative, and though we know that some reviews were undertaken in 1718, annual circuits only began from about 1720. However, under Cumberland's influence, reviewing proce-dures were intensified during the War of the Austrian Succession and extended in scope after 1748.

In the first instance, a review was intended to establish whether a regiment was in a fit state of military preparedness.[82] The generals proceeded from quarter to quarter, ordering units to pass in review before them, taking an exact account of the goodness of their men and horses and the condition of the clothing, weapons, accoutrements and regimental equipage. Each unit was put through its manual exercise of arms and military evolutions, the general taking note of any negligence and exhorting the officers to perfect the knowledge and discipline of their men. This completed the strictly military business, but then came an administrative chore that would grow in significance in subsequent decades. The reviewer was obliged to satisfy himself that the soldiers were punctually paid, not subject to any unwarrantable stoppages and that they paid their debts promptly in their billets. The inspection of clothing, arms and equipment was itself an administrative action, for any deficiencies in *matériel* were a reflection on the probity of the regimental proprietor, to whom responsibility for supply had been delegated. At the conclusion of the review the general made a detailed report to the King and suggested improvements for the general good of the service.[83] The general officer commanding in North Britain, whose regiments were too widely dispersed for him to see in person, was authorised to appoint subordinate officers to inspect on his behalf.[84] Troops in garrison were normally reviewed by their governor or lieutenant-governor.

After 1747, the reviewing generals were charged with additional financial responsibilities complementary to the reformed method of carrying out regimental musters.[85] They were instructed to call for lists of men discharged, dead, deserted, recommended to the Commissioners of Chelsea Hospital or enlisted since the previous muster, and to compare them with the regimental non-effective account and paymaster's books. If the unit was tolerably complete this was a formality, and it would be followed by a recommendation that any 'respites' (stops on regimental credit imposed by deputy commissaries of the musters) should be lifted. If, on the other hand, the unit appeared weak, a strict enquiry was to be made.[86] Rumour spread among the regiments that reviews would henceforth be very strict.[87] From 1750 the generals were also ordered to check whether the provisions of the Warrant of 19 June 1749 for Regulating the Necessary Stoppages from the Regiments of Dragoon Guards and Dragoons were being punctually observed.[88]

It was usual for reviews to be carried out in the spring and early summer, but from March 1750 until the spring of 1756 a spring circuit was followed by another in October, although in the opinion of Henry Fox, the Secretary at War, an annual review was sufficient for financial purposes.[89] In 1759, by which time the clearing of units by means of muster rolls had virtually ceased, review circuits were permitted to lapse and they were not resumed until October 1763.

At first some of the generals were not keen to look very deeply into regimental accounts[90] and the earliest reports extant are not very inspiring. Typically laconic comments include 'Kept according to Your Majesty's regulations' or 'kept according to order'. Lieutenant-General James Cholmondeley varied a brief 'Regularly kept' with an even more terse 'Kept regular,' perfunctory assessments which compare badly with the growing volume of comment on the appearance of a regiment, the quality of its recruits and its behaviour under arms. However, from 1755 we find included at the end of each sequence of reports a general declaration that the accounts were satisfactory and that the respites should be lifted, as well as an increased tendency to include a full statement of the regimental non-effective account for the year.[91] This is a strong indication that by the outbreak of the Seven Years' War the generals had become habituated to this innovatory aspect of their duty and that the devolved regimental accounting systems had been brought under stricter surveillance. Some caution is advisable, however, for it was always possible to dupe inspecting officers, even on the most obvious points of their duty.[92] The cynical Colonel Henry Hawley had long since suggested that although the King had his troops reviewed each year and demanded an exact report of their condition, in reality he knew little more than whether the men had clean shirts on their backs or made a decent attempt at their drill. For every fault detected, he insinuated, fifty were concealed.[93]

4. The problem of Ireland

Inevitably, any delegation of military authority beyond the walls of St James's or the favourite royal reviewing ground of Hyde Park resulted in a weakening of that authority. Nowhere was this more obvious than in Ireland.

Of all the great officers of state with devolved power over the army, the Lord Lieutenant of Ireland had the greatest direct influence. His full title, 'Lord Lieutenant and General Governor of Ireland', suggests the extent of his military authority. He had his own fifty-five-strong 'Company of Foot Guard, similarly uniformed to the Yeomen of the Guard and arm'd with Battle Axes to attend ye State'. His comings and goings were accompanied by displays of military pageantry; the streets of Dublin were lined with troops, a squadron of horse was in attendance and the thud of 'the Great Guns in His Majesty's Park the Phenix' mingled with answering 'vollies from the Regiments on Duty drawn out upon . . . [Trinity] College Green'.[94] To assist him he had a substantial military staff headed by a lieutenant-general commanding-in-chief, two additional lieutenant-generals, three major-generals and six brigadier-generals. He took advice from his own Board of General Officers, presided over by his commander-in-chief and independent of the home Board. He enjoyed the ascriptive right to nominate his own Adjutant and Quartermaster-Generals. His Chief Secretary in Dublin Castle and the latter's clerks carried out most of the business of a Secretary at War, and financial affairs were dealt with in the Muster Office, headed by the Muster-Master General and Clerk of the Cheque. The Lord Lieutenant had *aides-de-camp*, military clerks, a Master General of the Ordnance and principal officers, military engineers, officers of the train of artillery, artisans, storekeepers, major works of fortification, a chain of barracks and posts and, most important, a standing army of up to 12,000 officers and men.[95]

The destruction of the bulk of the Irish military records in the disastrous fire at the Four Courts, Dublin, in June 1922 leaves gaps in our understanding of the management of the Irish army that will never be completely filled,[96] but enough hints remain to suggest that under the first two Georges the Lord Lieutenant was more independent of British command than he later became, and that in terms of military efficiency the Irish Establishment left something to be desired.

It was certainly necessary for a viceroy to have a degree of military autonomy, for although the peasant population of Ireland tamely acquiesced in British rule throughout most of the period, the army was still an army of occupation. The roads of rural Ireland were unsafe; significantly, deputy commissaries of the musters were provided with an escort from quarter to quarter,[97] and in the depths of Cork and Kerry lurked '... the remains of the old popish clans who keep up a constant correspondence with France and Spain for smuggling, for recruits and our deserters, ... a very lawless people, mostly armed, frequently forming themselves into banditti, defying laws and magistrates and committing the greatest outrages'.[98] Moreover, beneath the placid surface of rural life, agrarian tensions were brewing which led, at the end of our period, to 'Whiteboy' risings in Tipperary, Munster and parts of Leinster and Connaught, and the 'Hearts of Oak' riots in Armagh, Tyrone and Derry. These disturbances, which were some of the most violent of their kind in Europe, resulted in considerable damage to property and querulous calls for military assistance. This was not easy to furnish effectively, for in order to pack the greatest possible number of regimental establishments into Ireland in peacetime, their quota of rank and file was kept as low as possible. Deploying these already precariously small units in penny packets over a wide area in response to public demand made it very difficult for their field officers to control and administer them. In time of war the situation worsened when the Irish regiments were called upon to fulfil their principal role as a strategic reserve. As they were hurriedly transferred to the British Establishment, often taking substantial drafts from the ranks of the remaining Irish regiments to bring them up to British numbers, the fund of trained men available to the government of Ireland to suppress internal disorder or resist invasion was seriously depleted. In December 1745, the most critical phase of the Jacobite rebellion in Britain, there were only three regiments of horse, three of dragoons and four of foot remaining in Ireland, a reduction of effective strength to well under 7,000.[99] In the winter of 1759–60 the defence of the whole of Ulster rested upon four raw companies of the 62nd Foot (about two hundred officers and men) with virtually no ball ammunition. Attention was drawn to this deficiency when a raiding party under Commodore Thurot forced the detachment to surrender at Carrickfergus on 21 February 1760.[100] It was hardly surprising that, when faced with constant demands for troops, Dublin Castle's response became distinctly shrill.[101]

It was doubly unfortunate therefore that the arrangement of forces on the Irish Establishment was not always dictated by strictly military considerations. Political pressure for the presence of soldiers resulted in an over-extended spread of detachments. Also, as the Irish Parliament was sufficiently independent to obstruct the government if it chose, it was inevitable that military commissions came to be included in the Lord Lieutenant's store of patronage. Even those viceroys most inclined to resist the demands of their Irish political allies were obliged to make concessions in favour of frightful lists of country cousins.[102] Also, like other politicians, they had clients of their own to promote, and attempts by their colleagues at home to interfere with their nominations were fiercely opposed.[103]

It was all the more regrettable that there was a noticeable dearth of military understanding in the Lords Lieutenant of our period. It was equally unusual to find a Chief Secretary with a military background.[104] With the frequent absence of one or both of these personages in England, pursuing their domestic political ambitions, much depended on the capability of the Irish staff. Here, alas, there was often little to commend, despite its size and cost. In the past, nominations had been sold or reversions granted which still governed the conduct of business years later: the important post of Muster-Master and Clerk of the Cheque was held in reversion by the Earls of Tullamore and two generations of Butlers had occupied the influential position of Adjutant-General. Colonel Thomas Butler, who succeeded his father James in 1743, was reckoned to be incompetent. An anonymous correspondent of Cumberland reported the opinion of General Gervais Parker, Irish commander-in-chief, that a review conducted by Butler at Kilkenny in 1750 'would make a dog spew'.[105] The commander-in-chief himself was very much subservient to the civil government,[106] and the general officers, discouraged by the relatively poor remuneration attached to their posts, were reluctant to serve in Ireland unless they had connections in the kingdom. On some occasions it was impossible to form a quorum of three for the Irish Board of General Officers, a body whose advice grew in significance when the Lord Lieutenant was not himself a military man. In the period immediately after the Seven Years' War it was necessary to commission the Earl of Drogheda as an acting major-general in Ireland to permit the Board to function at all. In peace and war there was a noticeable dearth of active young generals on the Establishment.[107]

In these circumstances it was not surprising to find doubts being raised about the efficiency of units quartered in Ireland. Although the Duke of Cumberland received covert reports from his Irish confidants, his authority to intervene in the sister kingdom was strictly limited by custom and propriety.[108] He had no direct command over the Irish army and officers there could not appeal to him over the heads of the Lord Lieutenant and Chief Secretary. The latter in particular determined to a large extent what military information reached Cumberland's distant ears, and even though Brigadier-General Lord George Sackville, Chief Secretary to his father, the Duke of Dorset (Lord Lieutenant 1750–55), was believed to be Cumberland's 'military man of confidence in Ireland' he guarded his prerogatives as jealously as any other Chief Secretary. His usefulness was further reduced by the number of political and military enemies he stirred up for himself in Ireland.[109] General orders for Ireland originated in Dublin Castle rather than in the orderly mind of Colonel Robert Napier, and were rambling and scrappy compared with the British model.[110] Despite Cumberland's wish to extend twice-yearly reviewing to Ireland the generals continued to make their circuits only once *per annum*, in June. Their reports were made to the Lord

Lieutenant and, though copies were certainly transmitted to London, it is interesting that they only appear with any frequency in the records after 1767.[111] For his part, the Secretary at War in London had no direct authority over officers serving on the Irish Establishment, no responsibility for the routine supervision of units quartered there, and he only dealt with them *via* the Chief Secretary or a Secretary of State. As for the Board of General Officers, it was not competent to intervene in any matter which fell within the terms of reference of the Irish Board.[112]

There is ample evidence to suggest therefore that the administrative division of the army into two Establishments was harmful to its efficiency. Regiments spending long periods of peacetime service there were relatively isolated from the revivified royal authority which prevailed at home, so that in some units the twin vices of military and administrative incompetence were allowed to linger into the 1750s and beyond.[113]

5. Officer discipline and resistance to authority

So far, we have been concerned with ways in which overlapping and inefficient executive agencies obstructed the full extension of the Crown's authority over the army, but that authority was also constrained by less tangible elements. It is a commonplace that all eighteenth-century government was hampered by the indifference and independent-mindedness of its own officials (isolated as they often were by distance and poor communications), and this was true of military as well as civil officers.[114] Beneath their veneer of technical professionalism the soldiers were often deeply insubordinate. They eagerly competed for royal grace and favour, but as members of the warrior fraternity of the European *ancien régime* and free-born Englishmen to boot, with the idea that no man, howsoever distinguished by lace and titles, had any greater merit than themselves, they were ready to criticise the throne itself if their pretensions to honour and preferment were not gratified and even to withdraw their services.[115] Besides sulking in their tents they also had, either in their own persons or *via* the good offices of friends and kinsmen, access to Parliament, to the press or even the courts of law, where, in one notorious instance, Lieutenant George Frye of the Marines sued members of a court-martial which had cashiered him and won £1,000 in damages.[116]

This 'stubborn English spirit'[117] was intrinsically hostile to any strengthening of military discipline associated with German influences (which were looked upon as mechanical and demeaning to Englishmen),[118] personified as it was by the forbidding presence of the Duke of Cumberland. Strict rules of conduct, it was urged, should '... be softened by gentle persuasive commands by which gentlemen, particularly those of a British constitution, are to be governed'.[119] Senior officers who did not observe this unwritten code of conduct were publicly excoriated. Pamphlets and broadsides highlighted the victimisation of Captain Robert Shafto of the Marines by his colonel, Edward Wolfe (a trivial complaint but one which was dredged up before the House of Commons committee on the land forces and Marines in 1746),[120] or the '... hairsbreadth escape from want and infamy' of Cornet Henry Belasyse, a victim of the apparently groundless enmity of Sir John Cope.[121] Lieutenant-General Humphrey Bland, author of the army's most influential textbook, *A Treatise of Military Discipline* (1727), was ridiculed for his despotism in the garrison of Gibralter,[122] and Lieutenant-General Philip Anstruther was arraigned on the floor of the House of Commons by one of his own subordinates on account of his so-called arbitrary behaviour as governor of Minorca. Under his benign command, it was alleged, officers '... were prohibited the social pleasure of making an afternoon visit above two miles without special licence'.[123] Henry Hawley and Edward Braddock, both favourites of the Duke of Cumberland, were depicted as oafs and bullies, ignorant to boot, a judgment which on the evidence of Hawley's surviving papers certainly cannot be supported.[124] Another notorious martinet, Colonel Sir Robert Rich of the 4th Foot, a man whose naturally severe temper cannot have been softened by being maimed in the hand and arm at the battle of Culloden, was shown in a cartoon as 'The Old Scourge', presiding over the flogging of his entire regiment.[125] This breed of martinet was given a nickname, 'Colonel Crushum', originally attributed to General Henry Grove on account of '... an expression perpetually in his mouth'. 'How,' enquired the author of *Seasonable and Affecting Observations on the Mutiny Bill*, 'is the poor captain and field officer, who has nothing but modest merit to support him, to put up with the insolence of office, the harsh command "Get to your quarters" or "Get you to your room!"?'

The main target of these accumulated resentments was Cumberland himself. The Duke's popularity did not long outlast his victory at Culloden, and the sympathies of Englishmen quickly shifted to the safely beaten Highlander. 'The person who *anno* 1745 was styled our deliverer,' cynically observed Henry Lowther in 1751, 'is now become the hatred of men of all ranks and conditions.'[126] For this the Duke was partly to blame. He did not suffer fools gladly and he was stubborn and difficult to anybody who opposed his wishes. Even to some of his best soldiers, who owed a lot to him, he could appear strangely limited. James Wolfe, for example, himself a meticulous regimental officer, found his '... sticking always to the same point, *vizt.* the battalion', extremely irksome.[127] He was surrounded by a coterie of sycophants whose behaviour sensitive spirits in the army found disobliging.[128] Worse, he was accused of having victimised a number of honourable and guiltless men, including Brigadier-General Richard Ingoldsby, superseded for disobedience to the Duke's orders at the battle of Fontenoy,[129] and the quixotic Brigadier-General James Edward Oglethorpe, who was prematurely retired for lack of zeal in pursuing the Young Pretender's army during its retreat from Derby in 1745.[130] Lieutenant-Colonel George Townshend, once a star in Cumberland's circle of *aides de camp*, considered himself such a marked man by 1750 that he resigned his commission, published a pamphlet critical of the Duke's generalship in the late war, snubbed his favourites in public, drew merciless caricatures of him, and was active in supporting parliamentary measures such as the reform of the Militia to which he knew his old master was hostile.[131] To his discredit, Cumberland retaliated by obstructing the military career of Townshend's younger brother, Roger.[132]

The political issue underlying these unsavoury skirmishes was: how great should be Cumberland's power as Captain General in peacetime? The conduct of previous Captains General, the Duke of Marlborough and James, Duke of Ormonde in 1714 had suggested that the office was a threat to the constitution. For the Duke's elder brother, Frederick Prince of Wales and his Leicester House courtiers, the fair promise of a future reign was distinctly clouded by the prospect of Cumberland remaining at the head of the regular army, and stealthy plans were made for his instant dismissal, the reduction of the land forces and a revival of the gentry-controlled Militia. Pending these happy events, Leicester House made do with polemical literature in which the hated enemy was characterised as '... a devil ... one of the proudest, haughtiest jackanapes that ever lived', obliquely compared with such historical villains as John of Gaunt and James II, '... tho' we are not to suppose that any such aspirer is now living', and in the scurrilous *Constitutional Queries* of 7 February 1751 to 'Crookback Richard'. This last production, '... sent by the penny post to many people of rank in town and left upon the table of several coffee houses by persons unknown', was believed to have come from the pen of the prince's chief adviser, the Earl of Egmont.[133]

Cumberland had been accused of aiming at the throne even while his brother was alive. After Frederick's sudden death on 20 March 1751, which left only the old King and the frail Prince George between the Captain General and the Crown of Great Britain, hostile tongues wagged more loudly than ever. Cumberland was evidently very upset by this,[134] and popular fear reached such absurd lengths that in 1757 it was even suggested that he had courted defeat in Germany to humiliate his father's ministers and promote his own dark domestic ends.[135]

Such attacks might have meant less to Cumberland if he had been more stoutly supported by his father's ministers, but in practice they were almost as suspicious of him as Prince Frederick had been. His growing authority, supported as it was by ambitious Whig politicians, Henry Fox, the Earl of Sandwich and the Duke of Bedford, was seen by the Duke of Newcastle as a threat. Newcastle's once benevolent view of Cumberland had been reversed by the latter's continuing favour to the detested Sandwich and by clashes over military patronage, and he grew particularly to distrust the Duke's protégé Fox, who was talented as well as ambitious. Fox's rash attack on Newcastle's political confidant the Earl of Hardwicke's Clandestine Marriage Bill in 1753 made him additional enemies among the influential Yorke tribe, and the infuriated Lord Chancellor henceforth regarded him as nothing more than the mouthpiece of arbitrary force.[136]

Cumberland was under no illusions as to the character of the Duke of Newcastle, but his relationship with the Duke's brother, Henry Pelham, Chancellor of the Exchequer and virtual Prime Minister, was more complex. He thought Pelham was an honourable man and had been pleased to find during negotiations over the reduction of the army in 1748 that Pelham appreciated the necessity of keeping the army in a better state of discipline and effectiveness than it had been in 1740.[137]

Pelham was ready to argue this point in Parliament. 'The preservation of discipline,' he declared, 'demands that His Royal Highness should retain his commission as Captain General, for without him, no inferior general would possess authority sufficient to enforce that discipline which is so necessary to render the troops serviceable against the enemy; and to prevent that laxity and sloth which peace would engender among them requires great authority in the commander.'[138]

But this did not mean that he was willing to go very far in sustaining Cumberland's authority when it was politically inconvenient. The Duke should have received ample warning of this in the adverse reaction to his plan to disband Major-General Philip Bragg's 28th Foot in 1748. In 1737 this regiment, then serving on the Irish Establishment, was reported as being '... in as good order as troops can be',[139] and in 1745 it was one of ten picked battalions summoned from Flanders to face the Jacobite rebels, but by September 1746 it was clearly in decline. 'The Old Braggs' behaved dismally during General St Clair's abortive raid on Port l'Orient that month,[140] and after seeing them in action for himself during the next campaign Cumberland reached the decision that they should be broken. 'Such an example,' he concluded, 'I can't help thinking is absolutely necessary for HM's service.'[141] An added attraction of disbanding Bragg's regiment was that by doing so he would be able to retain the services of an excellent battalion otherwise destined to be broken, Colonel Henry Seymour Conway's 48th Foot.[142]

In the uproar which greeted the premature disclosure of these measures in a leak from the Secretary of State, the Duke of Bedford's office it soon became clear that the matter of the military effectiveness of Bragg's was of little concern to those objecting to the plan.[143] It was the long-standing custom of the army to break regiments from the youngest backwards. Thus the property interests of those fortunate officers who had bought or fought their way into the 'old corps' of horse, dragoons and foot were protected. These units, like the 'old corps' of Pelhamite loyalists in the House of Commons who shared the nickname, had become a permanent feature of public life, and an attack on their precedence and seniority amounted to a direct attack on property. Colonel Joseph Yorke, who was perfectly aware of Cumberland's good intentions in disciplining the 28th, was nonetheless of the opinion that anyone trying to break up the corporate interest of the 'old corps' was making a rope to hang himself.[144] Moreover, the intention was seen as an act of vile favouritism in Conway's interest, for the latter had served on Cumberland's staff since 1745, and as he himself admitted, Cumberland scarcely knew Bragg, who had served much of his time in Ireland.

Meanwhile, Bragg was making it known that he could not be held responsible for his regiment's present poor condition. He had some justice on his side, for he had been one of the precariously small number of active general officers in Ireland and had lost touch with his unit when it had been ordered on foreign service.[145] He quickly won the support of his patron and former Lord Lieutenant, the Duke of Dorset, who viewed the imminent humiliation of Bragg not only as a slur on an honourable and diligent soldier, but as an insult to the man who had placed him in the service — himself. He wrote to Cumberland pointing this out, and successfully enrolled the Pelhams in support. (The cynical Joseph Yorke thought that his real concern was not poor Bragg but the reputation of his son, Lord George Sackville, who had been lieutenant-colonel of the 28th from 1740 to 1746, and that he would have intervened even if the regiment had been fifty times as bad.)[146]

Cumberland bowed regretfully to the powerful combination of his father's friends. Bragg's regiment escaped its justly deserved fate and was exiled to the Irish Establishment, whence came rumours of misbehaviour that must have been gall and wormwood to the Duke. At a review at Limerick in the summer of 1750, when it was going through the exercise in company with Hopson's 40th Foot, a shower of rain halted the firings. Some of Bragg's officers, it was reported, called out to their men to go home and, they promptly 'shift off' (*sic*), taking many of Hopson's with them. On 12 July, the day before the regiment quit Limerick, the officers kept such a slack rein on their men that the unfortunate inhabitants '... did believe Hell was broke'. The next morning the regiment was reeling drunk and the drummers incapable of beating a march.[147] This sort of thing made Bragg's a standing joke in the army for many years, something about which the regimental histories are demurely silent.[148] Meanwhile, at the same time as submitting tamely to the preservation of the 28th, Cumberland was obliged to swallow Henry Pelham's advice that it was politically expedient to order the disbandment of his own young regiment of dragoons, which had covered itself with glory at the battle of Laffeldt (2 July 1747).[149] Proprietary custom and political expediency had combined to save a bad regiment at the expense of a good one; the only consolation was that by juggling the overall number of non-effective men in Ireland it became possible to save Conway's 48th Foot after all.

In time, Cumberland's zealous regard for efficiency of the service was to bring about a far greater humiliation than the escape of Bragg's. Although he may have been defeated in his attempt to discipline a regiment, he still considered it absolutely requisite to bring about an improvement in officer discipline *via* the Mutiny Act and Articles of War, a view concurred in by the First Lord of the Admiralty, George Anson. The principal objectives of the reforms of 1749–50 were to establish the liability of half-pay officers to martial law and to provide for a revision of court-martial sentences that were insufficiently severe. Not surprisingly, such proposals were greeted as an assault on the liberties of the subject and an attempt to turn the army in general and the officer corps in particular into the creatures of a military tyrant. At first the King's ministers stood firm in support of the project, but in time they prudently backed off, leaving Cumberland at the mercy of the pamphleteers. He was now so violently unpopular that it became necessary to deny him the full powers he might otherwise have expected to enjoy in a Regency Bill made necessary by the sudden death of Prince Frederick in 1751. Cumberland was mortified by this slight, as was the old King, who thought it had been brought about by '... the Scotch, the Jacobites and the English that do not love discipline: and because all this is not enough discouraged by the ministry.'[150] By the time of his reluctant departure for Hanover in April 1757, where he was to taste defeat and public disgrace, his power was already waning, a situation for which he was partly to blame.[151]

The eclipse of Cumberland was a timely reminder that although he and his father and grandfather had significantly extended their control over the army, the balance of forces in the military machine was such that there was no high road to reform. There is evidence to suggest that Cumberland ultimately understood this. In the margin of a draft paper, possibly the brainchild of Napier, Fox or the Duke himself, which proposed the dismantling of the regimental economy and its replacement by a centrally administered non-effective fund for the whole army, is scrawled the pregnant endorsement, '... will cause too many disputes, too great an innovation'.[152] For the remainder of the period, reform of regimental adminis- tration would follow the path of least resistance, which led through the pockets of the junior proprietors, the captains of cavalry and infantry.

Notes

1 'The Duty of a Soldier in Two Letters to a Young Officer in High Command ... by a Field Marshal', *London Chronicle* (25 May 1758), p. 498. See, in general, N. Hampson, 'The French Revolution and the Nationalisation of Honour' in M. R. D. Foot ed., *War and Society*, London, 1973, pp. 193–212.

2 *Observations on the Prevailing Abuses in the British Army* 'by the Honourable ——, an Officer' attributed to Ensign Thomas Erskine 1st Foot, London, 1775, p. 17; Capt. Thomas Simes, *The Regulator*, London, 1780, pp. 1–2.

3 Lt. Col. James Wolfe, 20th Foot, to his mother, Mrs Henrietta Wolfe, 19 Jan. 1753; Wright, *Wolfe*, p. 253.

4 I. R. Christie, 'The Personality of George II', *History Today*, V, 1959, pp. 516–28.

5 'Messieurs d'Allemagne ...' who 'roll their red eyes, stroke up their great beavers and look fierce.' Horace Walpole to Sir Horace Mann, 29 April 1742, W. S. Lewis ed., *Correspondence of Horace Walpole*, New Haven, 1937–79, XVII, p. 410.

6 DRO. D86.X3, Henry Fox Secretary at War, to the Second Earl of Albemarle, 27 Nov. 1746.

7 Hervey, *Memoirs*, pp. 771–12.

8 BL. Add. MSS. 9176 f. 34, Horatio Walpole to Robert Trevor, 22 Feb. 1740.

9 BL. Add. MSS, 32889 f. 225, Newcastle to Lord Fitzwilliam, 24 March 1759.

10 Major James Wolfe, 20th Foot, to his mother, 29 March 1750; B. Willson, *The Life and Letters of James Wolfe*, London, 1909, p. 117.

11 BL. Add. MSS. 17493 f. 81, John Calcraft, regimental agent, to Col. John Stanwix, 10 July 1757; Add. MSS 17494 f. 129, Same to Maj.-Gen. John Griffin, 1 Sept. 1760.

12 Cathcart to John Earl of Stair, 1 Nov. 1733. J. Murray Graham ed., *The Annals of Stair*, Edinburgh, 1899, II, p. 200. Cathcart was gazetted colonel of the 3rd Horse on 7 Aug. 1733.

13 A. Lindsay, *The Lives of the Lindsays*, Wigan, 1840, II, p. 140.

14 *DNB*, 'Conway, Henry Seymour'.

15 Horace Walpole, *Memoirs*, III, p. 273, attributed the wording of the public general order disgracing Sackville to the King; R. H Whitworth, *Field Marshal Lord Ligonier*, Oxford, 1958, detects the influence of the Commander-in-Chief.

16 Horace Walpole, *Memoirs*, III pp. 64–5.

17 PRO. WO 4/58 f. 71, Viscount Barrington, Secretary at War, to Lt.-Col. John Clavering, 14 June 1759.

18 C. Dalton, *George the First's Army*, London, 1910, I, p. xxi.

19 Hervey, *Memoirs*, p. 176.

20 *DNB*, 'Temple, Sir Richard, Viscount Cobham'; Dalton, *op. cit.*, II, pp. 1–8.

21 Colley, *In Defiance of Oligarchy*, pp. 102–3.

22 *Parl. Hist.* IX, pp. 286 ff, 327 ff, 13 Feb. 1734.

23 *Stair Annals*, II, pp. 213–14.

24 B. Williams, *The Life of William Pitt*, London 1913, I, p. 67.

25 *House of Commons, 1714–1754*, 'Fane, John, Earl of Westmorland'.

26 A very general guide to the organisation of the Electoral army is provided by Niemeyer and Ortenburg, *op. cit.*, pp. 11–17, 41–4.

27 Frederick-William I of Prussia thought the Electoral troops were mollycoddled; R. Ergang, *The Potsdam Führer*, New York, 1941, p. 68.

28 These developments are examined by I. F. Burton in an article, 'The Committee of Council at the War Office', *Historical Journal*, IV 1961, pp. 78–84, and more briefly in his biography of Marlborough, *The Captain General*, London, 1968, pp. 166–91, *passim*. For the great amount of military business outstanding at the end of the War of the Spanish Succession, see Scouller, *The Armies of Queen Anne* pp. 44–51, For the Board of General Officers, see below, pp. 30–2.

29 The close personal interest shown by George in the detailed workings of his army was commended by Fortescue, *History*, II, pp. 30–1, but not explored in any detail. Disappointingly, R. M. Hatton in her otherwise exemplary *George I*, London 1978, does not discuss it. However, a few extracts from the first out-letter books of the reign show the extent of the king's concern: PRO. WO 4/17 f. 83, William Pulteney, Secretary at War, to Lt.-Gen. William Cadogan, 24 March 1715: 'I cannot but take notice to you sir of the great disposition I observe in His Majesty to make some example that may deter all officers in his service from showing so little regard for it. And that none of them may be encouraged to be negligent in recruiting by the advantage they may receive from it, his Majesty is pleased to direct that you give the strictest orders that the troops be allowed upon the musters for effectives only. His Majesty intending to judge himself what allowances to make them for recruiting ... which will be proportionate according to their behaviour in completing their regiments'; WO 4/17 f. 152. Same to General Thomas Erle, 30 July 1715, on the occasion of serious deficiencies being noticed in the complements of five regiments of foot; '... His Majesty has expressed so great a displeasure at such practices that for the future he will make a sure example of those who shall be guilty of such neglect of their duty'. Also WO 4/20 f. 225, James Craggs the Younger, Secretary at War, to Col. Roger Handasyde, 22nd Foot, 23 Sept. 1717, whose regiment was returned 102 men under strength; 'His Majesty is much surprised to find you so weak, and that he expects his forces to be kept in another condition, that he does not understand how your regiment can be so deficient, unless it be owing to the absolute negligence of the captains, who the colonels, who are supposed to be able to answer for their regiments, should correct'. Evidently, any difficulties experienced by the king with the English language did not extend to interpreting regimental returns or instructing his Secretaries at War.

30 M. A. Thompson, *Secretaries of State 1681–1782*, London, 1968, *passim*.

31 Appendix One. For the early history of the secretaryship, see O. Anderson, 'The Constitutional Position of the Secretary at War', *JSAHR*, XXXVI, 1958, pp. 165–99, also Thompson, *op. cit.* pp. 65–9, and the definitive study by I. F. Burton, 'The Secretary at War and the Administration of the Army during the War of the Spanish Succession'.

32 *DNB*, 'Pelham, Henry'. In 1757 there was a possibility that Maj.-Gen. Lord George Sackville would be given the appointment, but this came to nothing; A. Valentine, *Lord George Germain*, Oxford, 1961, p. 33.

33 PRO. WO 4/59 f. 82, Establishment for the War Office, Sept. 1759. The figure of twelve clerks is a maximum. At other times there were fewer clerks and all the desks were not necessarily filled. However, the *Court and City Register* for 1766 notes the existence of six 'extra clerks'. Five extra clerks are recorded in 1767 and 1768 but none before or immediately after. It is not impossible that such assistance had also been engaged during the Seven Years' War.

34 Henry Fox to his brother, Stephen, Earl of Ilchester, 29 April 1746; Earl of Ilchester ed., *Henry Fox, First Lord Holland*, London, 1920, I, p. 133; R. A. Cumb C 14/361, Sir William Yonge, Secretary at War, to the Duke of Cumberland, 10 May 1746. Yonge, who served as Secretary from May 1735 to July 1746, and his predecessor, Sir William Strickland (May 1730–May 1735) were martyrs to gout in the hands, a serious problem for an administrator. Yonge was superseded by Henry Fox in 1746 in order to prevent the imminent collapse of business.

35 Here I follow the conclusions of Burton, 'Secretary at War', *passim*.

36 PRO. WO 4/20 f. 131, James Craggs the Younger to Col. Richard Molesworth, 14 June 1717.

37 8 Geo. II, cap. 30, 'An Act for Quartering Soldiers at Elections'. It had long been customary for the Secretary at War to march soldiers out of town on polling day. The opposition argued successfully that keeping a battalion at Holyrood during the election of the representative peers of Scotland had amounted to an attempt to prejudice the poll and the custom was converted into a binding obligation; *Parl. Hist.* IX, p. 608.

38 Fox to Stephen, Earl of Ilchester, 29 April 1746, Ilchester, *op. cit.*, I, p. 132; same to same, 4, 11 Dec. 1746, *ibid.*, p. 141; DRO. D86.X3, Fox to Col. Joseph Yorke, 27 Feb 1748.

39 For Barrington and Cumberland see Shute Barrington, *The Political Life of William Wildman, Viscount Barrington*, London, 1814, pp. 18–26. For Barrington *v.* Ligonier see BL. Add. MSS. 17,493 f. 149, John Calcraft, regimental agent, to William Earl of Home, 2 April 1758; 'Things are on such a foot at present that one does not know whether he [Barrington] or who is the person to apply to on military business, for in the course of last week, Lord Lindores and old Parker had kissed the king's hands for invalid regiments when Bn. was in Berkshire and knew nothing of the matter at which he is violently enraged. Lord Ligonier and he often have rubs of this sort and altogether, 'tis a strange jumble'. See also PRO. WO 34/86 f. 110, Lt. Col. Isaac Barré to Maj.-Gen. Jeffery Amherst, 14 March 1761.

40 PRO. WO 4/981, Charles Townshend to Ligonier, 30 May, 28 July 1761; same to his brother, Maj.-Gen. George Townshend, 30 Sept. 1761; L. B. Namier, J. Brooke, *Charles Townshend*, London, 1964, p. 72.

41 BL Add. MSS. 40,759, 'Francis Report', *passim*.

42 See above, pp. 2–3.

43 PRO. WO. 24/127, Establishment of Guards and Garrisons, 1727; WO 26/25 f. 27, Establishment of General and Staff Officers in Great Britain and Germany, 1759–60.

44 BL. Add. MSS. 23,636 f. 31, A Correct List of HM's Officers ... on the Establishment of Ireland, 1726.

45 *Committee Report* (1746), p. 115.

46 PRO. WO. 26/21 F. 109, Warrant to Deputy Commissary Charles Hope Weir, 22 May 1747.

47 PRO. WO. 26/22 f. 324, Warrant to Thomas Pitcher, 29, Oct. 1754; WO 11 f. 59, Warrant for a deputy commissary, 10 Sept. 1756. Pitcher mustered the Oswego garrison on 4(?), 5 and 8 July, S. M. Pargellis ed.,*Military Affairs in North America 1748–65*, Hamden, Conn., 1969, pp. 201–3.

48 PRO. T 6808/41 f. 2, f. 185, f. 208; R. A. Cumb C20/127, Establishment of General and Staff Officers ... in the Low Countries, 1747. (Watson does not appear in the 1748 Establishment, R. A Cumb. C31/5); *House of Commons 1714–1754*, 'Watson, Thomas'.

49 *Committee Report* (1746), p. 115.

50 WO 7/124 f. 70, R. Veal to John Hesse, First Clerk in the Commissary General's Office, 18 Jan. 1763.

51 'We do hereby order and direct, that all officers and soldiers do peaceably and quietly submit, and suffer the ... commissaries to execute and perform all and every the rules, orders and directions herein contained, and if any officer or soldier shall presume to taunt, redicule [*sic*], obstruct or pick a quarrel with any of the commissaries, on account of the performance of his duty ... we shall look on them as contemners of His Majesty's authority, and disobeyers of our commands; for which they may expect severe punishment shall be inflicted.' 16th article, 'Orders, Rules and Instructions to be observed by the Muster Master General, and Clerks of the Cheque' given out by Lord George Sackville, Chief Secretary, Dublin Castle, 20 Dec. 1751, and printed in *Standing Orders (Ireland)*, p. 38. In 1771, after repeated solicitation, the commissaries' status was enhanced by a handsome blue and red uniform; PRO. WO 7/124 f. 226, Circular to deputy commissaries, Nov. 1771.

52 *Committee Report* (1746), pp. 116–18.

53 PRO. WO 8/3 f. 106,Warrant to the Lord Lieutenant of Ireland, 22 April 1746.

54 PRO. WO 7/124 f. 188, Hesse to Deputy Commissary Ker, 5 April 1759. The deputy for Jersey and Guernsey was only paid 2s 6d *per diem* and the deputy for the Scillies 1s 4d.

55 See below, pp. 74–80.

56 King George III to the Earl of Bute, 3 March 1763, R. Sedgwick ed., *Letters from George III to Lord Bute*, London, 1939, pp. 194–5.

57 George Baillie of Jerviswood to Lord Polwarth, 10 July 1723, *Hist. MSS. Comm. Polwarth*, III, p. 284; J. Lekeux to the Hon. John Molesworth, n.d. (1725?), *Hist. MSS. Comm. Various Collections*, VIII, 1913, p. 393. Cadogan had been appointed Master General of the Ordnance in 1722 after the death of Marlborough. In 1725 the brothers-in-law managed to have him replaced by the Duke of Argyll. Cadogan's career and political ambitions are examined in *DNB* 'Cadogan, William, 1st Earl Cadogan' and *House of Commons 1714–1754*, I, pp. 26–7. In PRO. SP 43/66 is a copy of a royal warrant of 30 May 1723 apparently appointing Cadogan commander-in-chief but subsequently struck out.

58 In February 1721, as a consequence of projected ministerial changes, there was a possibility that Lt.-Gen. James, Earl Stanhope, then Secretary of State, would succeed the ailing Marlborough as Captain General. These arrangements were upset by Stanhope's sudden death on 5 Feb.; *House of Commons 1714–54*, I, pp. 30–1.

59 For Cumberland's promotion see Whitworth, *Ligonier*, pp. 94–5.

60 See among his early papers R. A. Cumb. C1/247, 'Instructions for methodising the Papers of a General Commanding in Chief', March 1744.

61 E. Charteris, *William Augustus Duke of Cumberland: His Early Life and Times*, London, 1913, p. 165; *DNB*, 'Fawkener, Sir Everard'.

62 Robert Napier: Ensign, 5th Foot, 1722; Lt., 13 Oct. 1723; Quartermaster, 1725; subsequently adjutant, though he resigned this post through ill health in 1727 and was recorded as being on half pay in summer 1728. Lt., 2nd Foot, 1728; half pay, 1729; Lt., 2nd Foot, 1730; Capt. Lt., 1736; Capt., 1738; Deputy-Quartermaster-General to forces ordered to Flanders, 1742; DQMG to forces in the Austrian Netherlands, 1745; Col. and Adjutant-General of British forces in Flanders, 1746; Adjutant-General of all our Forces in England, 1748–63; Col., 53rd (later 51st) Foot, 1755–57; Maj.-Gen., 1756; Lt.-Gen., 1759; Col., 12th Foot, 1757 until his death, 23 Nov. 1766; biographical note by R. Jones, *JSAHR* XXII, 1943–44, p. 86.

63 The Duke of Newcastle to the Earl of Hardwicke, 23 Oct. 1757, P. C. Yorke, *The Life of Lord Chancellor Hardwicke*, London, 1913, III, p. 191; BL. Add. MSS. 32,911 f. 103, same to same, 6 Sept. 1760.

64 Lt. Col. James Wolfe, 20th Foot, to Charles, Duke of Richmond, 17 March 1756, R. H. Whitworth ed., 'Some Unpublished Wolfe Letters', *JSAHR*, LIII, 1975, p. 70.

65 BL. Add. MSS 40,759, 'Francis Report', f. 241. For remarks on the duty of the Adjutant-General in the field see Col. Humphrey Bland, *A Treatise of Military Discipline*, London, 1727, pp. 283–4.

66 G. H. Rose ed., *Selections from the Papers of the Earl of Marchmont*, London, 1831, I, p. 227.

67 See, for example, the allegations against the officers under his command made by Gen. James St Clair after the failure of the L'Orient expedition (September 1746), R. A. Cumb. C18/336, 19 Oct. 1746.

68 R. A. Cumb. 62/64, May 1755, printed as 'Standing Orders for the Army' in *JSAHR*, V, 1926, pp. 191–9; *ibid.* VI, 1929, pp. 8–10.

69 Pimlott, 'Administration of the British Army', pp. 41–2. The Quartermaster-General was the most important member of the military staff in time of war: it was in this office that William, Earl Cadogan had made his reputation under Marlborough. In time of peace his duties were much more mundane, consisting largely of advising the Secretary at War on march routes and prospective billets; BL. Add. MSS. 40,759, 'Francis Report', f. 253. The office was not at the forefront of administrative developments in our period. Junior officers appointed to Adjutant and Quartermaster-Generalships in Britain and Ireland were usually given the rank of colonel in the army.

70 Pimlott, *op. cit.*, pp. 43–6.

71 For the early history of the Board, see the comprehensive treatment by Scouller, *op. cit.*, pp. 44–51. For the situation in 1714, see PRO. WO 71/3 f. 46, 24 Nov. 1714.

72 PRO. WO 81/2 f. 139, King Gould, Judge Advocate General, to Richard Arnold, Deputy Secretary at War, 11 July 1734.

73 Records of the Board's proceedings can be followed in PRO. WO 26 and WO 71. See especially WO 26/14 f. 125, Warrant of 30 May 1714; WO 71/3 f. 41, 10 Nov. 1714; WO 71/3 f. 50, 'Rules agreed by the General Officers to be observed by them in future', 3 Dec. 1714; WO 26/14 f. 190, 25 Feb. 1715; *ibid.*, f. 196, 15 June 1715; WO 26/15 f. 38, 28 Oct. 1717; WO 26/16 f. 97, 30 Dec. 1720.

74 PRO. WO 4/20 f. 158, James Craggs the Younger to E. Hughes, 8 July 1717.

75 PRO. WO 71/3 f. 265, same to same, 17 Aug. 1717.

76 See below, p. 80.

77 See below, pp. 143–6.

78 Houlding, *Fit for Service*, p. 311.

79 The accession of George II inaugurated a succession of royal reviews; PRO. WO 4/29 ff. 69–76, 160, 181, 250, Circular letters to Colonels, 1727. The King saw regiments

almost every season around London, and the embarkations for Europe in 1742 gave him the opportunity of seeing many regiments as they passed near the capital; Houlding, *op. cit.*, p. 311.

80 *Ibid.*, p. 310.

81 PRO. WO 26/14 f. 257, Reviewing Instructions given by HRH the Prince of Wales (later King George II), 23 July 1716.

82 This aspect of the generals' task is explored in detail by Houlding, *op. cit.*, pp. 297–313.

83 PRO. WO 26/14 f. 257, Reviewing Instructions, 23 July 1716; WO 4/18 f. 201, Circular letter to colonels, 25 July 1716.

84 PRO. WO 26/15 f. 112, Robert Pringle, Secretary at War, to Brig.-Gen. George Preston, 27 Sept. 1718.

85 See below, pp. 78–9.

86 PRO. WO 4/45 f. 22, Fox to Maj.-Gen. James Cholmondeley, 31 May 1748.

87 JRL. B2.2.361, Capt. Thomas Levett, regimental agent, to Major Samuel Bagshawe, 39th Foot, 4 July 1748.

88 PRO. WO 26/21 f. 426, Fox to Lt.-Gen. Sir Philip Honywood, 26 March 1750.

89 DRO. D86/X3, Fox to Col. Robert Napier, 27 Feb. 1747; *ibid.*, same to same, 10 April 1747; PRO. WO 26/21 f. 426, Fox to Honywood, 26 March 1750; *ibid.*, f. 428, same to Lt.-Gen. Sir John Campbell and Lt.-Gen Richard Onslow, 26 March 1750.

90 DRO. D86/X3, Fox to Col. Joseph Yorke, 5 April 1748; PRO. WO 4/45 f. 22, same to Cholmondeley, 31 May 1748.

91 PRO. WO 27/3-6, Inspection Reports, 1754–59. The form of a declaration is as follows: 'The last year's accounts of the disposal of the money arising by non-effectives and the allowance borne on the Establishment to the captains of the foregoing regiments for keeping their troops and companies complete have been laid before me; and I find that the money arising therefrom for the year 1755 has been applied to complete the troops and companies of the said regiments. I am therefore most humbly of opinion that the respitts [*sic*] may be taken off to the 24th of June 1756, provided the balance of the stock purse and non-effective accounts to that time be brought forward and continue to be applied to complete the regiments with men and horses agreeable to the regulation' (PRO. WO 27/4). It may be that the relative completeness of regimental information post 1754 is due to some of the generals (or the regiments) having provided themselves with the blank 'Forms for General Reviews and Monthly Returns' produced by J. Millan 'opposite the Admiralty', publisher of the *Army List, Succession of Colonels*, regimental books and military treatises and '*A Catalogue of my Museum ... consisting of the most numerous and beautiful minerals etc. that ever were in the hands of any collector*' (1763).

92 A. J. Guy, 'Reinforcements for Portugal, 1762', *ARNAM*, 1977–78, pp. 29–34, *passim*.

93 NAM. 7411-24-16.

94 PRO. SP 63/423 f. 21, An account of the state arrival of the Duke of Northumberland, 22 Sept. 1762.

95 NAM. 7406-50-47, 'An Establishment of our Army, Ordinance [*sic*] and other Officers ... for Military Affairs ... for our Kingdom of Ireland, to commence from ye 24th of August, 1717'.

96 Appendix Two.

97 PRO. WO 8/3 f. 115, Instructions to the Muster Master General of Ireland, 12 Feb. 1748; Ferguson, 'The Army in Ireland', p. 82.

98 NAM. 6806-41-7-5, George, Viscount Townshend, Lord Lieutenant, to the Earl of Rochford, Secretary of State, 16 Oct. 1770.

99 *Cal. Treas. Paps. 1742–45*, pp. 729, 787. In an attempt to speed up the rate of recruiting the regiments of foot remaining in Ireland were provided with additional companies and divided into two battalions.

100 For this incident see in particular BL. Add. Mss. 32,902 f. 344, Strode to the Duke of Bedford, 22 Feb 1760; Add. MSS. 32,903 f. 37, Return of Officers and Men made Prisoners of War and also wounded by Lt.-Col. John Jennings, officer commanding at Carrickfergus; *The London Gazette*, No. 998, 26 Feb.–1 March 1760; N. C. E. Kenrick, *The Story of the Wiltshire Regiment*, Aldershot, 1963, pp. 14–19.

101 The Duke of Bedford in particular was always anxious to preserve 'our small pittance of infantry, that part of the army in which I put my chief trust', PRO. 30/8.19 f. 157, Bedford to Pitt, 29 Aug. 1758. When marching regiments were withdrawn, his anxiety was switched to the dragoons, WO 1/609 f. 69, same to same, 30 Jan. 1760. One solution, actively pursued after 1759, was to raise young corps among Irish protestants. This increased numbers of effectives to over 14,000 for a time in 1760 but as the men were raw and repeatedly drafted, the appearance of strength is misleading; *Journals HOC Ireland* VI Appendix cclxxxviii.

102 BL. Add. Mss. 17,495 f. 74, John Calcraft to Col. John Craufurd, 85th Foot, 22 July 1760.

103 BL. Add. MSS. 17,493 f. 156, Calcraft to Lt.-Col. Edward Sandford, 28–29(?) April 1758.

104 One exception was Lord George Sackville, see below. Another was Col. Henry Seymour Conway who went to Ireland with Lord Hartington in 1755. His tenure of office only lasted until the following year; *DNB* 'Conway, Henry Seymour'.

105 R. A. Cumb C44/99, 'Observations concerning military affairs in Ireland' by 'Mr Lovetruth', enclosed in C44/98, Col. Caroline Frederick Scott to Napier, 29 July 1750. There seems no reason to doubt that Scott, one of Cumberland's trusted coterie of officers, was 'Lovetruth'. For his career and notorious cruelty in suppressing the rebels after Culloden see P. R. Cadell, 'Caroline Frederick Scott', *Army Quarterly*, LXVII, 1953–54, pp. 233–44.

106 Ferguson, 'The Army in Ireland', p. 65.

107 PRO. SP 63/411 f. 196, The Earl of Harrington, Lord Lieutenant of Ireland, to the Duke of Bedford, Secretary of State, 1 Nov. 1749; SP 63/416/ f. 119, The Duke of Bedford, Lord Lieutenant of Ireland, to William Pitt, Secretary of Sate, 12 Nov. 1759; SP 63/431 f. 216, George, Viscount Townshend, Lord Lieutenant, to the Earl of Weymouth, Secretary of State, 5 May 1770; SP 63/432 f. 262, same to same, 20 Dec. 1770; R. A. Cumb. C. Vol. 9, 'Report of a Committee (of the Irish House of Commons) appointed to enquire into the Application of Money for and the State of the Irish Military Establishment, 1751–1767', 16 Feb. 1768.

108 A. J. Guy, 'A Whole Army Absolutely Ruined in Ireland: Aspects of the Irish Establishment, 1715–1773', *ARNAM*, 1978–79, pp. 34–35; Hayes, 'Social and Professional Backgound' pp. 17–20.

109 Philip, Earl of Chesterfield to Major John Irwin, 5th Foot, 1 Sept. 1751, J. Bradshaw ed., *Letters of Philip Dormer Stanhope, Earl of Chesterfield*, London, 1892, III, p. 993; R. A. Cumb. C.61/B12, 'Military Memorandum of Irish Affairs picked up by a Lover of Truth from one and other', 1749–50 'and after'; another anonymous production from Col. Caroline Frederick Scott, see note 105 above; HUL. DDHO 4.4, Major Thomas Gage, 44th Foot, to Charles Hotham, 13 Feb. 1750; A. Valentine, *Lord George Germain*, Oxford 1961, *passim*.

110 Compare HUL. DDHO4.285, *Standing Orders to be observed by His Majesty's Forces in Ireland*, Cork, 1764, and NAM. 6707–11–18, a manuscript *aide-mémoire* of standing orders, etc., kept by 'Lieutenant Hamilton', with R. A. Cumb. 62/C4, the digest of the Duke's orders issued by Robert Napier in May 1755 and the draft 'Regulations

proposed for Ireland' of 15 Dec. 1750, R. A. Cumb. C44/140. The rambling Irish official collection, incorporating orders issued in Dublin from 18 Oct. 1751 onwards, includes some of Cumberland's ideas of 1750 but is greatly dissimilar in content and, above all, method from Napier's work of 1755.

111 R. A. Cumb. C44/140, 'Regulations proposed for Ireland', 15 Dec. 1750; HUL. DDHO4.284, *Standing Orders, Ireland*, p. 3, 18 Oct. 1751; Major John Irwin, 5th Foot, to Lt. Col. Charles Whitefoord, 9 June 1752, W. S. Hewins ed., *The Whitefoord Papers*, Oxford, 1898, pp. 112–13.

112 PRO. WO 71/3 f. 116, William Pulteney, Secretary at War, to the Judge Advocate General, 19 April 1716.

113 This is an important issue in any discussion of the effectiveness of the army quartered in eithteenth-century Ireland, although explorations of it are seriously hampered by the destruction of so many critically important papers in 1922; see Appendix Two and Guy, 'A Whole Army Absolutely Ruined in Ireland'. Some fresh material is gradually being unearthed by Irish scholars, as reported by K. P. Ferguson, 'Military Manuscripts in the Public Record Office of Ireland', *The Irish Sword*, XV, 1982, pp. 112–15, but the sources are scattered and progress is slow. Meanwhile, for important evidence on the poor condition of resident units later in the century see G. A. Hayes-McCoy, 'The Government Forces which opposed the Irish Insurgents in 1798', *ibid.*, IX, 1959–60, pp. 16–28, and T. Pakenham, *The Year of Liberty: The Great Irish Rebellion of 1798*, London, 1969, pp. 50–6.

114 For a discussion of the shortcomings of mid-Georgian administration, see N. Baker, 'Changing Attitudes toward Government in Eighteenth Century Britain', A. Whiteman *et al.*, *Statesmen, Scholars and Merchants*, Oxford, 1973, pp. 202–19.

115 N. , Hampson, 'The French Revolution and the Nationalisation of Honour', M. R. D. Foot ed., *War and Society*, London, 1973, pp. 200–1; Dr Samuel Johnson, 'On the Bravery of the English Common Soldier', *Works*, Oxford, 1925, VI, pp. 150–1.

116 Baugh, *Naval Administration*, pp. 7–8.

117 *A Succinct and Impartial History of all the Regencies, Protectorships, Minorities and Princes of England or Great Britain and Wales that have been since the Conquest, with a proper Dedication to the Great Duke*, London, 1751, p. vi.

118 For an example of the English dislike of German discipline see the entertaining 'Fog's Scheme for an Army of Wax' ('... their exercise to be in the highest German taste'), reprinted in *Gents. Mag.* VI, 1736, p. 31. The essay has been attributed to the Earl of Chesterfield.

119 Cuthbertson, *System*, p. xxxix.

120 For the case of Capt. Shafto, see *Committee Report* (1746), pp. 144–52, and the anti-Cumberland pamphlet *Seasonable and Affecting Observations on the Mutiny Bill*, London, 1750, p. 37.

121 Belasyse was superseded after the battle of Dettingen (27 June 1743), as it had been suspected that he had absented himself from the fighting. In fact, he had been dangerously wounded in a cavalry melée and was subsequently vindicated by the Board of General Officers; PRO. WO 71/7 f. 156, John Earl of Stair to the Deputy Judge Advocate General, 22 Feb. 1745; *loc. cit.*, Report of a Board of General Officers, 26 Feb., 2 March 1745. The case is alluded to in two anti-Cumberland tracts: *Sesaonable and Affecting Observations on the Mutiny Bill*, London, 1750, p. 37 and *A Seasonable Letter to the Author of Seasonable and Affecting Observations*, London, 1751, p. ix.

122 For Bland's authoritarian behaviour, see Lt.-Col. James Wolfe, 20th Foot, to his father, 31 Jan. 1751, Wright, *Wolfe*, p. 143.

123 For the sensational House of Commons attacks on Anstruther in Feb.–March 1751, see W. Coxe, *The Administration of the Right Honourable Henry Pelham*, London, 1829, II, pp. 158–62, and *House of Commons, 1715–54*, 'Anstruther, Philip'. The remarks on his

Minorca regime are from *Seasonable and Affecting Observations'*, p. 37.

124 For both men, see *DNB*. Braddock has been substantially rehabilitated by L.J. McCardell, *Ill-starred General; Braddock of the Coldstream* Guards, Pittsburgh, 1958. Hawley's idiosyncratic papers are in the National Army Museum. His worst enemy is probably his own handwriting. Some notion of the singularity of his character can be obtained from the wording of his will, which was widely publicised after his death in 1759: '... as I began the world with nothing, I can dispose of it as I please. But first I direct and order (that as there's now a peace, and I may die the common way) my carcase may be put any where; 'tis equal to me; but I will have no more expence or ridiculous shew, than if a poor soldier (who is as good a man) was to be buried from the hospital. The priest, I conclude, will have his fee: let the puppy have it. Pay the carpenter for the carcase box ...', etc. *Gents. Mag.*, XXIX. 1759, pp. 157–8.

125 *DNB*, 'Rich, Sir Robert, 1714–1785'; L. I. Cooper, *The King's Own*, Oxford, 1939, p. 190.

126 Lowther to Viscount Irwin, 28 March 1751, *Hist. Mss. Comm. Various Collections*, VIII, 1913, p. 173.

127 Lt.-Col. James Wolfe to his father, 1 Sept. 1750, Wright, *Wolfe*, p. 152.

128 The treatment meted out to these unfortunate people by Cumberland's entourage was known as 'cherry bobbing': see the account of it by William, Earl of Shelburne in his 'Autobiography', quoted by E. Fitzmaurice, *Life of William Earl of Shelburne*, London, 1875, I, pp. 58–9. Shelburne only entered the army in 1756, so his opinions were probably formed from regimental gossip.

129 Ingoldsby was brought before a general court-martial on 25 July 1745 accused of disobedience to orders at Fontenoy, 11–12 May 1745. The charge was proved despite an inchoate prosecution and the absence of Cumberland, a material witness. Ingoldsby was suspended during the Duke's pleasure, in practice a period of three months, during which time he was allowed to sell a captaincy in the 1st Foot Guards (but not his majority) and retire. F. H. Skrine, *Fontenoy*, London, 1906, p. 232, suggests that Cumberland may have felt some qualms of conscience in dealing with this painful case, for the prisoner's contention that he had been perplexed by inconsistent orders was amply borne out by the evidence, but such qualms, if they even existed, do not seem to have softened his attitude towards Ingoldsby's piteous appeals for clemency. Indeed, as he revealed in his treatment of Brigadier-General Thomas Fowke, who failed to relieve Minorca in 1756, he was implacable against commanders he believed to have failed in their duty, Shute-Barrington, *op. cit.*, pp. 18–26.

130 When Cumberland returned to London in December 1745 after his abortive pursuit of the Prince through Cumbria he lodged a charge of misconduct against Oglethorpe, accusing him of having lingered on the road instead of harrying the retreating Jacobites at Shap. At a subsequent court-martial, Oglethorpe was acquitted but his military career was at an end and his regiment of foot in Georgia (rumoured to be in poor condition) was disbanded at the end of the war. Like George Townshend, Oglethorpe took an active role in Parliament in favour of a reorganised Militia, a Tory project to which Cumberland was hostile; A. A. Ettinger, *James Edward Oglethorpe, Imperial Idealist*, Oxford, 1936, pp. 266–70; *A Seasonable Letter, passim*.

131 George Townshend had served as a volunteer in the 'Pragmatic Army' in 1742–43 and in 1746 had been placed in the Duke's staff by the Pelhams in an attempt to counteract the influence of his Jacobite mother. He became *aide-de-camp* to Cumberland in 1747 and subsequently captain and lieutenant-colonel in the Duke's regiment, the 1st Foot Guards. It must have been some time after this that he began to earn the Duke's displeasure by his offensive caricatures, some of which can be enjoyed in E. Harris, *The Townshend Album*, London, 1974, and when in 1750, he was placed

under arrest by one of the Duke's lesser favourites, the martinet Col. Alexander Drury, after an attempt to absent himself from regimental duty to go on a hunting expedition to Belvoir Castle with the Marquess of Granby, he resigned his commission; NAM. 6806–41–1, 'Papers relating to the Services of Marquess Townshend'. (There is a less internally convincing account of the resignation in R. Glover, *Memoirs of a Celebrated Literary and Political Character*, London 1814, pp. 52–3.) Townshend only returned to the army in 1758 after Cumberland's disgrace. In the interim he was credited with the authorship of a tract critical of Cumberland's generalship, the *Brief Narrative of the Late Campaign in Germany and Flanders*, London, 1751, was active in Parliament in support of Militia reform and joined in the attack on the martinet Philip Anstruther.

132 For this unpleasant incident see Capt. Roger Townshend to Lord Townshend, 5 Nov. 1755, C.V.F. Townshend, *The Military Life of Field Marshal George, First Marquess Townshend*, London, 1901, pp. 129–31.

133 For these tracts and their authorship, see E. Charteris, *William Augustus Duke of Cumberland and the Seven Years' War*, London, 1925, p. 73; *Historical Memoirs of His Royal Highness the Duke of Cumberland*, London 1767, pp. 475–9; *DNB*, 'William Augustus, Duke of Cumberland'. The quotation denouncing Cumberland as '... a devil ... good-for-nothing jackanapes ...' is from *A Dialogue between Thomas Jones, a Life-Guard Man and John Smith, late a Serjeant in the First Regiment of Foot Guards, just returned from Flanders*, London 1749, pp. 7–8. The political background to the anti-Cumberland propaganda is described by A. H. Newman, 'Leicester House Politics, 1748–1751', *EHR* 76, 1961, pp. 577–89.

134 Horace Walpole, *Memoirs*, I, pp. 349–51.

135 BL. Add. MSS. 51, 387, Welbore Ellis to Henry Fox, 18(?) Oct. 1757.

136 Horace Walpole, *Memoirs*, I, pp. 349–51; Charteris, *op. cit.*, p. 85.

137 For the poor condition of the army before 1740 see king George III to the Earl of Bute, 3 March 1763, citing the opinion of Lord Ligonier; R. Sedgwick ed., *Letters from George III to Lord Bute 1756–1766*, London, 1939, pp. 194–5.

138 Coxe, *Pelham Administration*, II, 147–9 (4 Feb. 1751).

139 BL. Add. MSS. 32,690 f. 374, The Duke of Devonshire, Lord Lieutenant, to Newcastle, 30 Sept. 1737.

140 R. A. Cumb. C.18/336, St Clair to Col. Robert Napier, 19 Oct. 1746.

141 R. A. Cumb. C39/143, Cumberland to Newcastle, 16 Sept. 1748.

142 *DNB*, 'Conway, Henry Seymour'.

143 DRO. D86.X3, Henry Fox to Napier, 11 Oct. 1748.

144 BL. Add. MSS. 35,354 f. 397, Yorke to the Earl of Hardwicke, 28 Oct 1748.

145 PRO. SP 63/409 f. 107, Memorial of Major-General Philip Bragg, March 1746; *DNB*, 'Bragg, Philip'.

146 R. A. Cumb. C40/283, Dorset to Cumberland, 21 Oct 1748; BL. Add. MSS. 35,354 f. 397, Yorke to Hardwicke, 28 Oct 1748.

147 R. A. Cumb. C44/99, 'Observations concerning military affairs in Ireland' by 'Mr Lovetruth' enclosed in C44/98, Col. Caroline Frederick Scott to Napier, 29 July 1750.

148 PRO. WO 71/75, General Court Martial of Ensign Arthur Cole, 28th Foot, March 1766; F. Brodigan, *Historical Records of the 28th Regiment*, London, 1884; D. Scott Daniell, *Cap of Honour*, London, 1951.

149 R. A. Cumb. C36/104, Memorandum by Henry Pelham, 5 June 1748; C37/71, Cumberland to Pelham, 5 July 1748; C39/48, Pelham to Cumberland 29 Aug. 1748; C39/57, Cumberland to Newcastle, 2 Sept. 1748; C39/143, same to same, 16 Sept. 1748.

150 For a succinct account of a lengthy controversy see Western, *Militia*, pp. 120–1. Cumberland's rather indecorous zeal for reform of the Mutiny Act and Articles is

discussed by Charteris, *William Augustus Duke of Cumberland and the Seven Years' War*, pp. 37–9, 56. Some traces of the evolution of Cumberland's plans for 1749 can be traced in PRO. WO 4/43 f. 287, Fox to Gen. Sir Robert Rich, 4 June 1747; WO 4/44 f. 293, same to the Attorney and Solicitor Generals, 17 Feb 1748, and R. A. Cumberland C43–12, 13, 'Remarks of HRH The Duke on the proposed Articles of War', 1749. It is evident that a number of consultations were taken in advance of the reform and the latter document was intended for discussion by the Board of General Officers. The whole subject of Cumberland's proposed reforms of military law and his attitude toward courts-martial as carried out in the army at that time deserve a full treatment, drawing on the extensive records of the 1st Regiment of Foot Guards, of which he was colonel. Failing that, the controversy is best followed in the pamphlet literature, some of which has already been referred to as bearing on general attacks on arbitrary commanders. The most important anti-Cumberland tracts are: *A letter to a Member of Parliament in Relation to the Bill for Punishing Mutiny and Desertion*', London, 1749; *Seasonable and Affecting Observations on the Mutiny Bill*, London 1750, and *A Seasonable Letter to the Author of Seasonable and Affecting Observations*, London, 1751. The pro-Cumberland pieces, which dwell on the relative leniency of the English military code and the vital need to maintain discipline in a time of uneasy peace are: *The Ancient and Present State of the Military Law in Great Britain Considered*, London, 1749 and 1750, and *A Modest Defence of the Army by a Soldier*, London, 1753. For the rough treatment meted out to Lord Anson's similar proposals by belligerent naval officers see D. Erskine ed., *Augustus Hervey's Journal*, London, 1953, pp. 79–84. For the humiliation of Cumberland in the Regency Bill proposals see Coxe, *Pelham Administration*, II, p. 169.

151 Whitworth, *Ligonier*, p. 216; Sir R. Savory, *His Britannic Majesty's Army in Germany during the Seven Years' War*, Oxford, 1966, pp. 20–46.

152 R. A. Cumb. C43/14, 'Articles re. Musters etc. of HM's Forces', dated 1749 but containing material dealing with administrative position in 1747. The endorsement is undated.

3

The machinery of regimental finance
and its reform, 1714–66

To those accustomed to the course of office, the intricacies of regimental finance were reckoned to be 'easy and familiar',[1] but this is far from how historians have seen them. 'In mortal dread of distasteful discussions of the military estimates,' despaired Sir John Fortescue, 'the civil authority clothed every possible grant of money in the garment of pay for the men, and made it over to regimental officers to do their best or worst with it. Hence arose a chaos of strange terms which are the bewilderment and despair of every student.'[2] Indeed, the labrynth of regimental finance could be almost as confusing to contemporaries as it was to Fortescue. It only needed a little artfulness in the making up of accounts to render them so obscure that even senior War Office clerks could not penetrate them.[3] It is the intention of this chapter therefore to make the mysteries of the early Georgian regimental economy as seen from the point of view of the regimental officer intelligible, and to throw some light upon the ways in which it was reformed up to the end of the Seven Years' War and its administrative aftermath, to about 1766.

The reform of regimental administration began in the first years of the new dynasty. The impulse was provided by George I's dislike of the jumble of proprietary interest and individualistic custom which characterised his army, which he viewed as a potential screen for fraud and indiscipline. There was no systematic programme of reform in the modern sense, or even anything approaching the radical administrative changes of the 1780s. The reforms carried out by George I and his son were mostly pragmatic and limited in scope, remedying existing defects and tackling specific problems, but in their totality they effected a revolution in the character of proprietary soldiering as experienced by troop and company commanders. The integration of royal warrants regulating specific areas of the regimental economy, enquiries by the Board of General Officers, field reviews and musters had the cumulative effect of defining and fixing hitherto obscure custom, established precedents and exposed the mechanism of military finance to more comprehensive regulation. The culmination of this effort during our period was the suspension of open-ended dividends drawn by captains from their troop and company funds and their replacement by strictly controlled allowances.

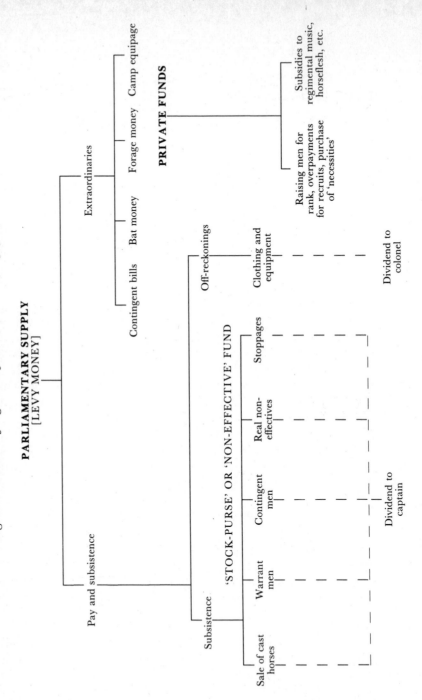

Fig. 3.1 *Structure of regimental finance, 1714–47 (simplified)*

The machinery of regimental finance

Table 3.1 *A regimental establishment (3rd Foot), 1762*; (PRO. WO 24/394)
Nine companies of 100 private men, in all 1034 officers and men

	s	d	Per diem £	s	d	For 365 days £	s	d
Field and staff officers								
Colonel as colonel	12	0		14	0		255 10	0
In lieu of his servants	2	0					255 10	0
Lieutenant-colonel as lieutenant colonel				7	0		127 15	0
Major as major				5	0		91 5	0
Chaplain				6	8		121 13	4
Adjutant				4	0		73 0	0
Quartermaster	4	0						
In lieu of his servant		8		4	8		85 3	4
			£ 2	12	4		955 1	8
One company								
Captain	8	0						
In lieu of his servants	2	0		10	0		182 10	0
Two lieutenants each 4s	8	0						
In lieu of their servants	1	4		9	4		170 6	8
Ensign	3	0						
In lieu of his servant		8		3	8		66 18	4
Four sergeants each 1s 6d				6	0		109 10	0
Four corporals each 1s 0d				4	0		73 0	0
Two drummers each 1s 0d				2	0		36 10	0
One hundred private men each 8d			£ 3	6	8		1,216 13	4
			£ 5	1	8		1,855 8	4
Allowance to the widows				1	4		24 6	8
Allowance to the colonel for clothing lost by deserters				1	2		21 5	10
Allowance to the captain for recruiting etc				1	0		18 5	0
Allowance to the agent					6		9 2	6
Seven companies more of the like numbers and rates			£ 5	5	8		1,928 8	4
as the company above mentioned			£36	19	8		13,498 18	4
One company of grenadiers								
Captain	8	0						
In lieu of his servants	2	0		10	0		182 10	0
Three lieutenants each 4s	12	0						
In lieu of their servants	2	0		14	0		255 10	0
Four sergeants each 1s 6d				6	0		109 10	0
Four corporals each 1s 0d				4	0		73 0	0
Two drummers each 1s 0d				2	0		36 10	0
Two fifers each 1s 0d				2	0		36 10	0
One hundred private men each 8d			£ 3	6	8		1,216 13	4
Allowance to colonel, widows, captain and agent			£ 5	4	8		1,910 3	4
as above				4	0		73 0	0
			£ 5	8	8		1,983 3	4
Total for this regiment			£50	6	4		18,365 11	8

Oeconomy and discipline

1. The Pay Office

To appreciate how the regimental economy operated it is first necessary to understand how money voted for the army was managed centrally.

The annual parliamentary grant to the land forces was formed on the basis of estimates of the gross expense of the various regiments of horse and foot to be maintained on the British Establishment during the ensuing year and presented to the House of Commons by the Secretary at War. Once a supply had been voted on the basis of these estimates, there came from the Treasury to the Pay Office the King's Sign Manual, directing the Lords Commissioners of the Treasury to issue part of that supply to the Paymaster General as an imprest. This was recorded in the Pay Office but the instrument itself was lodged in the Exchequer, where it gave the Paymaster credit for the sum specified. To obtain any part of it, he memorialised the Treasury, stating the sum required and the service for which it was intended, information supplied to him by the Secretary at War. The Treasury then authorised the Exchequer to issue the funds. When the sum covered by the Sign Manual was exhausted, the Paymaster obtained another, and so on until the last issue of the year, when the whole supply was confirmed and authorised by a Privy Seal. It was customary for the Paymaster General to apply for approximately one-third of what was termed the 'pay and subsistence of the army' every four months.

While the course of office was bringing this money into the Paymaster General's hands, the Secretary at War prepared 'establishments' based on the estimates but which, rather than simply indicating the whole number of officers and men in the regiment and the cost to the public, set out in detail their ranks and the distribution of pay. These establishments were extremely important papers. Copies of them were lodged in the War and Pay Offices and in the Treasury. They were to be '... the guide and direction to all the officers in everything that respects the pay, the strength and also the credit of each corps'. They were grouped in distinct services; these normally comprised the Guards, Garrisons and Land Forces in Great Britain, Gibraltar and Minorca and the Plantations. They included abstracts of a number of warrants, including those authorising a stoppage of 1s in the £ on all money disbursed by the Paymaster General (the so-called 'poundage'),[4] and a stoppage of one day's pay from all ranks to maintain the Royal Hospital Chelsea, but the bulk of the establishments consisted of lists of the regiments and other formations detailing their pay *per diem* and *per annum* without deduction. Also included were statements of a number of allowances which subsidised the regimental economy and boosted the personal pay of the officers.

The first of these allowances was granted to commissioned officers in lieu of mustering civilian servants in the ranks or making use of soldier–servants, and it was calculated at the rate of daily pay of a private man in each branch of the service; i.e. 2s 6d in the regiments of horse, 1s 6d in the dragoons and 8d in the foot. A captain was entitled to an allowance for three servants, and a subaltern to one or two. Field officers were credited with an allowance in their capacity as captains. These allowances were authorised in an establishment dated 15 June 1713, extended on 29 April 1714 to quartermasters of horse and dragoons and on 24 June 1718 to quartermasters of infantry. They were counted as part of the gross pay of the officers and liable to stoppages as such.[5]

The remaining allowances, as they appeared in British regimental establishments with effect from 11 August 1716 and Irish establishments from 2 April 1740, were as follows:[6]

1. The proprietary colonel was credited with the equivalent of one man's subsistence per troop or company *per diem* as a perquisite and a contribution towards defraying the cost of regimental clothing carried off by deserters.
2. The subsistence of two 'warrant men' or 'non-effective men' was credited to each proprietary captain's non-effective account as an aid to recruiting and a perquisite (there was provision in the establishments for this allowance to be withheld if the unit was not kept up to strength).
3. The subsistence of one warrant man per troop or company, the 'agent's man', was credited to the regimental agent as part of his salary.

The colonel derived additional benefit from these four non-effectives, for the balance of their nett pay was credited to him in lieu of off-reckonings. On the regimental establishment it was lumped in with his allowance of 'colonel's men', which increased the income from this source in each company of foot from 8*d per diem* to 1*s* 4*d*.

A final allowance was granted to the widows of commissioned officers. It originally consisted of the equivalent of the full pay *per diem* of one man per troop or company but by 1718 this had been augmented to two. The regiments and companies of invalids were excluded from this arrangement, as were the four household troops of Horse Guards and the two troops of Horse Grenadier Guards. In the latter two instances, a deduction was made at the Pay Office equal to the pay of two men in each of the troops of Horse Guards and one in the Horse Grenadiers and the money forwarded to the Paymaster of the Widows' Pensions, a War Office official, at two-monthly intervals. After a stoppage of 1*s* in the £ for salaries and contingencies, it was issued to the widows or their attorneys every four months. For much of our period the amount of money in the fund had exceded the demand for pensions.

In order to make a practical distribution of pay it was necessary for the Paymaster General to formulate a division of gross pay based on the establishments but not conforming to them exactly. His most important task was to issue the men's subsistence, the element of their pay intended to maintain them from day to day. Subsistence was normally issued every two months without deduction. The balance was known as the 'gross off-reckonings' for the rank and file and 'arrears' for the officers. From it, the Paymaster deducted the poundage, the one day's pay for Chelsea Hospital, 2*d* in the £ for the regimental agent and the widows' pensions. The balance owing to the rank and file was now termed the 'nett off-reckonings' and its main purpose was '... to reimburse the expense of clothes, accoutrements, their loss, repair, package, freight and insurance etc. for the non-commissioned officers and private men'. The men did not get to finger this money, rather it was issued periodically to the proprietary colonel or his assigns to provide uniforms, an operation which resulted in a substantial perquisite, to be examined in detail in a later chapter.[7]

Any outstanding balances of regimental pay, including the officers' arrears, were known as the 'clearings'. Habitual looseness of terminology in the eighteenth century has resulted in the term being applied to the arrears alone as well as the actual process of settling or 'clearing' the regimental accounts. The method of doing this was as follows. When a regimental account was closed up to a certain period, commonly midsummer or Christmas, the Treasury deducted the amount of subsistence actually issued, as well as any other advance made to the regiment from its credit against full supply, a sum arrived at by comparing the establishment with properly authenticated muster rolls or their equivalent. Any favourable balances or 'clearings' were issued to the corps, together with the officers' arrears. The unit was then understood to be 'cleared'. The Paymaster General stated a balance to the regimental agent, who returned him an acquittance which would be submitted in due course to the Auditors of the Imprest when the Paymaster's own accounts were audited.

The retention during the year of the arrears, clearings and nett off-reckonings was useful to government, in that it provided rudimentary insurance against the incompetence or corruption of officers and their agents. From the point of view of the officers, it became of critical importance to be able to provide verifiable muster rolls, for without them the clearing process could not be completed, and for the time being they would be deprived of their arrears.[8]

After it left the Pay Office, the subsistence was remitted to the regimental agent or, in the case of units serving overseas, remitted by a contractor and his agents to Deputy Paymasters in foreign stations, or else shipped out in specie. For example, at the height of the Seven Years' War, John Calcraft, premier agent on the British Establishment, only received full subsistence for his regiments serving at home. The subsistence of his regiments in Germany was remitted abroad by contract, as was the subsistence of rank and file in America, although in the case of the latter regiments he did receive a sum roughly equivalent to the officers' subsistence every two months. His regiments serving in the East Indies had their subsistence despatched in specie every six months and nothing remained in Calcraft's hands except deductions authorised by the officers to support their families. The officers' arrears were usually issued at six-monthly intervals; not surprisingly, they were claimed almost at once.[9]

The subsistence was issued by the agent or by the Deputy Paymaster (subject in the latter instance to ration stoppages for regiments in the field), to the regimental paymaster, who in turn issued it to the captains or commanding officers of troops and companies. They accounted with him for it and, as it became liable to additional stoppages at troop and company level, they periodically accounted with their men. The paymaster accounted with the regimental agent but the latter did not account direct with the Paymaster General; rather, his accounts lay within the inspection of the Secretary at War.[10]

Thus was the day-to-day management of large amounts of the public treasure devolved to semi-autonomous businesses, administered by nominees of the proprietary officers – the agent and the paymaster.

2. The regimental agent

The steady flow of subsistence from the Pay Office to the unit, the prompt issue of clearings and arrears, the settlement of the non-effective account and the assignment of the nett off-reckonings all depended to a large extent on the activity and effectiveness of the regimental agent. In many instances it was he who arranged for subsistence to be remitted to regimental headquarters and digested information sent by the regimental paymaster (who was not necessarily very professional in his accounting technique, a fault often shared by the captains with whom he dealt); he drew up regimental accounts for the information of the War Office and his colonel; he attended the War and Pay Offices to resolve any difficulties; he dealt on the colonel's behalf with clothiers, sword cutlers, gunsmiths, insurance agents and other contractors; he acted for the colonel and the other officers in numerous regimental and private concerns and, in the best agency firms, provided them, their patrons and kinsmen with a political, military and social post office.[11]

The agent was a civilian and the nominee and personal servant of the proprietary colonel. Only in the regiments of Foot Guards did he appear on the establishment as 'sollicitor' and not otherwise.[12] He was remunerated by a stoppage on the gross pay of the corps (but deducted from the gross off-reckonings) and by income from the 'agent's man' in each troop and company already described. It was customary for the colonel and agent to haggle over the actual payment of these allowances, with the result that agents' incomes were not uniform throughout the service.[13]

As a class of bureaucrat the agents were descended from the humble (and venal) Tudor company clerk. Even those appointed as recently as the post-Restoration period were insignificant figures, mere *commis* to the senior officers who chose them, but the military business generated by the wars of King William III and Queen Anne and its growing complexity enhanced their status and improved their opportunities. The difficulty of uniting the virtues of combatant officer and military accountant obliged colonels to rely more and more heavily on their agents, some of whom abused their charges cruelly.[14] The agents quickly established permanent offices, employed their own clerks and engrossed the business of several regiments at once. Some officers even took up the profession. One authority has suggested that this may have dignified it, but it is more likely that the growing importance of the job offered a profitable alternative to a career with the sword and where intricate details mastered during military service could be put to congenial use in the world ouside.[15] Until 1721 the officer-agents were permitted to combine their agency business with combatant commissions, often absenting themselves from their regiments for long periods, '... but ... in order ... to prevent any inconvenience of this kind in our service for the future and that every officer may have his just hour of duty in the regiment to which he belongs', an order was issued on 13 May of that year that they should either resign their agencies or their commissions by 1 June 1721 on pain of being superseded in the latter by half-pay officers.[16] A number chose to keep their agencies: four, Captain Thomas Levett, Major George Sawyer, Captain Alexander Wilkinson and Captain Alexander Wilson, were still in business in London in the 1740s. Four more, Captain Theophilus Debrisay, Captain Johnson, Captain Montgomery and Major Carlton Whitelocke, were regimental agents in Dublin. After 1721 a young man intending to make a career in agency served his apprenticeship in the War or Pay Offices, as secretary to a senior officer or clerk to an established agent.[17]

In theory, there could have been as many agents as there were colonels to employ them, but in practice the complexity of the business, the necessity of providing capital for bonds and securities and the excellent reputations and connections of some of the existing agents meant that trade was unequally distributed. John Calcraft provided the most striking example of pluralism in the period. From modest beginnings after the War of the Austrian Succession under the patronage of Henry Fox, Secretary at War, Calcraft was able to combine salaried places in the War and Commissary General of the Musters' Offices with the agency of sixty-three out of 160 regiments available for business at the height of the Seven Years' War. Moreover, he was not the first agent to gather a disproportionate number of appointments, for Captain Alexander Wilson of Queen's Street, Westminster, built up a business of twenty-four units out of eighty-eight available for business during 1746–47.

Unfortunately for the agents, such large empires were of brief duration, for with the coming of peace young corps were broken and old corps reduced, while other regiments were transferred to the Irish Establishment. The preponderance enjoyed by Calcraft was largely derived from regiments raised after 1759. In 1763 he lost at least twenty-three of his clients by breaking, eleven more by their being consigned to Ireland and a number of others as a result of changes of colonel. At the end of 1764 Calcraft let it be known that he was quitting the agency business to pursue a political career, although it is now known that he tried to keep a grip on what remained of his empire by going into partnership with his rather shady protégé and former clerk James Meyrick.[18]

Regiments on the Irish Establishment required agents locally to receive funds issued from Dublin Castle, to carry out in Ireland parallel functions to the English agents and to share with them the complicated business of adjusting accounts between the two Establishments.[19] As, however, most warlike business was conducted on the British Establishment, there were fewer agents operating in Dublin than in London; no more than six at any time after 1745 and as few as four in 1762, as opposed to nineteen on the sister Establishment. So, although the Irish agents enjoyed passing advantages from regiments raised or augmented in the kingdom before their transfer to Britain, their businesses were only put on a solid footing in time of peace, when a large number of regimental cadres were returned to Ireland. Naturally, the English business was in its most flourishing condition during time of war.

Although it was often necessary for the British and Irish agents to correspond with each other, there were apparently no formal partnerships between them. Indeed, there was even a reluctance to form partnerships at home, a fact which sometimes resulted in disastrous consequences when an agent died or was declared insolvent.[20]

Like so many of the brokers, stock-jobbers, government contractors, paymasters and commissaries who rose to places of profit and influence on the bandwagons of credit financing and inflated military budgets, the regimental agents were despised as '... state vultures that prey upon the vitals of the nation'.[21] Their dubious origin, their unsavoury historical record, the arcane qualities of regimental finance and the fact that their remuneration was settled by private treaty buttressed these suspicions. However, with the exception of the inevitable recriminations resulting from bankruptcies and the loss of regimental funds, there are remarkably few complaints about the behaviour of agents in our period. They were, after all, liable to the provisions of the Mutiny Act; one of them, Mr Thomas Fisher of Axe Yard, Westminster, was actually court-martialled in 1762 at the insistence of the troublesome Field Marshal Sir Robert Rich and his equally combative and litigious son, Lieutenant-General Sir Robert Rich,[22] and it was also to be expected that the pecuniary interest of the colonels would induce them to keep a close eye on their appointees. Moreover, with a few ignoble exceptions, agencies were in the hands of a group of honourable and efficient businessmen, some of whom used their own money to boost flagging regimental accounts, rendered services to officers (even very junior officers)[23] well beyond their formal obligations, and who ended up becoming trusted colleagues and friends of their clients. One of them, Mr William Adair of Pall Mall, received legacies valued at £16,000 from his colonel, General John Huske of the 23rd Foot, in 1761, and two of his clerks, Henry and Thomas Bullock, received £200 and £100 respectively.[24] Any residual dislike of agents was largely attributable to the fact that '... we are not angry at a soldier's getting riches because we see that he possesses qualities which we have not. If a man returns from a battle having lost one hand and the other full of gold, we feel that he deserves the gold, but we cannot think that a fellow, by sitting all day at a desk, is entitled to get above us.'[25]

3. The regimental paymaster

The regimental paymaster did not appear on the establishment. He was not a regimental staff officer in the strictest sense, therefore, but he was nonetheless indispensable. He received money remitted to the corps by the agent or by the Deputy Paymasters in foreign stations or in the field. In colonial garrisons it was usual for him to negotiate credit with local contractors for cash and supplies, the undertakers drawing on the agent in London. Within the regiment, the paymster issued money to the rank and file *via* their captains, accounting with them, the agent and sometimes the proprietary colonel. The duty was a highly responsible one, and it was not unusual to find captains or even field officers performing it, although the Duke of Cumberland certainly disapproved of the latter doing so.[26]

By the custom of the army the appointment of the paymaster was a regimental affair. The nomination lay with the captains, the colonel participating in his capacity of captain of a troop or company.[27] It is hard to imagine the captains going against any express wish of their colonel in making such an influential appointment.

To answer the paymaster's considerable trouble in the execution of his office, it was customary for the captains to allow him a sum equivalent to the subsistence of a man per troop or company *per diem*.[28] An alternative method of remuneration, an agreement with the agent that part of the latter's allowance would be made over to the paymaster, required the close co-operation of the colonel, who fixed such matters with the agent by private treaty.[29]

Persons nominating the paymaster shared the responsibility for any loss incurred as a result of his incompetence, misfortune or malfeasance during the time he continued to receive funds.[30] It was therefore customary for him to provide cash security or personal backers to stand surety for him.[31]

It was essential for the paymaster to be able to call upon the services of an experienced non-commissioned officer to act as paymaster-sergeant. This position, like the paymastership itself, did not appear on the establishments and little is known about the extent of the work or the remuneration. There is no doubt, however, that there existed an important substratum of petty administrators drawn from the ranks. The existence of troop and company clerks is well attested; there was a requirement for non-commissioned officers and even private men to assist in the drawing up and copying of regimental documents, and it was one of the prerequisites for obtaining the rank of sergeant that the candidate should be able to write a fair hand. It was alleged that sometimes too much power was delegated to these men by indifferent and inefficient company officers.[32]

4. Regimental non-effective and stock purse funds

The regimental 'non-effective fund' in the regiments of foot and the equivalent 'stock purse' in the cavalry was the foundation of the unit's interior economy.[33] Sometimes referred to as the 'bank', it was intended to answer the common financial occurrences of the regiment. In time of peace, most of its income was generated by the subsistence of non-effective men and horses and, in the cavalry, the sale of worn-out horseflesh. The regiment was regarded essentially as 'living of its own' and all routine costs were intended to be answered without recourse to Parliament. The main charge against the bank was the recruiting of men and horses; additional expenditure was necessary to answer a multitude of petty contingencies. The honest and efficient proprietary captain was entitled to a dividend on the annual surplus in the non-effective account.

The bank was a 'regimental' fund in that, in time of war, the Secretary at War was authorised to prohibit any distribution of dividends. He could put charges against it during war or peace[34] and, in any case, any division of the fund required the agreement of the colonel as trustee for the whole. However, the fund was stated by the troop or company and, although one company in a regiment might show a profit and its neighbour a deficit, the colonel had no authority to apply the one to the other.[35]

It was customary for the account and balances to be stated by the agent annually on 24 June, a date formally established by a royal warrant issued by George II from his field headquarters at Hanau on 24 August 1743,[36] reiterated in the Warrant for Regulating the Necessary Stoppages from the Regiments of Dragoon Guards, Dragoons and Foot of 19 June 1749[37] and in a regulation promulgated by the Duke of Cumberland in June 1750.[38] The 1749 warrant greatly restricted the payment of dividends in the cavalry, but for the time being the principle that the captains of infantry were allowed a dividend, '... partly in aid of their extraordinary expenses and partly as a reward of their care and diligence in completing their companies', was interpreted generously. If a company was not complete to establishment on 24 June, £5 was to be detained in the agent's hands for every man wanting but any balance was to be paid to the captains as a perquisite. Adverse balances were carried forward.

(i) Levy money

When it was proposed to raise a regiment from scratch or augment an existing one, the 'bank' which would answer this cost either did not exist, or was too small to finance the undertaking, so the enterprise was launched by an allowance of 'levy money'.

The usual method of providing levy money was to issue a warrant permitting the unit to be mustered as if complete from the date of the beating order which authorised the officers to raise recruits by beat of drum. The device of 'mustering complete' was also used to generate funds for a regiment which had been heavily drafted and had not been reimbursed (as it should have been) by the regiments which had received its men. It was also used to restore the buoyancy of a regimental bank depleted by heavy expenditure.

As an alternative to mustering complete, it was possible for the regiment to be credited with a lump sum of levy money, and in other circumstances the War

Office appealed to ambitious officers to provide their own bank of levy money in return for promotion into the new unit.[39]

(ii) 'Ideal' and 'real' non-effectives

Once the regimental bank had been launched, most of its income was supposed to be generated by the subsistence of non-effectives. It will be recalled that, historically, the widespread use of official non-effectives or 'dead pays' had opened the door to manifold abuses. These had persisted despite generous allowances made to the captains and frequent musters in the field or in quarters.

There were two general classes of non-effectives; 'ideal' non-effectives who were rarely, if ever, expected to appear in the ranks and 'real' non-effectives, the rank and file vacant between musters. Ideal non-effectives fell into two distinct categories, 'warrant men and 'contingent men', although, as usual in Georgian Britain, habitual looseness with nomenclature made them easy to confuse with each other.

Prior to the muster-period commencing 25 August 1716, warrant men in regiments on the British Establishment were provided by the ancient and grossly abused expedient of fictitious names in the muster roll of each troop or company. Their subsistence was divided among the colonel and captains as agreed among themselves and the balance of their gross pay after the deduction of poundage and money for Chelsea Hospital went to the colonel as off-reckonings.

George I was unhappy at the looseness of these arrangements, the connivance of government in the insertion of bogus names in official documents, and the difficulty in determining exact numbers of effective men at a glance. Reform of the regimental establishments in this respect had been already embarked upon in 1713 by stating distinct allowances for officers' servants in lieu of mustering them in the ranks,[40] but the King's warrant of 11 August 1716 suppressed all fictitious names in units on the British Establishment,[41] the troops of Horse and Horse Grenadier Guards excepted.[42] The prohibition was extended to these household formations on 11 August 1747 as a follow-up to the disbandment of the 3rd and 4th Troops of Horse Guards in December 1746.[43] Money equivalents to the pay of the fictitious men now appeared separately on the regimental establishments as already described. Fictitious names continued to be used on the Irish Establishment, however, notwithstanding an apparent desire to bring the custom to an end. The anomaly was rectified on 2 April 1740, and from that time Irish regimental establishments were ordered after the British manner.[44]

From the point of view of the captain, the most important source of company income was the subsistence of the two 'warrant men' for recruiting. This was worth £73 4s per troop *per annum* in the regiments of horse, £42 11s 8d in the dragoons and £18 5s in the foot. The equivalent income in Ireland was £48 3s 4d, £34 19s 7d and £11 14s *per annum* in Irish currency.

Additional credit was supplied by a second class of ideal non-effectives, the 'contingent men'. These were obtained by not recruiting the regiments to their establishment and were envisaged as only a wartime expedient. The royal warrant issued at Hanau on 24 August 1743 reserved £5 per man in the non-effective accounts to bring the unit up to full strength if ordered.[45] In time of war, a company of foot carried three or four contingent men and a troop of horse or dragoons two or three. It was usually found necessary to continue to subsidise the non-effective fund by allowing one or two 'contingents' even in time of peace.

In some regiments, income from contingent men was treated as an intrinsic part of the non-effective fund, in others it was paid over to the captain with the subsistence of his effectives and did not figure in the account.[46] In some instances, income from the contingent men was used to provide the customary remuneration of a man's subsistence per troop or company *per diem* to the paymaster.[47]

In addition to the two officially sanctioned classes of ideal non-effectives there was a quasi-legitimate allowance of the subsistence of 'hautboys' (oboe-players in the regimental music) in the two troops of Horse Grenadier Guards and in each troop of dragoons. This was a customary perquisite of the colonel and will be examined in a later chapter.[48]

Supplementary income was obtained from the subsistence of 'real' non-effectives, rank and file vacant between the two-monthly visits of a deputy commissary of the musters. The deputy commissary was supposed to inspect the corps in the presence of a Justice of the Peace and call-over each troop and company roll. If he was not satisfied that missing men were on furlough, detached duty or sick in the regimental infirmary, it was his duty to 'respite' them on the muster rolls which he forwarded to the Commissary General of the Musters in London. The captain's credit suffered accordingly when the regiment was cleared, and he ran the risk of having his official allowance of warrant men docked. However, if he supplied a recruit promptly, or obtained the benefit of a royal warrant whereby the regiment was regarded as having been mustered complete, he kept the benefit of the incidental vacant subsistence. In practice the mustering system did not operate as intended and in 1747 it was extensively reformed. This cleared the way for more stringent control of dividends and will be examined shortly.

(iii) Sale of cast stock

In regiments of cavalry this was an integral feature of annual income to the stock purse. It fluctuated according to prices currently given for cast nags. It was customary for a troop to cast an average of four horses *per annum* in peacetime, no horse being allowed to serve after its fourteenth year.

It was estimated that this transaction might bring in rather less than £20 per troop *per annum*.[49] In 1756 the 3rd Dragoon Guards disposed of eighteen horses for only £35 4s 3d, but the fact that in the same season the 1st Dragoons sold fifteen horses for £133 3s suggests that no cast iron estimate can be made of this source of income.[50]

(iv) Stoppages

It has been noted that the regimental bank was intended to answer a variety of contingent expenses. These includeed allowances to riding masters and rough-

Oeconomy and discipline

Table 3.2 'Computation of the Yearly Expenses a Company of Foot (in Ireland) is subject to for which the Captain is allowed Two Men's Pay.' c. 1727 (BL. Add. MSS.23636/43 f.4)

Charges attending Musters, writing Muster Rolls, etc	£ 4	15s	0d
Expense of burying Men, for a Coffin etc		10s	0d
Loss by Mens' dying or running away in Debt	£ 1	10s	0d
Charge of sending after and taking Deserters	£ 2	10s	0d
The mending and keeping in good order spare Arms left by Deserters, Dead and discharged Men		15s	
To nursing Men and extraordinary expenses in fluxing Men, etc	£ 1	0s	0d
Expenses of carriage of Gunpowder from ye places ye warrants upon etc to ye Company Quarters		10s	0d
To advertizing Deserters		5s	5d
For printing Furlows and Discharges			10d
Charge of sending *Dublin Gazette* twice a week to Quarters		2s	7d
Charge of receiving ye yearly Baggage money out of ye Treasury			10d
	£11	19s	8d

Two men's pay at 4d a day for a year comes to £12 3s 4d
But to deduct taking of the Check of these two men, 10s 8d and ye Colonel and Agent's Man, leaves £11 12s 8d

By ye above Accot. The Captain loses 7s

Upon a supposition yt a company may want yearly 4 Recruits to compleat it, And supposing ye Foure one with another are vacant Half ye Yeare, in yt

Case ye non-effective money of ye four Men comes to	£14	7s	2d
To 4 Recruits brought out of England at £5 English each, in Irish money is	£22	8s	0d
By which it appears ye Cap loses	£ 8	0s	10d

'Usual Stoppages made from each Company of Foot'

Each Soldier has stopped from him every Foure weeks 4d, for which he is not accounted with ye stoppage, from 34 men for a yeare

comes to	£7	7s	4d
To deduct Infirmary Surgeon's Chest,	£4	16s	8d
Remains	£2	10s	8d

The Sergeants, Corps, Drummers have stopped from them out of their aeeares 3d a week each which for a yeare comes to from 2

Sergeants, 2 Corporals, 1 Drummer,					£3	5s	0d
But to deduct for ye surgeon 4s each	£1	0s	0d }		£1	13s	9d
and for infirmary and surgeons chest		13s	9d				
Remains					£1	11s	3d

Each drummer has besides ye above stoppage 1½d per week stopt from him for ye drum major, which is paid to him, £4 1s 11d which £4 1s 11d is towards defraying ye charge of postage of abstracts and letters, for fetching of money, Paying a Sergeant Major and many unforseen charges as receiving light gold, buying clothes where men have deserted with their regimental clothes, money given baggage men on a march, ye charge when in some quarters as yt of Waterford of paying a post between yt place and Duncannon Fort, the prosecuting a man who murdered a soldier, £1 0s 9d, ye company carriage of sick men on horse back when not able to ride on a Carr, charge to double musters on Embarcation, charge of sending men to Regimental court martial when in a dispersed quarter, All of which one yeare with another doth more than sink ye above sume.

riders (discontinued in wartime), payments to the regimental surgeon to enable him to maintain his medicine chest, the charge of burying the dead, hiring storehouses and parade grounds, gratuities to soldiers who assisted in the alteration of newly arrived bales of clothing or the compiling and copying of muster rolls, the cost of printing regimental stationary and of advertising for and sending after deserters, fees on warrants for the issue of gunpowder and other stores and postage (including the cost of making sure that regimental head-quarters was constantly supplied with those essential publications the *Dublin* and *London Gazettes*) (Table 3.2). It was assumed that income from warrant and contingent men would cover some of this, although differing regimental methods of stating the non-effective account obscured the true level of contingent expenditure; for example, not all the income from contingent men was necessarily entered. Stoppages were supposed to answer any bills still outstanding, as well as a number of additional expenses associated with the management of the soldier, in particular the cost of replacing his 'necessaries' – shoes, stockings, linen and gaiters, items originally provided from a hefty stoppage imposed on his enlistment bounty of a guinea and a crown.

Stoppages on the soldier's already paltry subsistence had a history as long and shady as fictitious names and false musters and, like every deduction which did not show up in an account, they were a constant cause of discontent. George I was uneasy about them and referred the matter to the Board of General Officers in the summer of 1717.

The results of the Board's deliberations were registered in the Warrant for Regulating the Necessary Stoppages from the Regiments of Dragoons and Foot of 24 August 1717 and the Warrant for Regulating Necessary Stoppages from the Regiments of Horse of 10 September 1717.[51] In the regiments of horse a stoppage of sixpence a week was authorised from the subsistence of each corporal of horse and private man, applicable at the colonel's direction to the contingent charges of each troop, and to offset the cost of remounts. No other stoppage was permitted without express royal approbation. In the regiments of foot, 1s a week was stopped from the subsistence of each sergeant, and 6d from each corporal, drummer and private man to answer the captains's outlay on necessaries.

In the regiments of dragoons the structure of stoppages was more complicated. When the men were in winter quarters, 'in the house', where their horses were supplied with their landlord's corn, their lodging cost twice as much as during their summer camp. Conversely, the cost of the summer grass contract was greater by nearly half than the cost of winter corn. The weekly saving during the summer months (1s 9d from the pay of every sergeant, corporal and dragoon) was known as 'grass money'. An allowance of 2d a week was paid to the surgeon out of it and the balance was applied to the cost of necessaries and contingencies.

The captain of dragoons was under orders to account with his men for their grass money within fourteen days of the horses being taken up from grass. Any balances in their favour were supposed to be distributed to them. In the regiments of foot the men were accounted with every two months. The temptation to the captain to engross the full amount of these stoppages, plus the fact that the original cost of equipping a man with necessaries put him almost permanently in debt to his captain, meant that he was unlikely ever to see much of this money. It was said that any man who tried to claim his just balance got short shrift from his officer.[52]

Subsequent royal warrants reiterated the general principles to be observed in applying these stoppages and made only minor adjustments to the amounts of money involved and the exact method of distribution. The Warrant for Regulating the Necessary Stoppages from the Regiments of Dragoons and Foot of 28 June 1721 was a consequence of a small increase in dragoon pay made to quieten the complaints of their landlords that they were too expensive to billet.[53] These arrangements were confirmed by the Warrant for Regulating the Necessary Stoppages from Weekly Pay of 29 April 1732 (Table 3.3).[54] In the 1721 and 1732 warrants, sums of money had been appropriated for riding masters in the dragoons. The final warrant in this sequence, the Warrant for Regulating the Necessary Stoppages from the Regiments of Dragoon Guards, Dragoons and Foot of 19 June 1749, made a further subdivision of stoppages to provide additional funds for the surgeon's medicine chest.[55]

In time of war, stoppages were applied differently. They were governed by the movement of men in and out of winter quarters, by times during which they were being supplied from magazines, by changes in currency values between the war zones and the need to generate extraordinary supplies of cash to answer the contingencies of active service.

When the army was sent to Europe in 1742 it was intended to base field administration on the precedents of Marlborough's campaigns. The records of the War Office and the regimental agents were applied to in order to ascertain what these had been, but the facts were elusive and the service did not admit of delay. The army commander, John, Earl of Stair, was hurried away without the business having been settled, and he soon discovered that things were already on a far different and adverse footing.[56] The army's quarters were proving to be much more expensive than they had been in Queen Anne's time, baggage horses were twice the price, and the captains of dragoons were angry that, having been given the honour of serving His Majesty overseas, their annual grass money income had been disrupted. Complaints poured into Stair's headquarters, setting him the unenviable task of trying to ease the service without departing too much from the old arrangements.

A satisfactory arrangement was not reached until 2 October 1744, when Field Marshal George Wade issued a regulation of stoppages from his headquarters at Huy. This authorised a stoppage of 6d *per diem* from the pay of every non-commissioned officer and private man of the dragoons from the day the army took the field until the day it went into winter quarters. The declared reason for this stoppage was to offset the cost of a daily horse ration of forage, consisting of

Table 3.3 *Warrant for Regulating the Necessary Stoppages from Weekly Pay,*
29 April 1732 (PRO. WO 26/18 f. 78)

In winter quarters or in the house

				Remains to be paid weekly
Dragoons				
Sergeant, full pay per week			15s 9d	
Deductions { To his landlord Diet	3s 6d			
Hay and Straw	3s 6d	7s 0d		
For corn		1s 5½d		
To farrier		3½d		
			8s 9d	7s 0d
Corporal and Drum each			12s 3d	
Deductions as above			8s 0d	3s 6d
Dragoon			9s 11d	
Deductions as above			8s 9d	1s 2d

At grass

Sergeant, full pay per week			15s 9d	
Deductions { To his landlord for Diet	3s 6d			
For grass	2s 4d			
To farrier		3½d		
To riding master		7d		
Grass money here aforementioned		1s 10½d		
			8s 7d	7s 2d
Corporal and Drum each			12s 3d	
Deductions as above			8s 7d	3s 8d
Dragoon, full pay per week			9s 11d	
Deductions { To his landlord for Diet	3s 6d			
For grass	2s 4d			
To farrier		3½d		
To riding master	7d		6s 8d	3s 2½d
Of which 3s 2½d there being paid to the dragoon weekly				1s 4d
there will remain				1s 10½d
Commonly called *Grass Money*				

Out of which the sergeant, corporal drum and dragoon may be furnished with all such necessaries as are not (by the Regulation for Cloathing) supplied by the colonel and pay 2s a year to the surgeon for medicines, out of which also such losses may be made good as may happen by exchange of money in the remittance of their pay. And it is humbly offered that the captains do find the dragoons with the aforementioned necessaries at the rate before set down, both in the house and at grass, taking the same at all hazards equally in all regiments and that they be required to acompt with them for the remainder within 14 days after the horses are taken up from grass.

Foot			Remains
Sergeant, full pay per week	7s 0d		
paid weekly	6s 0d		1s 0d
Corporal and Drum each	4s 6d		
paid weekly	4s 0d		6d
Private soldier	3s 6d		
paid weekly	3s 0d		6d

Out of which remainders of pay the captains may deduct for shoes, stockings, gayters, medicines, shaving, mending of arms, loss by exchange of remittance of their pay but nothing else except such things as may be lost or spoiled by the soldier's negligence and the captain is to accompt with them for the residue every two months.

sixteen pounds of hay, six pounds of straw and about three-quarters of a peck of corn, but during the summer these rations were supplied to the unit at zero cost, and the produce of the stoppage accumulated in the hands of the regimental agent. Fourpence of it was credited to the stock purse, and twopence reserved to answer the cost of camp necessaries for the next campaign. Additional stoppages were made of 1s 6d a month for the farrier, 5¼d a month for the paymaster and the same amount for the surgeon. Any balances were paid to the men, often considerably in arrear. A winter stoppage, also of 6d *per diem*, was made for any horse rations received, but if these were not actually supplied, the money was credited to the stock purse.

Meanwhile the non-commissioned officers and private men of the infantry were stopped 4d a week from the day they entered winter quarters to the day they took the field. This money was applied to offset the cost of camp necessaries, baggage horses and a pair of grey gaiters per man. The soldiers were to be accounted with for these stoppages at the regulation two-monthly intervals.[57]

These arrangements afforded the precedent for stoppages imposed during the Seven Years' War, but after 1758 the German campaigns of that conflict became so prolonged and expensive that the dragoon regimen almost broke down. The winter stoppage of 6d *per diem* was imposed whether forage was supplied or not, as part reimbursement to the Treasury for the initial cost of forming magazines. The outraged cavalrymen demanded credit of these sixpences and some colonels actually entered them in the stock purse accounts, but the Treasury would only agree to this in return for a *quid pro quo* of not charging the public for horses lost in action. The War Office dithered over this deal, then allowed the offer to lapse, and the war ended without the matter being resolved.[58]

5. Contingent bills and their regulation

It was axiomatic that many regimental contingent expenses would be paid out of internally generated income, but there was an additional range of charges that were entered in contingent bills and paid for out of parliamentary votes of contingencies or 'Extraordinaries of the Army.' These included:

1. A refund for costs incurred in troop movements;
2. The carriage of ammunition;
3. The cost of 'fire and candle' in quarters;
4. Payment for horses lost on service;
5. Payment for equipment lost on service;
6. The replacement of camp necessaries if the colonel had provided them in the first instance.[59]

In time of peace, expenditure on troop movements was usually the largest item in any contingent bill.[60] Deeply ingrained suspicion of the standing army had left it without its own means of transport, and for movement around the kingdom on strictly designated march routes it relied on the co-operation of the civil power and locally requisitioned rustic carts.[61] The rates of hire for these vehicles were fixed by successive Mutiny Acts; 1s a mile for the use of a cart and five horses or a wagon with six or four oxen, 5d a mile for a cart with four horses, and so on down the scale. In Britain it was possible to collate the cost of these marches against the routes laid down by the War Office, but in time of war the clerks only had time to check the computations.[62] They were in much the same situation when it came to reviewing other charges entered in wartime bills, sums of money which soon outran the modest sums for contingencies voted by Parliament in advance and which had perforce to be answered by retrospective votes of 'Extraordinaries of the Army'.

The bills submitted by regiments during the Seven Years' War were riddled with inconsistencies. After the war a few were subjected to close examination, '... but to very little purpose, as these matters seem to have gone upon an arbitrary footing, every agent giving a different price for the same article. This disagreement is not very easy to be accounted for, as there is no obvious reason why the cloak, the saddle, or any other article belonging to a dragoon of one regiment should cost more than the same article for the dragoon of another, excepting where there is a known difference in the equipment ... This being the case, it is useless to give any table of the price of replacing accoutrements lost on service, as there is no charge, however exorbitant, whereof there may not be found a precedent in the books of the office.'[63]

This was not the first time that confusion had been noted in the making up of contingent bills, but a determined attempt was now made to clarify which charges should be entered in them and which should be charged to the regimental banks. The Warrant for Regulating the Stock Purse Funds of the Regiments of Dragoon Guards, Dragoons and Light Dragoons of 19 February 1766, and the Warrant for Regulating the Non-effective Funds of the Several Regiments of Infantry, also of 19 February 1766, declared that no charge should be levied on the banks other than those incurred in recruiting, issuing bounty money to discharged soldiers to maintain them until they reached their home parishes, the cost of subsisting invalid soldiers pending their appearance before the Board of Governors of the Royal Hospital, Chelsea, fees attending pay warrants and the cost of reclaiming deserters. All oher expenses were to be entered in contingent bills, to be submitted to the War Office at midsummer and Christmas.[64] All expenses were to be entered under their true heads and nothing more charged than what had actually been paid. Only the customary charges were to be set down and no extraordinary charges would be accepted unless they were vouched for by an order from the War Office. All marches itemised in the bill were to be stated against the original order for making them. As an additional check on the system, all captains were to submit accounts of their contingencies to the regimental paymaster, to be scrutinised and vouched for by him, and then examined by the commanding officer and sent by him 'upon honour' to the War Office and the agent with a declaration that the account was accurate.[65]

6. 'Bat money' and camp necessaries

These were additional cash injections or issues of equipment to enable a regiment to take the field without damaging its economy.

Each company of foot had a requirement or a number of 'bat' or 'bas' horses to carry its equipment.[66] A company of seventy private men was allowed one animal, and a company of 100 two, plus a horse to carry the regiments's medicine chest. The allowance was issued in cash or kind. During the War of the Austrian Succession Captain Edward Johnson of the 33rd Foot received '... for himself and his company, a Bas Mare valued at £7 10*s* and £7 10*s* in money; and that he had his choice, either to take the mare, or the money at which she was valued ...'.[67] Supplications were made that there should be an allowance of £10 an animal, and this was the rate paid during the Seven Years' War. The original cost of the bat horses was answered out of the Extra-ordinaries of the Army, but after the first campaign it was understood that they would be replaced out of money from the winter stoppages.[68]

Camp necessaries comprised a multitude of essential and expensive items: tents, tent poles, tent pegs and mallets, camp kettles, canteens, hatchets, shovels, wheel barrows, drum cases, powder bags, knapsacks and haversacks. Regiments of cavalry also needed picket poles, nosebags, mangers, corn sacks, scythes, horse cloths and saddle covers.[69] This equipage was either furnished out of government stocks at HM Tower of London or provided by a contractor, who submitted his bill to the War Office together with a certificate of delivery provided by the colonel or his agent. In due course, the cost would be answered from parliamentary votes of Extraordinaries, but it was the custom for two-thirds of the cost of the equipment to be paid on account and the balance on delivery.[70] The repair and replacement of the equipment was intended to be paid for out of stoppages, unless it had either been lost in action or had been originally provided by the colonel, in which case details were to be inserted in the regiment's contingent bills. Any surplus money on the enterprise was understood to be a perquisite of the colonel.[71]

7. Other income

There were several additional sources of regimental income, some generated within the unit or obtained from the equivalent funds of other regiments, and some of which were entirely out of the purview of the War Office.

(i) Refunds for drafts

It was customary for regiments receiving drafts to refund the cost of the men to the parent corps out of their own non-effective funds. The price of men fluctuated according to the general availability of recruits, and it was sometimes necessary for the Secretary at War to appoint a senior officer to carry out the sensitive task of inspecting the drafts and determining the charge on the non-effective funds of the receiving units. It was entirely another matter whether the latter could stand the cost.[72]

(ii) Private credit

The most conspicuous use of private credit occurred after midsummer 1759 when a general dearth of recruits induced government to tempt ambitious officers with the bait of preferment in new units if they engaged to recruit men from their own resources. This they did, sometimes with minimal administrative competence, and at rates double the usual price of £5 a man. Over sixty independent companies of foot were raised by this method, and over thirty regiments (some of more than one battalion), into which many of the companies were later drafted. But, this massive exercise apart, it was already entirely routine for officers to subsidise their commands. For example, it was one of the distinguishing marks of a good colonel that he spent his own money on the regimental music, on additional clothing or accoutrements for his men, on superior-quality horseflesh, or board and lodging for his lowly paid subalterns. The captains also helped fund the regimental music, provided gratuities for a teacher to school the regiment's children and, most commonly, advanced their own money for recruiting or soldiers' necessaries, an outlay which it would take a long time to recoup from stoppages.[73]

At least one regiment had a private credit structure entirely separate from its public account. The 1st, or Royal, Regiment of Dragoons had had a private reserve fund since 1749, kept by the colonel, Lieutenant-General Henry Hawley, for emergencies and for recruiting the regiment, and which was nothing to do with the regimental paymaster or the captains. In 1759 there was a balance of £464 13s 2d in this fund.[74]

(iii) Subscriptions

The threat posed by the 'Forty-five' evoked a novel concern among the public for the soldiers defending it from Popish tyranny, and during the winter campaign of 1745–46 a subscription was launched by the Westminster and Middlesex Association to provide them with comforts. The parish of St James's also provided palliasses, while a committee presided over by the Lord Mayor of London and Samuel Smith of Old Jewry undertook to provide watch-coats, warm caps and waistcoats.[75]

Similar schemes were promoted during the Seven Years' War, affording relief to regimental funds as well as to the men. Samuel Smith was again prominent in a committee of peers and businessmen known as 'The Society for the British Troops Abroad and for the Orphans of Soldiers Slain in Battle'. At one time the society raised over £7,000 in three months, thanks largely to the merciless weather of January 1760. A consignment of long flannel waistcoats, woolly caps, gloves and half-gaiters valued at £3,700 reached the army at Osnabruck on 5 February. Ten thousand pairs of shoes were sent out to the army in North America in April 1760, with £500 in specie for charitable distribution. Another

£500 was sent to Germany for the relief of orphans belonging to the British contingent.[76]

8. The mustering system and the reform of 1747

Mustering remained the central problem of military finance. The Crown was determined that the captain should not be allowed to manipulate non-effective income for his own benefit. In theory, the continuance of his allowance of warrant men, his legitimate dividend and his personal arrears were dependent on his troop or company being kept 'complete' to the number expected to appear against the establishment. He was answerable to the service for every penny of public money passing though his hands,[77] and any attempt to embezzle it was regarded as '... a scandalous breach of trust'.[78]

Two administrative procedures were used in conjunction to enforce financial control: (i) monthly returns of the effective stength of the unit, made by the officers 'upon honour'; (ii) periodic musters by the civilian deputy commissaries.

The commanding officer of each corps was under a standing order to transmit a monthly return of effectives to the War Office, the peacetime equivalent of the wartime practice of submitting returns of effective strength to the brigade or army commander. Information obtained from returns had alerted George I to the weakened state of the army at the opening of the reign.

The returns were made by troop and company. By 1764 the commanding officers were also required to send a regimental abstract of returns to the Adjutant–General.[79] In Ireland, returns were sent to the Chief Secretary's office in the first post after the end of the month and were then forwarded to the Adjutant-General of Ireland.[80]

Apart from providing a regular statement of effectives, returns were also valuable in that they provided a running check on the muster rolls. These were taken in the quarters of each regiment or detachement by the Commissary General of the Musters or one of his small staff of deputy commissaries. Each of the deputies travelled a circuit of considerable extent, adjusted at rather infrequent meetings at the Commissary General's office. It was intended that each deputy should keep within his own circuit.[81]

Before 1747 musters on the British Establishment were made retrospectively every two months, covering periods of sixty or sixty-one days. After the system was reformed, they were made twice-yearly for 182 and 183 days and integrated with the general officers' reviewing circuits as already described.[82] In Ireland the deputies made four circuits *per annum*, setting out on the first day of January, April, July and October. This practice continued after 1747, regardless of the new method adopted in Great Britain.[83]

It was the intention that musters in the forces abroad should also take place every two months, but this proved impracticable. Governor Edward Cornwallis of Nova Scotia petitioned that it was impossible to enforce the system there and the reformed British method was adopted in 1751.[84] Deputy Commissary

The machinery of regimental finance

Thomas Pitcher, who experienced similar problems mustering Braddock's army in Virginia in 1755, requested that six-monthly musters be introduced in North America; Cumberland agreed, provided Braddock had no objection.[85] Deputy Commissary Richard Veal's retrospective musters of the British contingent in Germany during the Seven Years' War were also made on a six-monthly basis.[86] However, the two-monthly muster survived in the garrisons of Gibraltar and Minorca.[87]

On his arrival at quarters a deputy commissary was under instructions to advise the officers that he intended to commence mustering the next morning. He had the men drawn up, and called over the roll, satisfying himself that any absentees were either on furlough, on detached duty or sick, in which instance he collected a certificate endorsed by the regimental surgeon. By his oath of office he was obliged to 'respite' the pay of vacant officers and men, as well as anybody absent without leave.[88]

In Ireland it was also the custom to impose respites on the warrant men. These could only be lifted by paying a fee equal to two days' subsistence. Respites were also slapped on the pay of officers away recruiting in Britain, requiring the payment of a fee of £1 2s 6d per muster to have each one lifted. It was not unknown to find a respite imposed on the pay of an officer temporarily doing duty in another company. These practices were cynically referred to by the officers as 'The Country Exchange', and it was alleged that the income went straight into the pockets of the Muster-Master General and Clerk of the Cheque and the Chief Secretary, '... contrary to equity and justice, ... contrary to the opinion of any honest man of all men, those who gain by the fraud excepted'.[89] Lord George Sackville, Chief Secretary 1751–55, would be taunted with the memory of these exactions at the time of his disgrace in 1759.[90] Confusingly, respites in Ireland were known as 'cheques'.

After the muster, the deputy commissary closed the rolls 'with all convenient speed' and, after giving a copy to each captain, despatched another to the Pay Office, one to the Commissary General and one to the Comptrollers of the Accounts of the Army.[91] In Ireland one copy was left with the captain, one sent to the Chief Secretary and one delivered by hand to the Muster-Master and Clerk of the Cheque.[92]

The deputy commissary was bound by clauses in the Mutiny Act directed against false musters. If he connived at the falsification of the rolls he was liable to dismissal, a fine of up to £100 and was debarred from ever holding office under the Crown. As a check on his activities, he was obliged to summon the civil power, in the person of a Justice of the Peace or the local equivalent, to the muster ground in order to view the proceedings and countersign the completed rolls.

It will be remembered that some of the income of the regimental bank was obtained from the subsistence of real non-effectives between musters. As the musters were taken retrospectively, subsistence for the period of the muster had already passed through the captain's hands or into his pocket. If his unit was 'complete' on the muster day his credit would remain unharmed. If not, the respite was imposed on the growing income of his command. When the regiment was cleared at midsummer and Christmas, the respites were computed, charged back to the respective troops and companies, and deducted from credit of subsistence.[93]

Before 1747 there was only one method of getting respites lifted on the British Establishment, and that was by petitioning the Crown for permission to muster complete, regardless of gaps in the rolls which would then be solemnly filled with fictitious names in the Commissary General's office. In time of war, when regiments were liable to heavy drafting, this expedient was justified, although MPs were understandably dubious about it. In Ireland, predictably, the method of lifting 'cheques' was different. Muster rolls were lodged in the office of the Muster-Master and Clerk of the Cheque. Every three months, abstracts of them were issued to the Dublin agents, who memorialised the Castle for their regiments to be cleared. After the rolls had been examined and the necessary fees paid, some respites were lifted and the remainder accounted a saving to the public.[94]

The weakness of the unreformed system of mustering was that, as long as the unit was complete on the muster day, it was impossible to tell how long between the musters any vacancies had actually been allowed to stand and thus how much vacant subsistence had been engrossed by the captains. Worse, there was ample evidence from a comparison of muster rolls and returns to show that the former were not being compiled in the regulation manner.

Brief reference has already been made to the distinctly unsteady quality of the gentleman-amateur deputy commissaries. To the frustration of the Commissary General they frequently delayed the transmission of the rolls, ignored or forgot their instructions and, most damningly, introduced customary muster arrangements of their own. It was usual for them to accept the word of the officers that absent men were on furlough or detached duty, and it was rare for them to imspect the sick. There was also cause for concern over the payment to them by the troop and company officers of customary gratuities, a guinea or half a guinea per muster. There was more than a suspicion that this money was given in return for the favour of mustering the unit complete, but this was not a simple case of what today would be regarded as 'corruption'. Rather, it was a tacit recognition by the deputy commissary that without maximum benefit of vacant subsistence it was often impossible to fill up the troop or company more than once a year.[95]

Moreover, to be fair to the deputy commissaries, their task was by no means easy. Their circuits were too extensive for a two-monthly perambulation. A conscientious man might hardly have arrived home before he was obliged to set out again.[96] A regiment might arrive in his area without notice, obliging him to make an impromptu journey. He might completely miss a detachment marching from one station to another.[97] Frequently, on his arrival at regimental headquarters, he would find the officers unprepared, or the muster rolls drawn up wrongly.[98] It was virtually impossible for him to tell the difference between real soldiers and officers' servants who had been put into the ranks for the occasion. Criticisms of the officers were badly received by them. Justices of the Peace or mayors of boroughs, far from being eager to turn out and keep an eye on the nefarious doings of the military, frequently failed to turn up at the muster, obliging the deputy commissary to have the rolls endorsed later in chambers, thus flying in the face of the Mutiny Act. This was not only a feature of military life in the provinces, for even in London the Justices did not bother to turn up for musters of the Foot Guards, despite a payment of 10s a muster for a messenger.[99]

Even if a muster was completed correctly there were still obstacles to be overcome. The rolls travelled to London *via* commercial carriers, and while they were in transit they were at the mercy of the weather, including rain, which obliterated the contents.[100] The luckless commissary was equally at odds with the weather. During his winter circuit of 1757 Deputy Commissary Barrow reported from Norwich that '... the roads are as unfrequented now as the roads in Siberia. Deputy muster-masters, stage-coachmen and post-boys are the only persons who do face such weather: if I had been twenty years older I should have been found upright on the Norfolk Heaths, stiff and dead.'[101]

Such arduous work came as an unpleasant surprise to gentlemen seeking easy employment; they either paid a substitute or hired a neighbouring deputy to do the job. There was no check on the handwriting of the person who endorsed the rolls.[102]

Deficiencies in musters taken abroad were, if anything, even more glaring. The Commons committee on the land forces and Marines of 1746 heard allegations that the deputy commissary for Gibraltar was absent from his post, that the deputy for Minorca had last been seen in Bath and that no rolls had been received from Annapolis Royal for seven years.[103] The lack of any muster-master in New York had opened the door to incredible abuses,[104] while similar frauds were believed to be taking place in Georgia and the Carolinas.[105]

The revival of parliamentary interest in army affairs was an inevitable consequence of the deteriorating military situation. The European campaign of 1744 had been dismally uneventful. The great battle of Fontenoy on 11–12 May 1745, although glorious for the British contingent, had ended in a bloody tactical and strategic reverse. Prince Charles Edward Stuart's Jacobite army had destroyed Sir John Cope's forces at Prestonpans on 21 September 1745, brought the pick of the British army scampering home from Flanders, advanced to Derby and had then deftly withdrawn to the safety of the Highlands, leaving King George's generals, including his favourite son, the Duke of Cumberland, clutching at thin air. On 17 January 1746 the royal army suffered a fresh humiliation when Henry Hawley, a favourite of Cumberland, allowed himself to be caught napping at Falkirk. On 6 February the Hon. Alexander Hume Campbell moved for a House of Commons Committee to enquire into the state of His Majesty's land forces and Marines.

Oeconomy and discipline

This was the second Commons initiative on the army in less than a year. The first, an address to the throne on 8 April 1745, had been easily contained. Its objective had been to modify the mustering procedure in the Americas by allowing officers to present a document easier to obtain than a muster roll, but of equal validity, so putting a stop to the over use of the dubious expedient of mustering regiments complete. The Crown responded by issuing the Warrant for Regulating the Pay of the Forces in the Plantations of 17 September 1745. This instructed officers in America or the West Indies to remit, in lieu of musters, a certificate identical in form to a muster roll, but subscribed to by themselves on oath before the nearest civil magistrate, signed by two subordinate officers and accompanied by a statement of how the non-effective money had been spent.[106]

Campbell's proposal was much more sinister, however, for the committee's brief was extensive, touching on the distribution of money throughout the army, on mustering, clothing, recruiting and on numbers of effective men. The Secretary at War, Sir William Yonge, was apprehensive that the enquiry would broaden into a general assault on the King's administration. Cumberland agreed with him. He was well aware of weaknesses and shortcomings in the organisation of the army, but he was strongly of the opinion that parliamentary inquests were not the way to tackle them. He and Yonge hoped that enough friends of the administration and military MPs would turn up to keep the committee within bounds.[107]

The committee met for the first time at 5 p.m. on 6 February 1746 in the Speaker's chamber. Between then and 6 June, when its report was presented, it met frequently, calling for extensive documentation and listening to expert testimony. When it thought that its enquiries were being obstructed the committee did not lack toughness: on 14 April Edmund Jones, cashier to the Paymaster of Marines, was placed in custody for prevaricating in his evidence.[108] Ultimately, however, the report made very tame reading. It was little more than a survey of miscellaneous financial arrangements with virtually no analysis or comment, and as such it was left to lie on the table of the House. Only on one point had the committee come to any definite conclusion, namely that '... the method of mustering practised by the commissaries ... by no means appears to answer the intentions of the legislature'.[109] The inadequacies of the deputy commissaries had been cruelly exposed and it had been discovered besides that the Comptrolllers of the Accounts of the Army, who, according to their instructions of 1703, were supposed to keep the mustering machinery under review, had long since made only the most cursory inspection of the rolls, never checked the computations of respites and were currently preoccupied with examining the government victualling accounts.[110]

Cumberland's resounding victory over the rebels at Culloden on 16 April 1746 effectively wiped out any threat presented by the committee and its badly digested report, and early in 1747 the Duke and his advisers, Henry Fox and Colonel Robert Napier, formulated a scheme for musters which would comprehensively deter any fresh criticism. From now on, the deputy commissaries would make their circuits at six-monthly intervals. The dates on which any men joined or left the regiment were to be plainly indicated in the rolls, and any pay for the intermediate vacancies or 'broken times' was to be strictly respited. The new mustering cycle was to be integrated with the general officers' reviewing circuits, and the generals, after perusing the regimental accounts, were to give their opinion as to whether any respites should be lifted. All customary gratuities to deputy commissaries were forbidden.[111]

This package was received with approbation by the House of Commons and inaugurated in a circular to deputy commissaries issued by the Commissary General on 15 June 1747. Substantial sums in respites quickly showed up in the records.[112]

Unfortunately, however, the long-term results of the reform fell well short of what had been hoped. The Commissary General's venal and essentially amateur staff was neither increased in number nor improved in quality and, as the procedure for compiling the rolls had actually been made more complicated by the reform, blunders proliferated. Military events then intervened to further undermine the new regime. When extensive operations began in North America during 1755–56 it quickly became impossible, notwithstanding the heroic efforts of Commissaries Pitcher and Billings, to satisfy even the minimum requirements of a civil muster laid down by the warrant of 17 September 1745. In the West Indies it was complied with rather longer, but once island-hopping campaigns began in 1758 it became increasingly difficult to lay hold of civil magistrates in front of whom muster rolls could be sworn.

Such failures to comply with the requirements of a muster immediately put the officers' arrears in jeopardy, and a clamour broke out for the 'impracticable warrant' to be waived. This concession was granted to units in North America on 2 August 1758.[113] Meanwhile, as war-fronts broadened, the regular mustering machinery was faced with disintegration even at home. One night in May 1758 Deputy Commissary Thomas Sadleir missed the tide at Lymington and with it the last chance of mustering the expeditionary force then assembling in the Isle of Wight until Deputy Commissary Richard Veal caught up with elements of it at Osnabruck in 1763.[114] By that time the only units on the British Establishment still being cleared by means of muster rolls were the garrison companies of Invalids.[115] For all other formations, warrants were issued to the Paymaster General authorising him to make out debentures (certificates of the amount of pay due to a unit in a particular period), which were then transmitted to the Secretary at War, who prepared additional warrants enabling the regiments to be cleared. To satisfy the forms of office, spurious muster rolls were fabricated in the Commissary General's office or taken, as in the case of Veal's trip to Germany, for long periods in retrospect, using the regimental books. As a corollary to what the War Office clerk Philip Francis called 'this scandalous farce', units in the field were subsisted on the basis of current lists of effectives and, from about midsummer 1757, all non-effective balances were carried forward from year to year until it could be decided what access to them should be enjoyed by the proprietary captains, presently empty-handed.[116]

9. The regulation of dividends, 1749–66

The prospect of netting a legitimate, open-ended dividend from the management of his command was the distinguishing mark of the proprietary soldier, whether he was the colonel of a regiment or the humble captain of a troop or company, but, in the case of the latter, it was about to enter a terminal decline. The dividend issue was broached in a detailed questionnaire submitted by Henry Fox to a Board of General Officers who were also colonels of regiments of dragoon guards and dragoons on 2 May 1749. The generals were asked to comment on a proposal that there should be a fixed annual allowance out of the stock purse to captains for contingencies, and to state what should then be done with any balance in the account.[117] On 9 May the Board responded by recommending a contingent allowance of £25 *per annum*, resolving in addition that provided sufficient money was reserved in the account of each troop to recruit three horses each spring at £21 apiece, any surpluses should be paid to the captains as a dividend. However, having sounded his generals' opinion on this point, George II specifically dissented from it, and his Warrant for Regulating the Necessary Stoppages from the Regiments of Dragoon Guards and Dragoons of 19 June 1749 established the rule that stock purse balances should be automatically carried forward. Reviewing generals were instructed to see that this was done.[118]

Although the contingent allowance of £25 *per annum* was not embodied in the wording of the 1749 warrant, the generals' recommendation was evidently adhered to[119] until the Seven Years' War, when it was augmented to £35. A claim by the captains that an additional £65 *per annum* was required to offset the high cost of campaigning in Germany was not admitted.[120] The Warrant for Regulating the Stock Purse Funds of the Regiments of Dragoon Guards, Dragoons and Light Dragoons of 19 February 1766 conceded a peacetime dividend of £30 *per annum*, but there was to be no return to the custom of flexible, open-ended allowances.[121]

The captains of foot, poorly remunerated in contrast to their comrades in the cavalry, were by implication more deserving of their dividends. This was recognised in the Warrant for Settling their Recruiting Accounts, issued by George II from his wartime H.Q. at Hanau on 24 August 1743. Subject to a drawback of £5 for every man wanting to complete the unit to establishment, any non-effective balances were divided among the captains after the annual adjustment of the account on 24 June.[122]

The provisions of the 'Hanau Regulation' were reaffirmed by the Duke of Cumberland on 18 June 1750,[123] but it was not intended that the captains should have such generous access to the substantial non-effective balances building up after midsummer 1757 while the army was cleared by debentures, all the more so as it was believed that the non-effective accounts of regiments serving abroad, especially in North America, had been very loosely kept.[124] Instead, the Warrant for Applying the Non-effective Balances of the Regiments of Infantry of 17 March 1761 stated that, in the units now serving abroad, the balance of any non-effective account would in future be divided *equally* among the captains up to a limit of £30 to each captain whose company consisted of 100 private men, and in proportion if the company was at a lower establishment. In the regiments serving at home the ceiling was reduced to £20 or less, and all surpluses were brought to account as a saving to the public.[125] The Warrant for Regulating the Non-effective Funds of the Regiments of Infantry of 19 February 1766 reinforced this trend towards restricted dividends by directing that, after £5 had been set aside for every man wanting to complete the unit at the spring review, any non-effective balances would be shared equally by the captains up to a maximum of £20 *per annum*, and entered as the final charge on the non-effective account.[126]

Throughout this time the liquidation of the large wartime balances had been going forward. On 23 November 1767 the regimental agents were ordered to refund any balances oustanding from midsummer 1757 to midsummer 1765, subject only to unsettled claims under the provisions of the 1761 warrant.[127] A final adjustment was made on 30 March 1768. This supplemented the 1761 warrant by authorising a dividend of £100 on the account of every company which had served abroad for the duration of the war, £80 for every company which had served partly abroad and partly at home, and £60 for a company which had remained in Great Britain. This money was to be shared between the captains who had commanded each company from midsummer 1757 to midsummer 1765 according to their periods of service, and was regarded as their final recompense. All captains who had received payment under the terms of the 1761 warrant were debarred from entering a new claim unless the money they had already been allowed was not equal to their fair share under the new settlement.[128]

Notes

1 *Fifth Report of the Commissioners Appointed to Examine, Take and State the Public Accounts of the Kingdom*, 28 Nov. 1781, *Journals, H.O.C.*, XXXVIII, p. 576
2 Fortescue, *History*, II, p. 589
3 PRO. WO 1/609 f. 185, Maj. Gen. John Adlercron, colonel of the 39th Foot, to W. Hamilton, 30 Oct. 1761.
4 The 'Poundage Warrant', which was entered in the establishments, authorised the Paymaster General to deduct 'twelve pence out of every twenty shillings' passing through his hands. The money was applied to a number of purposes, notably fees owing to the officers of the Exchequer for monies issued for the pay of the army. Part of the balance was used to maintain the Royal Hospital, Chelsea.
5 *Committee Report* (1746), pp. 76–7. Cavalry subalterns had the larger allowance.
6 PRO. WO 4/18 f. 222, William Pulteney, Secretary at War, to the Commissary General of the Musters, 11 Aug. 1716; R.A. Cumb., C.Vol.9/1, Report of a Committee (of the Irish House of Commons) appointed to Enquire into the

Application of Money granted for the Support of the Military Establishment, 1751–67, 16 Feb. 1768.

7 See below, pp. 147–57.

8 General account based on: PRO. SP 41/48 f. 357, 'On the Manner of Paying the Army', n.d., *temp.* George II; BL. Add. MSS. 40,759, 'Francis Report', f. 223; PRO. WO. 30/105, 'Custom and Practice of the Army concerning Off-reckonings', 25 April 1772; *Fifth Report of the Commissioners Appointed to Examine, Take and State the Public Accounts of the Kingdom*, 28 Nov. 1781, *Journals, H.O.C.*, XXXVIII, pp. 575–76. The allowance of widows' men had been raised to two per troop or company by 1718; *Abstracts of the Number and Yearly Pay of the Land Forces*, p. 6.

9 BL. Add. MSS. 17,495 f. 40, Calcraft to James, Lord Tyrawley, 11 June 1760. The purpose of Calcraft's exposition was to refute any idea that he had large balances in his hands. During the War of American Independence, however, it is known that some agents carried very large regimental balances indeed; *Tenth Report of the Commissioners for Examining*, 2 July 1783, *Journals H.O.C.*, XXXIX, p. 545.

10 *Ibid.*, p. 525

11 For a full study of the agent and his business see A. J. Guy, 'Regimental Agency in the British Standing Army, 1714–1763', *Bulletin of John Rylands University Library of Manchester*, LXII, 1980, pp. 423–53, LXIII, 1980, pp. 31–57.

12 *Abstracts of the Number and Yearly Pay of the Land Forces*, p. 5. The full pay *per diem* of the sollicitor was 4s and the subsistence 3s; *The Succession of Colonels of All His Majesties Land Forces from their Rise to 1742*, London, 1742.

13 The implications of these bargains are explored below, pp. 143–6.

14 Scouller, *Armies of Queen Anne*, pp. 135–6.

15 J. Hayes, 'The Military Papers of Colonel Samuel Bagshawe', *BJRL*, XXXIX, 1956–57, p. 373.

16 PRO. WO 26/16 f. 197, Circular to regimental agents, 13 May 1721. The officers who opted to keep their agencies were allowed to dispose of their commissions at the regulation price.

17 Some case histories are sketched by Guy, *art. cit.*, *BJRL*, LXII, pp. 425–31.

18 DRO. D86.X3, 'Articles of Co-partnership between John Calcraft and James Meyrick in the Business of Agents to Regiments', 27 Sept. 1763; Guy, *art. cit.*, *BJRL*, LXIII, pp. 42–6.

19 Hayes, 'Bagshawe Papers', pp. 377–9.

20 See below, pp. 122–3.

21 'The Amorous Agent and Miss Bide', *Town and Country Magazine*, October 1769, a satire on 'Crafterio' (John Calcraft) and his weakness for actresses.

22 Guy, *art. cit.*, *BJRL*, LXII, pp. 449–50.

23 *Memoirs and Anecdotes of Philip Thicknesse, late Lieutenant Governor of Landguard Fort*, London, 1788, I, pp. 68–9. The agent Henry Popple advanced six months' salary to Thicknesse without agency deduction after the latter inadvertently gave the entire contents of his pockets to chairmen after a heavy night out in Covent Garden, '. . . and the name of Popple has ever since been respectable in my ears'. This was just as well, for Popple went disastrously bankrupt in 1739; Guy, *art. cit.*, *BJRL*, LXII, pp. 434–7.

24 'Copy of the will of the late Lieutenant General Huske', *Gents. Mag.*, XXXI, 1761, p. 22. I am grateful to my colleague, Mr Peter Boyden, of the Department of Records, National Army Museum, for bringing this reference to my attention.

25 R. W. Chapman ed., James Boswell, *Journal of a Tour to the Hebrides with Samuel Johnson, LL.D,.*, Oxford 1930, p. 381.

26 BL. Add MSS., 17,495 f. 120, John Calcraft, regimental agent, to Lt.–Col. Commandant John Hale, 18th (Light) Dragoons, 28 Aug. 1760.

27 PRO. WO 4/56 f. 520, William, Viscount Barrington, Secretary at War, to Lt.–Col. Cyrus Trapaud, 3rd Foot, 1758.

28 JRL. B2.2.251, Lt.–Col. Matthews Sewell, 39th Foot, to Major Samuel Bagshawe, 13 Feb. 1749.

29 *Committee Report* (1746), p. 95. See below, p. 144.

30 PRO. WO 4/57 f. 447, Barrington to Maynard Guerin, regimental agent, 2 April 1759.

31 SRO. HA 174.1206.36.293, Considerations on the Case of Capt. Robert Shafto, 1759; PRO. WO 4/61 f. 487, Barrington to Henry Fox, Paymaster General, 25 July 1760.

32 'J. Railton', *The Army's Regulator or the British Monitor*, London, 1738, *passim*.

33 Some cavalry regiments divided their stock purses into recruiting and remounting funds; *Committee Report* (1746), p. 128.

34 These impositions were usually small; BL. Add. MSS. 40,759, 'Francis Report', f. 261.

35 *Committee Report* (1746), pp. 121–31, *passim*. This system did not operate in the regiments of Foot Guards. Guardsmen campaigned abroad in detachments, and the companies on active service incurred much heavier charges than those on metropolitan duty at home. Equity was obtained by forming a general account for each regiment, charging up the total cost of all recruiting and making an equal division of any balance among the captains; HUL. DDHO4.142, William, Second Earl of Albemarle on the Non-effective Accounts of the Regiments of Foot Guards, *c.* 1748; *ibid.* 149, 'Some Remarks on the Non-Effective Fund of the Guards', *c.* 1748.

36 PRO. Adm 96/3 f. 425, Attested copy of 'His Majesty's Order of the 24th of August 1743 for settling the Recruiting Accounts of the Infantry' given in camp at Hanau, and not entered in the War Office warrant books.

37 PRO. WO 26/21 f. 369.

38 PRO. Adm 96/3 f. 425, Attested copy of a warrant from the Duke of Cumberland affirming the 'Hanau Regulation', 18 June 1750.

39 PRO. WO 4/28 f. 257, Circular to colonels of fourteen regiments of foot, allowing them to be mustered complete and authorising a grant of £120 each for levy money, 27 April 1727.

40 *Committee Report* (1746), pp. 76–7.

41 PRO. WO 4/18 f. 222, William Pulteney, Secretary at War, to the Commissary General of the Musters, 11 Aug. 1716.

42 Twenty-six fictitious names were continued in each troop. They were distributed as follows; six to the colonel, two to the first lieutenant-colonel, one to the second lieutenant-colonel, one to the the cornet, one to the guidon, three to the four exempts, one to the four brigadiers, one the the four sub-brigadiers, one to the adjutant, one to the riding-master, four to the agent, two to the widows and two to the 'superannuated gentlemen'; *Committee Report*, (1746), p. 100.

43 PRO. WO 24/529, Establishment of Guards and Garrisons, 1747. The full pay of six private men per troop was substituted as a recruiting fund in lieu of fictitious names. An augmentation was made to the pay of the officers, an exception to the usual rule; PRO. WO 4/45 f. 7, Henry Fox to the Lords Commissioners of the Treasury, 16 May 1748. For long-standing peculiarities in the administration of the Horse Guards see J. L. Pimlott, 'The Reformation of the Life Guards, 1788', *JSAHR*, LIII, 1975, pp. 194–209.

44 PRO. WO 4/20 f. 261, James Craggs the Younger to the Lord Lieutenant of Ireland, 10 September 1717; WO 4/35 f. 225, Sir William Yonge to the Lord Lieutenant of Ireland, 6 November 1739; PRO. WO 8/56 f. 7, Warrant to the Lord Lieutenant, 2 April 1740. This arrangement was confirmed by a royal letter of 18 July 1749 and

reaffirmed by George III on 20 April, 1763; R.A. Cumb. C.9/1, 'Irish Committee Report', 1768.

45 PRO. Adm 96/3 f. 425.

46 *Committee Report* (1746), p.121. In Sir John Ligonier's regiment of horse, one contingent man appeared in the stock purse account of each troop, but the other was paid direct to the captain, *ibid.*, pp. 120–7.

47 *A Treatise on Military Finance*, attributed to John Williamson, London, 1782, p. 10.

48 See below, pp. 142–3.

49 R.A. Cumb C44/147, 'Memorandums for Dragoons, humbly proposed by Genl. Hawley to HRH', *c.* 1748–51; PRO. WO 71/9 f. 66, Report of a Board of General Officers whose members were colonels of regiments of dragoon guards and dragoons, 9 May 1749.

50 PRO. WO 27/4, Inspection Returns, 1756–57.

51 PRO. WO 26/15 f. 26; *ibid.*, f. 134.

52 J. Railton, *The Army's Regulator*, pp. 2–3.

53 PRO. WO 26/16 f. 145.

54 PRO. WO 26/18 f. 78.

55 PRO. WO 26/21 f. 369.

56 PRO. SP 87/10 f. 225, Heads of a Memorial from the Paymaster General, 17 Dec. 1742.

57 BL. Add. MSS. 41,148 f. 114, Orderly Book of the English Forces, 1744; *Committee Report* (1746), pp. 97–9.

58 BL. Add. MSS. 32,896 f. 82, John, Marquess of Granby, commander of the British contingent in Prince Ferdinand's army, to Newcastle, 25 Sept. 1759; *ibid.*, f. 268, Barrington to Newcastle, 4 Oct. 1759; PRO. WO 4/62 f. 93, Barrington to Granby, 12 Sept. 1760; BL. Add. MSS. 40,759, 'Francis Report', f. 247.

59 *Ibid.*, f. 251.

60 *Loc. cit.*

61 R.C. Jarvis, 'Army Transport', *Collected Papers on the Jacobite Risings*, I, Manchester, 1971, pp. 48–74.

62 BL. Add. MSS. 40,759, 'Francis Report', f. 251.

63 *Loc. cit.*

64 *A Collection of Regulations, Orders and Instructions formed and issued for the Use of the Army*, London, 1788, pp. 163–70.

65 Instructions for making out Contingent Bills, 20 Nov. 1765, Simes, *Military Medley*, pp. 47–8; PRO. WO 4/1044 f. 51, Circular from Col. Edward Harvey, Adjutant General, on compiling contingent bills, Jan. 1766.

66 A 'bat' in this context was a pack-saddle, hence 'bat' or 'bas' horse.

67 *Committee Report* (1746), p. 99.

68 BL. Add. MSS. 40,759, 'Francis Report', f. 243.

69 *Ibid.*, f. 259; JRL. B2.1.114, Camp Equipage for Col. Samuel Bagshawe's 93rd Foot, 19 June 1760.

70 PRO. WO 4/35 f. 551, Sir William Yonge to Maj.-Gen. John Armstrong, 7 May 1740.

71 *Committee Report* (1746), p. 99.

72 See below, pp. 126–7.

73 PRO. WO 4/1044 f. 59, Col. Edward Harvey, Adjutant-General, to Col. Robert Cunninghame, Adjutant-Gerreral of Ireland, 6 Feb. 1766.

74 PRO. WO 27/6, Inspection Returns, 1758–59.

75 At least £5,000 was raised for 'the poor soldiers'; R.A. Cumb. C7/221, Samson Gideon to Sir Everard Fawkener, 3 Nov. 1745; *ibid.*/22, James Waller to Fawkener, 30 Nov. 1745; *ibid.*/271, Smith to Fawkener, 17 Dec. 1745.

76 PRO. WO 34/100 f. 76, Advertisement for Subscriptions, 10 Jan. 1760; *ibid.* f. 74,

Samuel Smith to Maj.-Gen. Jeffery Amherst, 16 April 1760; *ibid.*, f. 78, William Thomas to Amherst, 17 April 1760; *ibid.*, f. 90, same to same, enclosing an octavo volume giving details of the subscription and how the money was spent. (This enclosure has not survived.)

77 JRL. B2.2.186., Major Samuel Bagshawe. 39th Foot, to Capt. Francis Forde, 25 Sept. 1750.

78 PRO. WO 4/58 f. 500, Barrington to Maynard Guerin, regimental agent, 5 Sept. 1759.

79 BL. Add. MSS. 40,579, 'Francis Report', f. 228.

80 *Standing Orders* (Ireland), p. 32, 16 Dec. 1761.

81 PRO. WO 7/122 f. 132, J. Gumley, Commissary General, to Deputy Commissary Peter Davenport, 18 Nov. 1727; WO 7/123 f. 191, Commissary General's circular to deputy commissaries, 20 March 1756; *Committee Report* (1746), p. 115.

82 PRO. AO 16/3, Computations of Musters, 1745; WO 7/122, Commissary General's Circular to deputy commissaries, 15 June 1747. See above, pp. 33–4.

83 PRO. WO 8/99, Lord Lieutenant of Ireland's warrant to the Muster Master General and Clerk of the Cheque, 9 April 1744; *ibid.*, same to same, 12 Feb. 1748; *Standing Orders* (Ireland), p. 35, 20 Dec. 1751; R. A. Cumb. C. Vol. 9/1, Irish Committee Report, 1768.

84 PRO. WO 7/123 f. 24, Thomas Gore, Commissary General, to the deputy commissary for Nova Scotia, 25 Nov. 1751.

85 PRO. WO 7/123 f. 104, Henry Fox, Secretary at War, to Thomas Gore, 10 April 1755.

86 PRO. WO 7/124 f. 13, John Calcraft, Deputy Commissary General of the Musters, to Barrington, 17 July 1760.

87 PRO. WO 25/3211, Computations of Musters, 1748–49.

88 BL. Add. MSS. 40,759, 'Francis Report', f. 222.

89 R. A. Cumb. C61/B12, 'Military Memorandum on Irish Affairs, picked up by a Lover of Truth from One to Another', 1749–50 'and after.'

90 *Consolatory Letter to a Noble Lord*, London, 1760, pp. 35–6.

91 *Committee Report* (1746), p. 114.

92 *Standing Orders* (Ireland), p. 36, 20 Dec. 1751.

93 *Committee Report* (1746), p. 128.

94 JRL. B2.2.263., Lt.-Col. Matthews Sewell, 39th Foot, to Major Samuel Bagshawe, 20 Feb. 1752; R. A. Cumb. C. Vol. 9/1, Irish Committee Report, 1768.

95 PRO. WO 7/122 f. 95, J. Gumley, Commissary General, to Deputy Commissary Richard Cullyford, 10 March 1724; *ibid.*, f. 111, Commissary General's circular to deputy commissaries, 26 July 1736; *ibid.*, Thomas Gore, Commissary General, to Cullyford, 4 Aug. 1747; *ibid.*, same to same, 18 Jan. 1748; WO 7/123 f. 298, Robert Napier to Gore, 24 May 1758; *ibid.*, f. 299; John Hesse, First Clerk in the Commissary General's office, to Deputy Commissary Ayliffe; *Committee Report* (1746), pp. 114–19. For some interesting observations on the difficulty of keeping a company complete without full advantage of vacant pay between musters, see the marginal notes in the Bodleian Library copy of J. Railton, *The Army's Regulator or the British Monitor*, London, 1738, (Bod. 8°, Rawl. 579), pp. 71–5.

96 PRO. WO7 123 f. 104. Hesse to Deputy Commissary C. Balderston, 27 April 1756.

97 *Committee Report* (1746). p. 117; PRO. WO7/123 f. 27, Commissary General's circular to Deputy Commissaries, 20 June 1751.

98 PRO. WO 7/123 f. 185, Deputy Commissary Barrow to Hesse, 18 Feb. 1756; *ibid.*, f. 242, Deputy Commissary George Overend to same, 4 Feb. 1757; WO 7/124, Deputy Commissary Thomas Sadleir to same, 4 Jan. 1761.

99 *Committee Report* (1746), pp. 114–19.

100 PRO. WO 7/123 f. 83, Deputy Commissary Overend to Hesse, 15 March 1754; *ibid.*,

f. 317, Deputy Commissary William Hope Wier to Hesse, 25 Oct. 1758.
101 PRO. WO 7/123 f. 240, Barrow to Hesse, 15 Jan. 1757.
102 *Committee Report* (1746), pp. 115, 118.
103 *Ibid.*, p. 115.
104 S. M. Pargellis, 'The Four Independent Companies of New York', *Essays in Colonial History presented to Charles M. Andrews by his Students*, New York, 1933.
105 These stories should be treated with care, for they were propagated by a gentleman anxious to be made one of two muster masters for North America and the West Indies; BL. Add. MSS. 32,709 f. 126, J. Hammerton, Secretary to the Council of South Carolina, to Andrew Stone, Private Secretary to the Duke of Newcastle, Secretary of State, October 1746.
106 PRO. WO 26/20 f. 292, Warrant for Regulating the Pay of the Forces in the Plantations, 17 Sept. 1745.
107 R. A. Cumb. C10/115, Sir William Yonge to Cumberland, 8 Feb. 1746; C11/16, Sir Everard Fawkener, to Yonge, 20 Feb. 1746. The committee members are listed in *Journals, H.O.C.*, XXV, pp. 57, 90, 99.
108 *Ibid.*, pp. 65, 67, 77, 79, 123–4, 157, 166.
109 *Committee Report* (1746), p. 119.
110 *Ibid.*, pp. 119–20; PRO. 30/8/76 f. 7, 'Observations relating to the Office of Comptroller of Accounts of the Army', n.d. (1746?).
111 For the decision-making process see DRO. D86.X3, Henry Fox to Col. Robert Napier, 27 Feb. 1747, 17 March 1747, 3, 10, April 1747. The clause prohibiting deputy commissaries accepting gratuities was inserted in the *Articles of War* for 1748; PRO. WO7 2/2. In HUL. DDHO4.149 there are printed *Instructions for Making Out Musters Rolls*, 1756, and a *Pattern of a Muster Roll*, intended for the instruction of deputy commissaries. A more accessible guide to the format of the new rolls is provided by Deputy Commissary George Overend's 'Instructions for Making Out Muster Rolls' in Capt. Robert Hinde's *The Discipline of the Light Horse*, London 1778, pp. 359–70.
112 PRO. WO 7/122. Circular from the Commissary General to Deputy Commissaries, 15 June 1747. For sums of money respited see PRO. WO 25/3211, Computations of Musters, 1748–49. In a 182 day muster of Lord George Sackville's 20th Foot, taken at Glasgow on 15 July 1749, Sackville's own company had respites imposed to the value of £34 16s; the lieutenant-colonel's company, £28 19s 4d; Major James Wolfe's company, £35 5s 8d, and the remaining seven companies amounts between £18 19s 4d and £30 3s 8d.
113 BL. Add. MSS. 17,494 f. 174, John Calcraft, regimental agent, to Brig.-Gen. William Whitmore, 8 June 1758; PRO. WO 26/23 f. 458, Warrant for suspending the Warrant of 17 Sept. 1745 regulating the pay of the forces in America, 2 Aug. 1758.
114 PRO. WO 7/123 f. 100, Sadleir to Hesse, 28 May 1758.
115 BL. Add. MSS. 40,759, 'Francis Report', f. 237.
116 *Loc. cit.*
117 PRO. WO71/9 f. 65, Henry Fox to the Judge Advocate General, 2 May 1749.
118 PRO. WO 71/9 f. 75, same to same, 22 June 1749; WO 26/21 f. 369. The members of the Board were Gen. Sir Philip Honywood, 1st Dragoon Guards (President), Lt.-Gen. Sir Charles Howard, 3rd Dragoon Guards, Lt.-Gen. Henry Hawley, 1st Dragoons, Lt.-Gen. the Earl of Crawford, 2nd Dragoons, Lt.-Gen. Humphrey Bland, 3rd Dragoons, Lt.-Gen. Sir Robert Rich, 4th Dragoons, and Lt.-Gen. Sir John Cope, 7th Dragoons.
119 PRO. WO 4/48/20, Circular from Henry Fox to regimental agents of dragoon guards and dragoons, 23 March 1751.
120 Paper on the allowances for contingencies by Lt.-Col. Flower Mocher, 3rd Dragoon Guards, 1760, annexed to PRO. WO 4/64 f. 399, Charles Townshend, Secretary at

War, to the Marquess of Granby, 21 May 1761.

121 *A Collection of Regulations*, pp. 163–4.
122 PRO. Adm 96/3 f. 425, Attested copy of 'His Majesty's Order of the 24th of August 1743 for settling the Recruiting Accounts of the Infantry'.
123 PRO. Adm 96/3 f. 425, Attested copy of a warrant from the Duke of Cumberland affirming the 'Hanau Regulation', 18 June 1750.
124 BL. Add. MSS. 40,759, 'Francis Report', f. 237.
125 PRO. WO 26/24 f. 387.
126 *A Collection of Regulations*, pp. 176–8.
127 PRO. WO 26/27 f. 448.
128 PRO. WO 26/28 f. 6.

4

Personal pay and private perquisites

The income of field officers, captains and subalterns

On 22 July 1752 Alexander Duroure, recently appointed colonel of the 38th Foot, joined his regiment in St Johns, Antigua. He brought with him special orders from the Duke of Cumberland to inspect the regiment and report on its condition, which was notoriously poor. It had been sent to the Leeward Isles in 1707 and had rarely been out of trouble since. Its recruits had died 'like rotten sheep'. Many of the effective men carried on civilian occupations, subsidising their comrades to stand their guards for them. The island's legislature, entrusted with the responsibility of caring for the men, had neglected to do so; their quarters were squalid and the barracks were falling down. Officers who could find an excuse for not joining the corps stayed well away from it. The late colonel, Lieutenant-General Robert Dalzell, had defrauded the men of their clothing and had been cashiered. The regimental agent, Captain Alexander Wilson, had gone bankrupt, leaving the regimental accounts in a state of utter perplexity. Altogether, reported Duroure, '... There is not a regiment in His Majesty's service whose condition is more to be lamented'. Being a man sensitive about the honour of the army, what moved him most was the plight of his subalterns. Most of them, he discovered, were younger sons, '... at a time of their life when their experience has taught them little oeconomy'. Their situation was worsened by the high cost of lodging and provisions in the islands. Some of them had kept up appearances only with the help of well-disposed residents. Others, horrible to relate, '... after pinching long in dread of such a catastrophe betook themselves to employments which elsewhere would not be thought compatible with their rank or duty'.[1]

In this and the following chapter we will explore the circumstances in which such a humiliating state of affairs could come about, assessing the value of personal pay and customary dividends against the background of administrative reform explored in the previous chapter, and examining conditions of service where attractive investments and proprietary incomes threatened to dwindle to nothing.

In order to put the officers' career prospects in perspective, however, we must first know a little more about their origins.

1. Officer material

There were no formal educational requirements to trouble the head of the aspiring officer, a deficiency which some observers thought made a bad contrast with the growing professionalism of the Royal Navy.[2] However, as the land forces were believed to pose a greater constitutional threat than naval forces, criteria governing the choice and preferment of officers were social rather than intellectual. The opinion of Henry Pelham on this subject, as voiced in Parliament in December 1744, prefigured the more notorious pronouncements of the Duke of Wellington: 'I have always heard it admitted that our liberties can never be in danger as long as they are entrusted to men of family and fortune, and the reason is obvious as well as unanswerable. The security of property must always depend on the preservation of liberty. Under a despotic government there is neither property nor liberty, for every man's estate, as well as his life, depends upon the rapine of an arbitrary sovereign. Has not then a man of fortune more reason to avoid such a melancholy predicament than a man of no estate? Has it not always been with good reason urged that our liberties are in no danger from our standing army because it is commanded by men of the best families and fortunes?'[3]

The implication contained in Pelham's speech, that the best places in the military hierarchy would be reserved for men of birth and fortune, was in general correct. Most colonelcies were held by men of noble birth or independent means, who gave their sons in large numbers to officer their regiments at lower grades, and this made them the most influential officer-producing group in the army.[4] The price of commissions and the expenses of command were thus not of overwhelming importance to this group. Nevertheless, the existence of such a social elite should not lead us automatically to assume that as a breed these officers were 'wealthy, idle and corrupt'.[5] Superior patronage–leverage and '. . . connections [which] in a constitution like that of England must ever be submitted to' imposed heavy obligations on those promoted young to high command,[6] while strict family settlements which kept landed property secure in the grasp of the firstborn thrust siblings into the world armed only with life annuites and the hope of obtaining genteel yet profitable office.[7] Neither these gentlemen nor their parents would be entirely indifferent to such mundane issues of income and expenditure, as may be seen in the concern shown by Lord Hardwicke over the mounting expenses of his Coldstream Guardsman younger son, Joseph Yorke.[8]

Moreover, from the time of the unprecedented expansion of the regular army under Queen Anne onward, most regimental commissions were held by officers who were gentlemen by virtue of a modicum of education, rather than by money and acres. This mixed grouping (which, by the Seven Years' War, included representatives of families which had been supplying officers to the army for several generations) comprised men from the middle classes (sometimes cadets of good families who had branched out earlier into trade and commerce), sons of the clergy, a significant number of sons of Huguenot refugees, a growing number of Irishmen, a contingent of old and experienced subalterns drawn from the ranks of the non-commissioned officers, and the ubiquitous Scotsmen, who by the mid-1760s were providing the army with between a fifth and a third of its officers. The dictum enunciated by Henry Pelham meant that their prospects of rising high in the service were less bright than those of the elite; rather, they lived with their battalions and by dint of long and patient service made those battalions into a formidable war machine. Rates of personal pay, the prompt payment of arrears and the annual division of non-effective balances were matters of understandable concern to such men.[9]

2. Investing in command

There were two basic methods of investing in command. The first, and most common, was to purchase a commission in a regiment and promotion thereafter. The second, which became widespread in the latter part of the Seven Years' War, was to raise a quota of recruits without government levy money. The only other method of obtaining promotion was to seek opportunities of service where local commanders had authority to fill up vacant commissions without purchase. Alternate periods of war and peace during the period meant that the majority of officers obtained preferment by a combination of these methods, although they were only entitled to sell those commissions they had actually purchased. The base value of the commission was that it represented a capital sum that could be realised on the officer's retirement from the service.

At the beginning of the eighteenth century the British army was the only army in Europe which operated a system of merchandising commissions through all the regimental grades. The traffic and originated in the high Middle Ages when groups of military entrepreneurs had pooled their cash resources to recruit soldiers for the king in return for pay and plunder, the distribution of which was governed by the amount each person had first laid out. In time, each rank in a band or company had an associated monetary value, and could be disposed of like a share in some more humdrum commercial venture. From 1684 the state benefited directly from this traffic by extorting buyers' and sellers' premiums of five per cent (gleanings which were assigned to the upkeep of the Royal Hospital, Chelsea), and there was also a more general and indirect benefit to the state in that as long as superannuated officers could generate capital by disposing of their commissions, it was relieved of any obligation to provide them with pensions. But, from the reign of William III, the Crown increasingly took the view that a network of private treaties, engagements and interests in the army detracted from its authority. From 1695 to 1700 trading in commissions was forbidden by statute, and from 1693 to 1695, and from 1705 to 1711, it was interdicted by royal warrant. Traffic was kept going, however, thanks to the overwhelming desire of existing commission-holders to protect their property rights, and for much of Queen Anne's reign, royal policy wavered between complete prohibition and the issuing of various regulations governing the disposal of commissions, such as preventing them being purchased on behalf of juveniles (1705), refusing to allow officers who had sold out once to buy in again, only allowing officers to sell after twenty years' service, or raising the buyers' and sellers' premiums to 12*d* in the £ (1711).

Coming from the German states, where the custom of purchase and sale of commissions was in decline, George I strongly favoured the policy of prohibition. His uncompromising view was that officers who had become unfit for service should either be dismissed or relegated to half pay to make way for fitter candidates, and so intense was his aversion to '... the abuse of buying and selling commissions like other merchandise'[10] that his Secretaries at War were extremely reluctant to submit proposed deals for consideration.

Such inflexibility did not long prevail, however. A combination of discontent among the officers, promotion stagnation in the regiments and sheer inability to suppress so widespread a custom led to the policy of prohibition being replaced on 21 February 1720 by one of regulation. The centrepiece of this policy was an official tariff of commission prices from subaltern to colonel (a considerable innovation in itself), a declaration that no officer should involve himself in choosing his successor by private negotiation, a declaration that commissions could only be sold to officers next in rank and an insistence that no man should be commissioned captain until he had been ten years a subaltern.[11] In March 1722 the drive against over-regulation prices was intensified by the demand that colonels should guarantee that officers buying into their regiments did so only at the regulation prices.[12]

The 1720 tariff stated prices as high as £9,000 for a regiment of horse to as little as £170–£200 for an ensigncy in a marching regiment–not perhaps the bargain-basement price levels of the War of the Spanish Succession, but not too exorbitant a first step for the younger sons of impoverished gentry and offering, at £66 18*s* 4*d per annum*, a distinctly more attractive prospect than some miserable curacy at £20 or less. To rise farther through the commissioned ranks, the young officer either purchased by laying out the difference between the price of his existing grade and the next, or obtained preferment gratis on active service. Thus, although Major William Burrard of Colonel William Gooch's American regiment loathed his meat saturated in brine and salt, his bread which swarmed with maggots as it lay upon the table '... and the water here that fluxes us all', he still wished that his younger brother George had ventured out with him to the West Indies in 1741, for had he done so '... he must now have been an old first lieutenant, we are in so great want of young gentlemen to fill up vacancies'.[13] In time of peace this bonanza of preferment came to an abrupt halt, resulting in immediate commission price inflation and stagnant promotion opportunities.[14] Towards the end of the century this factor became more acute, and it was stated that between the termination of the American War of Independence in 1783 and the year 1787 not a single promotion was made in the army without purchase.[15]

3. Personal pay and subsistence

The robust survival of the purchase system into the eighteenth century in the face

Table 4.1 *Daily pay of each rank in the Horse and Horse Grenadier Guards*

| | Horse Guards | | | | | | Grenadier Guards | | | | | |
| | Full pay | | | Subsist | | | Full pay | | | Subsist | | |
	£	s	d	£	s	d	£	s	d	£	s	d
Captain and colonel	1	16	0	1	7	0	1	10	0	1	2	6
Lieutenant and lieutenant-colonel {1st	1	11	0	1	3	3						
{2nd	1	7	0	1	0	6	1	2	6	0	17	0
Cornet and major (H.G.), major (G.G)	1	6	0	0	19	6	1	0	0	0	15	0
Guidon and major	1	4	0	0	18	0						
Exempt and Capt. (H.G.), Lieut and Capt. (G.G.)	0	16	0	0	12	1	0	17	0	0	13	0
Brigadier and lieut. (H.G.), sub-lieut. (G.G.)	0	11	0	0	8	2	0	10	0	0	7	6
Guidon and captain							0	16	0	0	12	0
Sub-brigadier and cornet	0	6	0	0	4	0						
Chaplain	0	6	8	0	5	0	0	6	8	0	5	0
Adjt. and lieut (H.G.), sub-lieut. and adjt. (G.G.)	0	11	0	0	8	0	0	7	0	0	5	6
Surgeon	0	8	0	0	6	0	0	8	0	0	6	0

Table 4.3 *Full pay* per annum *of commissioned officers on the British Establishment* (*Army List*, 1740)

| | Horse | | | Dragoon Guards, Dragoons, Light Dragoons | | | Foot Guards | | | Foot and Marines | | |
	£	s	d	£	s	d	£	s	d	£	s	d
Colonel and Captain	748	5	0	638	15	0	711	15	0	438	0	0
Lt-Col and captain	538	2	6	447	2	6	520	2	6	310	5	0
Major and captain	492	15	0	374	2	6	447	2	6	273	15	0
Captain	392	7	6	282	17	6	301	2	6	182	10	0
Lieutenant	273	15	0	164	5	0	142	19	2	85	3	4
Cornet	255	10	0	146	0	0	–			–		
Ensign, 2nd and 3rd Lts	–			–			106	9	2	66	18	4
Quartermaster	155	2	6	100	7	6	73	0	0	85	3	4
Chaplain	121	13	4	121	13	4	121	13	4	121	13	4
Adjutant	91	5	0	91	5	0	73	0	0	73	0	0
Surgeon	109	10	0	109	10	0	73	0	0	73	0	0
Surgeon's mate	–			–			63	17	6	63	17	6

Table 4.2 Pay and subsistence per diem of the officers of HM land forces on the British and Irish Establishments (*Army List*, 1740)

	British Establishment								Irish Establishment					
	Horse		Dragoon Guards, Dragoons, Light Dragoons		Foot Guards		Foot and Marines		Horse		Dragoons		Foot	
	Pay £ s d	Subce £ s d	Pay £ s d	Subce £ s d	Pay £ s d	Subce £ s d	Pay £ s d	Subce £ s d	Pay £ s d	Subce £ s d	Pay £ s d	Subce £ s d	Pay £ s d	Subce £ s d
Colonel and captain	2 1 0	1 11 0	1 15 0	1 6 6	1 19 0	1 10 0	1 4 0	18 0	1 18 0	1 8 9	1 11 4	1 3 8	1 4 6	18 4
Lt.-Colonel and captain	1 9 6	1 2 6	1 4 6	18 6	18 6	11 6	17 0	13 0	1 5 0	19 1	19 4	14 7	16 6	12 6
Major and captain	1 7 0	1 1 6	1 0 6	15 6	14 6	18 6	15 0	11 6	1 2 6	17 11	17 4	13 1	13 6	10 4
Captain	1 1 6	16 6	15 6	11 6	16 6	12 6	10 0	7 6	17 0	13 0	12 4	9 2	9 6	7 1
Lieutenant	15 0	11 6	9 0	7 0	7 10	6 0	4 8	3 6	10 6	8 0	6 2	4 9	4 6	3 4
Cornet	14 0	11 0	8 0	6 0	–	–	–	–	8 6	6 8	5 2	3 1	–	–
Ensign, 2nd or 3rd Lts	–	–	–	–	5 10	4 3	3 8	3 0	–	–	–	–	3 6	2 10
Quartermaster	8 6	6 6	5 6	4 0	4 0	3 0	4 8	3 6	5 0	4 8	3 0	2 9	–	–
Chaplain	6 8	5 0	6 8	5 0	6 8	5 0	6 8	5 0	6 8	5 0	6 8	5 0	6 8	5 0
Adjutant	5 0	4 6	5 0	4 6	4 0	3 0	4 0	3 0	–	–	–	–	4 0	3 0
Surgeon	6 0	4 6	6 0	4 6	4 0	3 0	4 0	3 0	4 0	3 0	4 0	3 0	4 0	3 0
Surgeon's mate	–	–	–	–	2 6	2 0	2 6	2 0	–	–	–	–	2 6	2 4

of attempts to suppress or curb its pervasive influence was a reminder of the mercenary origins of professional officership. The military entrepreneur still looked for a cash return from his investment comparable to an income from stocks[16] and, from time to time, even enthusiastic soldiers pondered whether they would be better off sinking their reserves of cash in some less demanding enterprise.[17]

The first point of reference for estimating the value of the investment was the going rate of personal pay. In 1766 the Board of General Officers fixed a new commission price tariff by first determining a reasonable price for subaltern ranks and then estimating the increase in prices through the grades after the rate of £100 for each shilling of personal pay *per diem*.[18]

Daily and annual rates of pay of officers of land forces and Marines are stated in Tables 4.1–3. These rates had not changed in essentials since the reign of William III and only marginal improvements were made during our period to the pay of some grades on the Irish Establishment.[19]

In 1759 the social statistician Joseph Massie assessed the income of the majority of military officers at £100 *per annum*, equal to that of the better sort of freeholder and 'persons professing the law', and comfortably above the £60 for 'persons professing liberal arts' or the £50 *per annum* of the inferior clergy, but well below the £200-£600 of the merchant or even the income of many prosperous tradesmen.[20] After stoppages and delays in the payment of arrears, the annual income of many officers dropped well below the figure of £100. It was thought that in general the pay of the officers of the Horse and Foot Guards was fixed at a generous enough level, as also the pay of many grades in the horse and dragoons, but that the pay of the officers of the marching regiments, upon whom the burden of conquering and garrisoning the Empire chiefly fell, was distinctly meagre.[21] Dr Roy Porter has recently estimated that it required £300 *per annum* to keep a Georgian gentleman in any style;[22] the full pay of a captain of foot was only £182 10s *per annum*. An ensign's full pay meanwhile was only £66 18s 4d.

Computing his 'Scheme of an Ensign's Constant Expenses' for publication in 1768, Captain Thomas Simes allowed his young officer a personal balance of £15 17s 7d *per annum*, and that only on an assumption that arrears would be paid (Table 4.4).[23] In a later variant, Simes allowed his ensign to eat supper, which reduced the balance to a dismal £8 2s 11d.[24]

Social pressures made it virtually impossible for a young gentleman to exist on such a regimen. Sooner or later he would be obliged to return compliments received from comrades of ampler fortune, or pay his share of the regimental mess bills. Lieutenant Nicholas Delacherois (9th Foot) lived in terror of these 'extraordinary expenses'. On duty in Dublin '... with strange officers and gentlemen ... I have been obliged to live in the same manner with them,' he complained. 'My eating here costs me my pay.'[25] In the 23rd Foot, Ensign Percival Stockdale and his friends found it impossible to bear the cost of messing with the captains and formed a mess of their own, which they soon bankrupted by calling for too much port wine.[26]

Table 4.4 *The Scheme of an Ensign's Constant Expenses* (Captain Thomas Simes, *The Military Medley*, London, 1768, pp. 197–8)

	By a day			By a week			By 4 weeks			By 52 weeks		
	£	s	d	£	s	d	£	s	d	£	s	d
Breakfast	0	0	6	0	3	6	0	14	0	9	2	0
Dinner	0	1	0	0	7	0	1	8	0	18	4	0
Wine and Beer	0	0	6	0	3	6	0	14	0	9	2	0
Four shirts, four stocks, four handkerchiefs a week	0	0	2	0	1	2	0	4	8	3	0	8
Four pairs of stockings, two nightcaps a week	0	0	1	0	0	7	0	2	4	1	10	4
Hair powder, pomatum, soap, blackball, pens, paper, ink, wax, wafers	0	0	2	0	1	2	0	4	8	3	0	8
Soldier to dress your hair, shave you, etc	0	0	1	0	1	0	0	4	0	2	12	0
Total	0	2	6	0	17	11	3	11	8	46	11	8
Your subsistence										54	15	0
Balance										8	3	4
Yearly Arrears										7	14	3
Total Balance										£15	17	7

Pecuniary embarrassment did not end with meat and drink. Captain Simes published an awesome list of things requisite for active service, many of which would be needed even for a summer camp at home.[27] No man could expect to furnish this immense kit out of an annual balance of eight or fifteen pounds (Table 4.5). When he was ordered to America in the spring of 1771, Ensign Jeremy Lister (10th Foot) had no choice but to call on his fond parent for aid. He warned his father that his equipage would 'amount to a great deal more than you expected'. He spent £36 6s 7½d on a profusion of small but important items, all of which, he was assured, would be much dearer in the colonies; these included thirty-six pairs of silk-thread worsted stockings, six pairs of shoes and one of boots, six cotton nightcaps, two hats, a cane, shaving utensils, a pocket glass, scissors, gloves, curling irons, an inkstand, sealing wax and papers. A fusil and sword cost five guineas more, and his regimentals another fifty.[28] It is not to be wondered at that in these circumstances there were numerous applications for advances of pay in regiments ordered abroad. Not every parent could afford to provide his son with an equipage valued at £400 (including two horses and a brace of silver-mounted pistols), as did Lord Townshend when his son George went out as a volunteer to the Low Countries in 1742.[29] Even senior officers were sometimes hard pressed to equip themselves decently. In 1741 Captain William Burrard complained from Jamaica that 'our expenses here are so excessively high that we are as poor as Job', and he entreated his brother to send him a few shirts.[30]

Table 4.5 *A List of Things Necessary for a Young Gentleman to be furnished with upon obtaining his first commission in the Infantry* (Captain Thomas Simes, *The Military Medley*, London, 1768, pp. 195–6)

A suit of clothes
Two frock suits
Two hats
Two cockades
One Pair of leather gloves
Sash and gorget   all Regimental
Fuzee or espontoon
Sword, sword knot and belt
Two pairs of white spatterdashes
One pair of black tops
One pair of gaiters
One pair of boots

A blue surtout-coat
A portugal cloak
Six white waistcoats
One dozen of stocks
Eighteen pairs of stockings
1 black stock
One pair of leather breeches
Six pairs of shoes
Two dozen shirts
Six towels
Three pairs of sheets
Three pillow cases
Six linen night caps

A field bed-stead, a pointed canvas bag to hold it, bed-curtains, quilt, three blankets, bolster, pillow, one mattress and a palliass. These articles should be carried in a leather valise; a travelling letter-case, to contain pens, ink, paper, wax and wafer; a case of instruments for drawing; and Muller's works on fortification etc. It is also essential that he have a watch, that he may mark the hour exactly when he sends any report.... If he is to provide a tent, the ornaments must be uniform, according to the facings of the corps.

It was hardly to be expected that government would pay any particular regard to the interests of individual officers in this matter. An order for foreign service sent them scurrying to buy their field equipage. If the order was countermanded, then it was up to them to make what bargains they could with the men going in their places.[31] The provision of horses was another case in point. It was very useful, even for an infantryman, to keep one or two horses on campaign to carry his equipment and sometimes himself. It is hard to imagine how the sickly James Wolfe and his brother Edward would have trudged into Germany through knee-deep snow in Feburary 1743 without the nag they purchased between them.[32] But, at the end of a war, when the sole objective of the government was to bring regiments home as cheaply as possible, these privately owned beasts were expendable. Only the major and adjutant, whose duty in action required them to be mounted, were permitted to embark a horse on the transports.[33] All other steeds had to be disposed of in a depressed market without any government compensation. Expensive animals were virtually given away, a situation which bore especially hard on the captains and subalterns of marching regiments, 'the sinews of the army'.[34] Meanwhile the circumstances of war itself were scarcely friendly to valuable personal equipment. Successful actions were characterised by a general dumping of gear, and unsuccessful engagements correspondingly more so,[35] while even a daily march was potentially hazardous for the 'little field equipage'. 'Frank Townsend has had his cart broke down,' sniggered Lieutenant-Colonel Charles Russell of the 1st Foot Guards, 'and all his baggage in the dirt. It has cost him four pounds to have it repaired, and he says he now begins to be sensible of the pleasures of his profession.'[36]

Moreover, lest it be thought that captains and subalterns of foot were the only sufferers by lowly amounts of pay, rates of subsistence of 11s 6d *per diem* for a major of foot, and 13s for a lieutenant-colonel (both inclusive of 7s as captain of a company), were clearly not in proportion to their responsibilities. In the habitual absence of the colonel they commanded the battalion, they were obliged to cut some sort of figure socially and had paternal obligations towards their fledgling subalterns that extended to entertaining them at table, yet, at the beginning of 1749, James Wolfe, newly appointed major of the 20th Foot, was moved to complain, 'I'm half undone with these expenses. The common demand for my horses, servants, washing, lodging, diet is no less than £3 10s a week. Judge then what there is left over for my things not less requisite of £15 a month.' He found himself no better off as lieutenant-colonel and was greatly disheartened by the prospect of foreign service. 'If,' he confided in his mother, 'we are ordered on board the fleet, either to cruise, or to Virginia, it will be absolutely necessary that I get myself furnished with a quantity of coarse shirts, and how to do it I really am at a loss to know, and if we were to take the field I should be totally ruined. This is the state of my affairs – I am eight-and-twenty years of age, a lieutenant-colonel of foot, and I cannot say I am the master of fifty pounds.'[37] His father, Lieutenant-General Edward Wolfe, himself an officer of very restricted means, promised help and gave his son a letter of credit, but his period as Quartermaster General to Sir John Mordaunt's attack on Rochefort (September 1757) left him with a new debt of £200, and as he prepared to go to America in 1758 he looked forward gloomily to spending another £500 or £600.[38]

More evidence of penury is provided by Lieutenant-Colonel Samuel Bagshawe of the 39th Foot. It is taken from a period when he was not engaged in active service, merely attempting to live honourably in a home posting in Ireland and carry out the duties associated with his rank. He had survived the loss of a leg during St Clair's raid on L'Orient (September 1746), and had obtained the lieutenant-colonelcy of the 39th with the help of a loan of £1,000 from his uncle. Many men raised money in this way, and without a private income to support their pretensions once in place they were at a chronic disadvantage. Some time during 1749 Bagshawe drew up his accounts for his uncle's benefit, possibly in the hope of changing the character of debts which

Table 4.6. *Lieutenant-Colonel Samuel Bagshawe's account of his income and expenditure* (JRL. B2.3.148, Bagshawe to his uncle, William Bagshawe of Ford, undated draft, *c*.1749)

My yearly income as subsistence paid me as Lt Col being money I can depend on is	£229	2*s*	11*d*
My arrears for the year, the payment of which is uncertain is	£ 51	14*s*	2*d*
£51 08*s* 10*d* true arrears			
	£280	17*s*	1*d*
Payments to be discharged by the above income:			
Interest of £1,000 at 5 per cent being £50 English is Irish money	£ 54	3*s*	4*d*
Ditto of £350 at 5 per cent at £17 10*s* English is Irish money	£ 18	19*s*	2*d*
Allowance to my sister at £30 English	£ 32	10*s*	0*d*
	£105	12*s*	6*d*
The keeping of two Horses, shoeing etc upon an average of 3*s* a day is	£ 54	15*s*	0*d*
Whenever I am in Dublin, I am obliged to keep two servants on account of my horses, in the country I keep one: their wages, board and clothes upon an average is	£ 34	12*s*	6*d*
Lodging when in Dublin (which as the government are generally attended by one Field Officer of a regiment I suppose half the year) at a Pistole, that is 18*s* 3*d* a week	£ 24	14*s*	6*d*
Coach and chair hire when in Dublin at a Pistole a week	£ 24	14*s*	6*d*
Coals and candles, about	£ 4	10*s*	0*d*
A new cane for my leg every year four guineas is is			
	£145	17*s*	0*d*
	£251	10*s*	0*d*
Supposing the arrears paid, there remains for my own diet, clothes and other expenses	£ 29	7*s*	1*d*
The method of an officer's diet in general is breakfast at his own lodging, dinner and supper in a tavern. I will suppose his breakfast 6*d*, dinner 13 pence (no officer dines cheaper in any part of the kingdom), supper and different kinds of drinkables one day with another two shillings and sixpence			
The diet of one day will be 4*s* 1*d* which for a year is	£ 74	10*s*	5*d*
A suit of regimentals a year is	£ 20	0*s*	0*d*
A frock suit with several pair of breeches as I wear them out fast occasioned by the cane of my stump leg is	£ 13	10*s*	0*d*
Five shirts coarse and fine and stocks	£ 6	0*s*	0*d*
Four pairs of stockens	£ 2	11*s*	5½*d*
Two pairs of shoes	£	10*s*	10*d*
Washing and mending my linen	£ 6	10*s*	0*d*
Books, Pen, Ink, Paper and other trifling articles	£ 10	0*s*	0*d*
	£133	12*s*	8½*d*

Expenses exceed the income *£104* 5s 7½d

now stood at £1,600 (Table 4.6). His conclusion was that by going nowhere except to his duty and treating nobody, he would still exceed his annual income by £104 5*s* 7½*d*.

Soon afterwards Bagshawe became engaged to Miss Catherine Caldwell, sister of Sir James Caldwell of Castle Caldwell, Co. Fermanagh. The young lady's portion was £2,000 settled to her advantage; in addition, the Dowager Lady

Caldwell agreed to pay off £350 owed by Bagshawe in Dublin. The marriage took place on 25 March 1751 but failed to bring an end to Bagshawe's financial problems. He found himself unable to pay his uncle an instalment of interest on his debt, while the high cost of establishing a home in Dublin, a journey to London to solicit preferment and his bride's ill-health soon added £200 to his liabilities. Although domestic expedients prevented his finances from failing completely, Bagshawe was in dire straits until he inherited the manor of Ford from his uncle in 1757.[39]

The part of gentleman and field officer was equally hard to play even for men with more substantial resources at command than Samuel Bagshawe. On inheriting the estate of Hebburn near Gateshead in 1726, Major Cuthbert Ellison of the 8th Dragoons turned the management of the manor over to his careful brother Henry and, in the best traditions of the mounted arm, devoted himself to expensive horseflesh, made a flashy tour as *aide-de-camp* to the Lord Lieutenant of Ireland and, to add spice to life, lengthy visits to the western spas in search of a cure for his hypochondriacal 'old disorder'. He was unable to do this without 'tolerable credit' from home, and, although he assured Henry that he took as little as he could from Hebburn, 'as small a share as perhaps any person who has the name of gentleman can of such a fortune in England', years of being bailed out of quarters made his position 'almost desperate'. Debt service swallowed the greater part of his income, and he was eventually obliged to sell part of his estate to secure the remainder. In bleaker moments he began to think the quality of gentleman a great inconvenience.[40] As Ensign Thomas Erskine (1st Foot) acidly remarked, 'Officers in the army, even in the most subaltern grades, have the misfortune to be considered as gentlemen which in England, as in other countries, implies a denomination of persons who from accidental circumstances of office or property are divided from the common herd of mankind and are obliged to form a barrier between those two orders, (as there is none in nature), by the luxuries of dress, equipage and attendance, but as the superfluities of life are the only props to this order of society, it is evident how distressing it must be to be installed in it unfurnished with the very article to which it owes its existence.'[41]

Professor Geoffrey Holmes has recently argued that notwithstanding the modest sums involved (Table 4.7), half pay provided the officer temporarily out of service with a lifeline, ensured the cohesion of a military profession and provided the state with a pool of military talent and experience against any future emergency.[42] For many old and wounded officers who had chosen not to realise the capital value of their commissions or lacked one to sell, a transfer to the half-pay list in the room of a fitter man offered the only tangible reward they were likely to receive for their services apart from one of the limited number of commissions in the Invalids or lieutenant-governerships of petty garrisons.

Half pay was used to provide a retainer for future services as early as 1641. It was at first an act of royal grace and favour, but in 1699 the House of Commons took notice of it, and from that time onward attempted to lay down rules as to who

Table 4.7 Half pay per annum of the officers of HM army on the British and Irish Establishments (Army List, 1740)

	British half pay						Irish Half pay					
	Horse		Dragoon Guards, Dragoons, Light Dragoons		Foot and Marines		Horse		Dragoons		Foot	
	pd.	py.	pd.	py.	pd.	py.	pd.	py.	pd.	py.	pd.	py.
	£ s d	£ s d	£ s d	£ s d	£ s d	£ s d	£ s d	£ s d	£ s d	£ s d	£ s d	£ s d
Colonel	13 0	237 5 0	13 0	237 5 0	12 0	219 0 0	19 0	346 15 0	12 6	228 2 6	12 3	223 11 3
Lt.-colonel	11 0	200 15 0	10 0	182 10 0	8 6	155 2 6	11 3	205 6 3	9 8	176 8 4	8 3	150 11 3
Major	11 5	209 17 6	8 0	146 0 0	7 6	136 17 6	8 6	155 2 6	8 8	158 3 4	6 9	123 3 9
Captain	7 0	127 15 0	5 6	100 7 6	5 0	91 5 0	5 3	95 16 3	6 2	112 10 10	4 9	86 13 9
Lieutenant	5 0	91 5 0	3 0	54 15 0	2 4	42 11 8	4 3	77 11 3	3 1	56 5 5	2 3	41 1 3
Cornet	4 6	82 2 6	2 6	45 12 6	—	—	—	—	2 7	47 2 11	—	—
Ensign, 2nd, 3rd Lts	—	—	—	—	1 0	33 9 2	2 6	45 12 6	—	—	1 9	31 18 9
Quartermaster	3 0	54 15 0	2 0	36 10 0	2 0	36 10 0	2 6	45 12 6	1 6	27 7 6	—	—
Adjutant	—	—	2 0	36 10 0	2 0	36 10 0	—	—	2 0	36 10 0	2 0	36 10 0
Surgeon	—	—	2 0	36 10 0	2 0	36 10 0	—	—	2 0	36 10 0	2 0	36 10 0
Chaplain	3 4	50 16 8	3 4	50 16 8	3 4	50 16 8	3 4	50 16 8	3 4	50 16 8	3 4	50 16 8

might be eligible for it, besides urging the Crown to lower the cost of the army by appointing half-pay officers to vacant commissions wherever possible. Meanwhile the half-pay list was increasingly being used as a refuge for shattered officers, and proper objects of mercy were actually nominated to it by the House of Commons. This trend was intensified with the influx of disabled officers from the War of the Spanish Succession and ratified by the House in April 1719, when the King was authorised to make use of funds voted for half pay to relieve '. . . such officers who were maimed or lost their limbs in the late wars, or to such others as by reason of their long service or otherwise His Majesty shall judge to be proper objects of charity'.[43] By 1749 the character of the half-pay list as a retired list was so well established that it was possible for enemies of the Duke of Cumberland to make good headway with the argument that by seeking to extend the provisions of the Mutiny Act and Articles of War to officers on half pay he was threatening a group of veterans who should be left in honourable repose.

There were some modest pension facilities available in addition to the half-pay list, notably a Compassionate List for deserving cases such as veterans without a commission they were entitled to sell. Persons on the list were paid out of a surplus in the half-pay fund. Each grant was regarded as a particular act of grace and gave no precedent for any other payment.[44] It was also possible to place officers temporarily on the out-pension of Chelsea Hospital[45] or make use of such places in the royal gift as the Poor Knighthoods of Westminster.[46]

Some officers were allowed to retire on full pay. This inflicted damage on the regimental economy, as it was the responsibility of officers who had profited by the change to pay for it. A captain might agree to make his predecessor an allowance from the profits of the company; Captain John Wilson was obliged to part with £1,200 of his own money to make good and engagement with Major Cookman of the 23rd Foot during 1717–27.[47] Alternative arrangements included the junior officers of each grade making over a portion of their pay to support the pensioner,[48] or the youngest ensign or cornet serving entirely without pay.[49] The Duke of Cumberland strongly disapproved of these arrangements as a burden on the regiment but they were made nevertheless.[50]

4. Allowances, dividends and perquisites

There were number of allowances paid to officers for special duties and, more importantly, to enable them to take the field.

Subaltern officers in charge of working parties on the military roads in Scotland were allowed a bonus of 2s 6d *per diem*, although some of this money was intended to defray the extraordinary cost of building shelters for the men and bringing provisions into isolated areas.[51]

Officers of the royal army serving with the land forces of the East India Company were given bonus payments to put them on the same footing with the company's troops. These amounted to 2s *per diem* for a captain and 1s *per diem* for subalterns. Fortunately for them, these officers also had access to the opulent and confusing gratuities of 'batta', 'double batta', 'revenue money' and the 'bazar'.[52]

'Batta' was a cash allowance which enabled the officer to take the field. Regiments on the home Establishments had similar but less opulent allowances of 'baggage money' and 'forage money'. Baggage money was paid to officers at the beginning of the campaigning season in lieu of horses to carry their equipment. The allowance to subalterns was £3 15s, the allowance to regimental staff officers was £5, captains and field officers were allowed £7 10s, and colonels £8 5s. Forage money was paid in lieu of a certain number of rations per diem as determined by rank. Subalterns and staff offficers of the marching regiments were allowed 6d per diem (the equivalent of one ration of horse forage), captains were allowed five rations, majors seven, a lieutenant-colonel nine and a colonel seven (he was understood to give up four additional rations to his captain-lieutenant, who would otherwise have received only one). It was customary to pay two hundred days' worth of forage money per annum in two issues of a hundred days. If the money was issued at home, it was liable to a deduction of 2d in the £ for agency. Abroad, the money was provided from the contingencies of the army and would eventually be paid for out of parliamentary votes of Extraordinaries.[53]

Officers were understandably reluctant to talk too much about their annual dividends, or the method of obtaining them. In early Georgian Britain (as now) it was more natural to dwell on some loss, hardship or grievance, so that we hear a lot from Captain Charles Whitefoord (18th Foot) about being obliged to borrow out his credit and next to nothing about the 'pickings' he obtained from managing his company, or in later life, the 'pious fraud' of drafting tall drummer boys into the ranks to deceive the deputy commissary of the musters.[54] Likewise, the sufferings of the poor subalterns of the 38th Foot in Antigua made a great noise, but not so the profits made by their captains from non-effective money during the War of the Austrian Succession.[55]

A useful starting point for a discussion of dividends was provided in 1963 by I. F. Burton and A. N. Newman in their important study of the career of Sir John Cope. Taking account of varying circumstances dictated by patterns of service, they estimated that the annual 'profits' of a captain of foot during the War of the Spanish Succession averaged about ten per cent of the subsistence of his company.[56] This was roughly equivalent to £60 per annum, a substantial addition to a full pay of £182 10s. Even extending this estimate to regiments on a low peacetime establishment produces dividends of approximately £70 per annum for a captain of dragoons and £50 for a captain of foot, sums appreciably higher than the contingent allowance of £25 per annum from the stock purses of the cavalry after 1749 and the dividend ceiling of £20 per annum imposed on the infantry in 1766.

In practice, regimental custom, local circumstance and a dearth of personal accounts make it virtually impossible to chart the going rate of dividends, especially when we remember that the most potentially lucrative commands were those posted beyond the range of effective administrative supervision. Antigua

Table 4.8 *Extracts from the Stock Purse Account of Sir John Ligonier's 8th Horse,* 1744–45 (*Report of a Committee appointed to consider the state of His Majesty's land forces and marines,* 1746)

Captain Madan's Stock-purse	Dr.			Per contra	Cr.		
1744				1744			
To paid for Exchange of a Trumpet	7	14	4	By 366 Days Pay for Two Warrant-men, from the 25th April 1743, to the 24th April 1744, at 4*s* a Day	73	4	0
To 9 Troop-horses, at £31 5*s* 3*d* each	281	7	3				
To 13 Men recruited, at £6 15*s* 6*d* each	88	1	6	By One Man's Vacancy for the same Time, at 2*s*	36	12	0
	£377	3	1	By Non-effectives, to the 24 August 1743	27	13	10¾
				Ditto to 24 Dec.	50	2	5½
				Ditto to 23 Feb.	34	14	7½
				Ditto to 24 April 1744	21	0	7¾
				By Net Allowance for Two Horses killed at Dettingen	29	16	8
					273	4	3½
				Balance carried to next Year's Account	103	18	9½
					£377	3	1
1745				1745			
To balance the above Account	103	18	9½	By 365 Days Pay for Two Warrant-men, from the 25 April 1744, to the 24 April 1745, at 4*s* a Day	73	0	0
To Six Months Interest on ditto	2	12	6				
To complete the Recruitmen for last year	23	3	7	By One Man's Vacancy for the same Time, at 2*s*	36	10	0
To Three Trumpet-horses, at £16 each	48	0	0	By Non-effectives, to 24 Dec 1744	52	17	8
To another Trumpet-horse	14	17	6	Ditto to 23 Feb	13	17	9
To paid for a Troop-horse	21	15	9	Ditto to 24 April 1745	7	10	9¾
To paid for another Trumpet horse	25	0	0		183	16	2¼
To Five Troop-horses, at £31 0*s* 11½*d* each	155	4	9½				
To Three Men recruited, at £3 3*s* 3*d*	9	9	9	Balance carried to next Year's Account	220	6	5¼
	£404	2	8		£404	2	8

Table 4.8 – *continued*

Captain Armiger's Stock-purse	Dr.			Per Contra	Cr.		
1744				1744			
To balance the last Year's Account }	25	5	10¼	By 366 Days Pay for Two Warrant-men, from the 25th April 1743, to the 24th April 1744, at 4s a Day }	73	4	0
To Six Months Interest on ditto }	0	12	6				
To paid for Exchange of a Trumpet }	7	14	4	By One Vacancy for the same Time, at 2s a Day }	36	12	0
To paid for a Trumpet-horse }	29	15	0				
To Six Troop horses, at £31 5s 3d each }	187	11	6	By Non-effectives, to the 24 August 1743 }	42	2	6½
To 11 Men recruited, at £6 15s 6d }	74	10	6	Ditto, to 24 Dec	62	2	3½
				Ditto, to 23 Feb	34	11	6
	325	9	8¼	Ditto, to 24 April 1744	22	8	0
Balance carried } to next Account	35	0	7¾	By Net Allowance for Six Horses killed at Dettingen }	89	10	0
	£360	10	4		£360	10	4
1745				1745			
To a Hessian Trumpeter	5	19	0	By Balance of the above Account }	35	0	7¾
To complete the Recruits for last Year }	14	14	5½	By 365 Days Pay for Two Warrant-men, from the 25 April 1744, to the 24 April 1745, at 4s a Day }	73	0	0
To 5 men recruited this Year, at £3 3s 3d }	15	16	3				
To 5 Troop horses, at £31 0s 11½d }	155	4	9½	By One Man's Vacancy for the same Time, at 2s }	36	10	0
	191	14	6	By Non-effectives, to 24 Dec 1744 }	25	14	4½
To paid the Captain to Balance	14	19	9¼	Ditto to 23 February	12	19	11
				Ditto to 24 April 1745	23	9	4
	£206	14	3¼		£206	14	3¼

was believed to be profitable for the captains and Georgia likewise.[57] In New York the plundering reached outrageous proportions.[58] More representative, however, are the perquisites of officers serving in units subject to the constraints of muster and review, and where no obvious fraud was being attempted. Even here it must already be evident that the shortcomings of the mustering system prior to the 1747 reform makes it impossible to determine how much non-effective subsistence went straight into the captain's pocket without being registered in any troop or company account as a dividend: likewise, the payment of some or all of the allowance for contingent men with the subsistence of the company's effectives meant that this also need not have showed up in the accounts. Surviving non-effective accounts should be examined with these considerations in mind.

The most complete set currently available, extracts from which form the basis of Table 4.8, belong to Sir John Ligonier's 8th Regiment of Horse, and were submitted as evidence to the Commons committee of 1746 by the agent, Henry Taylor. The return on the six troops looks unimpressive. General Ligonier's personal troop had a deficit of £67 11s 1¾d in 1744 and £24 19s7½d in 1745. The lieutenant-colonel's troop had a deficit of £3 0s 2d in 1744 but a dividend of £18 15s 2¼d was paid in 1745. The major's troop was in deficit both years, £40 7s 2d and £64 4s 8½d respectively. Captain Madan's troop was in particularly dismal straits, £103 18s 9½d in deficit in 1744 and £220 6s 5½d in 1745. Captain Armiger meanwhile had a favourable balance of £35 0s 7¾d carried forward in 1744 and a dividend of £14 19s 9½d paid in 1745. Captain Stuart's stock purse registered deficits of £27 3s 4½d in 1744 and £108 1s 8d in 1745. The adverse balances were all carried forward.[59]

A far healthier picture is obtained from sequences of regimental abstracts of non-effective accounts of units serving in Great Britain during 1754–59. Here can be found balances of several hundred pounds, and in one regiment over £1,000.[60] However, it is important to remember that now, after the reform of mustering, amounts of non-effective subsistence were being more accurately assessed and the captains' access to their balances was either already restricted (as in the introduction of the £25 *per annum* contingent allowances in the cavalry after 1749) or was about to be, first by suspending dividends throughout the army (from midsummer 1757) and then strictly defining their peacetime range (1761–68). Money which once had passed almost unnoticed into the captains' hands, and which may well have pushed their incidental incomes up to and beyond the ten per cent of subsistence postulated by Burton and Newman, was now either reserved for regimental purposes, drawn back as a saving to the public or filched by those better placed to pocket it.[61]

5. Prize money

Prize money was a major attraction of the naval service, and a sea officer who hoisted his flag in a cruiser in time of war looked forward to easy and substantial pickings.[62] The only form of prize money routinely anticipated by officers of the land service was an allowance of part of the value of contraband seized in anti-smuggling operations.[63]

Officers of the army and Marines serving aboard the fleet took shares of prize money as commanders of detachments, but not a great deal of money was involved. Captain David Hepburne (39th Foot) made several cruises in the *Invincible* man-of-war in 1747 and 1748, but his prize money only came to £60–£70. Given the great discomfort and expense of shipboard life and Hepburne's ingrained pessimism, it is uncertain what this meant to him in real terms.[64]

Regulations for the division of prize money promulgated in 1740 were greatly to the advantage of commanders of HM ships, and captains of land forces and marines were reduced to sharing one-eighth of any booty with sea lieutenants and ships' masters. Lieutenants, ensigns and staff officers divided their one-eighth with such humble personnel as boatswains, gunners, pursers, carpenters, masters' mates and surgeons. A regulation of 7 July 1756 was almost identical to the warrant of 1740.[65]

Major foreign expeditions appeared to offer better pickings. Prize money for the army, classically associated with the storm or ransom of some rich city, was rarely awarded in our period. All the plunder taken by Amherst's army in Canada was reserved to the public.[66] It was doubly unfortunate therefore that on those occasions when 'His Majesty's most gracious present' was granted, juggling with the dividends resulted in bitterness, recrimination and a very uncertain reward.

Lieutenant-Colonel Samuel Bagshawe of the 39th, whose precarious finances were noted above, knew enough about fortunes to be made in Bengal to relish going there in 1754. He hoped to obtain '. . . ten thousand pounds'. 'My family wants it,' he declared. If he died, situated as he was at present, they would be reduced to poverty.[67] He took with him a regulation of prize money fixed by Admiral Edward Boscawen and a council-of-war aboard the *Namur* off Mauritius in 1748 in the (forlorn) hope of taking booty from Pondicherry. It was similar to the regulation of 1740, and, in an independent command such as Bagshawe hoped to obtain, would have produced a very respectable return. Bagshawe clearly expected similar arrangements to be made for the 39th.[68]

In the event he was foiled in his hopes of command and disabled by an infection which, with his habitual ill luck, cost him the sight of an eye and a trip home to England. The tremendous prospect opened by Robert Clive's compact with Mir Jafar and the overthrow of Suraj ud Dowla at Plassey (23 June 1757) was described instead by one of his subordinates, Lieutenant John Corneille. The immense sum of 25 lakhs of rupees was the prize. 'As we had no such precedent for such a gift falling to the land army,' reported Corneille, 'it was therefore necessary to settle the proportion each rank ought to have received. This certainly should have been done before we set out on the expedition when the prospect of money being but distant would have given justice a fairer play. But our hopes of success seemed then too great a chimera for us seriously to take into account.'[69]

Uncertainty rose when the rumour spread that only half the sum promised to the army would be paid at the present time, the Nawab's treasury being unequal to the demands made upon it. The balance would be paid only in three yearly instalments. Not unnaturally, the officers of the land forces felt that their claims would be weakened as soon as they were dispersed on other services, and mutinous noises were heard, but Clive subdued their objections by declaring that as a servant of the East India Company he would be open to censure if he indulged the army with its full share, and that in any case their prize money had not come about as a direct result of Plassey but was thanks to the care he had taken of their interest in his negotiations with Mir Jafar.[70] Dissatisfaction now arose as to the method of making a division. The sum awarded to each of the captains, £3,000, although not inconsiderable in itself, was infinitely below their expectations, while field officers on the other hand appeared to have benefited out of all proportion. It was said that one of them, Captain Archibald Grant of the 39th, who held local rank as major, made a crore of rupees, 'upwards of twelve thousand pounds in sterling', from his share of the spoil, as well as a number of unregistered private donatives.[71]

This pattern of high expectation, frustration and subsequent bitterness was duplicated after the fall of Havana in 1762. This time at least, the joint commanders, Lieutenant-General George, third Earl of Albemarle, and Admiral Sir George Pocock, had sat down together in advance to fix a distribution of any loot with the help of prize regulations made for expeditions to the West Indies in 1694 and 1702. 'His Majesty,' declared Albemarle on the fall of the city 'has made the army very happy, as it is the first time either in this war or in the last (excepting in the East Indies) that they have had any share of the prize money . . . His Majesty's most gracious present is at this time the more acceptable as the officers are greatly discouraged in their circumstances from the constant service they have been upon and the extravagant dearness in the different parts they have been in, particularly in Martinique and this place, [Cuba], where they pay two-thirds more for everything than in any country I ever was in.'[72]

But he deluded himself. The cost of the gruelling summer siege had been high. Of a force of more than 12,000 men, 4,708 succumbed to disease, 253 died of wounds and 305 were killed in action between 7 June and 18 October 1762.[73] Many of the survivors were wasted by illness. Major-General Jeffery Amherst was stunned at 'the most deplorable state' of the officers and men disembarking in New York.[74] Immense plunder had been taken in the fall of Havana – a Spanish fleet, gold and merchandise worth £3 million and the share to be divided by the army was £368,093 11s 6d, so those who had suffered expected a reward in proportion. However, the scheme agreed between Albemarle and Pocock resulted in them dividing two-fifteenths of the whole between themselves, which meant that Albemarle received £122,697 10s 6d, as compared with only £564 14s 6d for a field officer, £184 4s 7½d for a captain and £116 3s 0¼d for a subaltern. The suspicion was voiced that the principal officers had refrained from ordering an early escalade which would have saved many lives in order to prevent these riches falling into the hands of the storming parties.[75]

Similar disappointment ensued from the capitulation of Manila to Rear-Admiral Samuel Cornish and Sir William Draper, colonel of the 79th Foot, on 6 October 1762. The attacking force was small. Draper's own regiment, a young corps certain to face disbandment at the peace, formed the largest contingent: 974 officers and men. The balance of the little army of about 2,000 was made up of seamen and Marines, a company of artillery, a detachment of the East India Company's sepoys and 'a motley composition ... [of] ... Cafres, Lascars, Topasses, French and German deserters'. Such banditti, Draper admitted, had scarcely been assembled since the time of Spartacus.[76] It proved impossible for the colonel to restrain his troops during the assault on the city and this provided the justification for the Spanish government to repudiate the lucrative ransom terms agreed between the British commanders and Archbishop Rojo, Governor of Manila. Only 526,306 dollars in specie and plate were gathered in the city from the original demand for four million. The soldiers were impatient for reward, having been thwarted of plunder in Pondicherry the previous year, and they soon found fault with a division of spoil proposed by Draper and Cornish by which the colonel was to share three-eighths with the captains of the naval squadron while captains of the land forces were reduced to dividing a mere one-eighth with sea lieutenants and ships' masters. The subalterns were to divide one eighth with the naval warrant officers.

As Draper knew, many of his officers were desperate men. They knew their regiment was doomed and a number '... from the usual and too sanguine hopes of their profession have already anticipated their supposed profits and may live to repent their fatal success in jail'.[77]

The Spaniards having reneged on the ransom deal, it is uncertain how much plunder, if any, ever reached the hands of Draper's officers. The colonel was suspected of having reached an accommodation with the government in return for not raising the claims of his officers for justice from Spain. This accusation was vigorously refuted by Draper in pamphlets published in 1764, and in 1769 after public savaging by 'Junius' and a *soi-disant* 'Half-pay Subaltern' of the 79th. Draper claimed that far from having made a profit out of the Manila fiasco he had lost £25,000 by the Spanish default and was worse off than he had been before the expedition sailed.[78]

Taken together, these wretched disputes suggest that for the majority of officers under field rank there was little to be expected in the way of prize money, even from the most dramatically successful expeditions of the period.

6. Sharp practice and fraud

'The custom of the army' was such a vital, anomalous and organic feature of regimental life that it was difficult to draw a clear line between legitimate profit and outright corruption. It is not clear to what extent we should regard a loosely kept non-effective account as fraud, although after 1748 giving a gratuity to a deputy commissary of the musters to wink at it most certainly was. To illustrate the general point: Matthews Sewell (39th Foot) claimed an agreement by the War Office for his inserting £20 in the contingent bills of the regiment under the headings 'fire, candle and carriage of ammunition' in order to generate an additional perquisite for himself as major. When Lieutenant-Colonel Samuel Bagshawe cast doubt on the validity of this, Sewell retorted that it was '... a constant practice of the army ... so publicly known that it can be no secret to the Secretary at War', and cited two other majors and Mr Edward Lloyd, First Clerk in the War Office, in support of his claim.[79] Another dubious source of income was obtained from the appointment of non-commissioned officers. It was common for a delay to take place between the death or discharge of one n.c.o. and the appointment of his successor, but it was customary for the colonel to backdate the promotion, indulging the captain by permitting him to pocket the interim vacant pay.[80] Another widespread and equally shady practice was the pocketing of vacant subsistence between the days on which the paymaster issued funds to the company.[81] It is impossible at this distance to determine how much of this sort of thing went on, but it seems reasonable to suppose that such sharp practice under the cloak of custom was widespread.

False mustering as such was a very serious military crime and there were dire threats issued against it in the Mutiny Act. Officers presenting false statements of men sick, on furlough, recruiting or on detached duty were liable to a fine of £50 for each offence, cashiering and disqualification from ever holding a civil or military appointment under the Crown. Those who fabricated and signed spurious muster rolls would, on proof before a general court martial, be cashiered, disqualified from future employment and ordered to pay a forfeit of £100 to the informer. The money was to be seized from the officer's clearings (in their role as insurance for good behaviour), and if these proved insufficient, the court-martial was empowered to distrain the criminal's personal effects and even commit him to jail for six months.

Accusations were made that false mustering was widespread and that there even existed a body of 'fagots', labourers, tradesmen and others who, for a fee, stood in at musters and reviews to enable the officer to pocket the bulk of the vacant subsistence,[82] but the almost complete lack of official enquiries into the problem during the period leads to the conclusion that false mustering was not perpetrated on the grand scale of the previous two centuries. A few potentially promising scandals brought to light on the British Establishment peter out as instances of individual malice or misjudgment.[83] Abroad, it was sometimes a different story, New York providing the most glaring example, but even this outrage did not escape retribution, for in 1756 Lord Loudoun, commander-in-chief in North America, court-martialled the leading offender, Captain Hubert Marshall, and tactfully accepted the resignation of some of his partners in crime.[84]

There were some other types of fraud, which all collapsed as soon as some witness or thwarted accomplice denounced them, a fact which suggests that if false mustering was blatant and widespread during the period, we would indeed have heard more about it.

The first of these misdemeanours smacks of inept private enterprise. In August 1744 a rumour reached the War Office that weapons belonging to the Invalid garrison of Plymouth had been hired to a privateer. The Invalids were organised in independent companies, their dury was sedentary and it was highly unlikely that they would be sent on some urgent service where their lack of firelocks would be noticed. Sir William Yonge ordered the Governor to investigate but, alas, no more is heard of the alleged crime.[85] However, in a similar case in November 1746, Lieutenant Lewis Brown (3rd Foot) was tried for having sold sixteen muskets, twenty bayonets and nineteen cartouch boxes to a Mr William Burleigh of Newcastle the previous June. He was found guilty and cashiered.[86]

A second example of fraud was not the product of foolish opportunism but a piece of calculated profiteering by speculators who took advantage of the complex system of forage distribution. It was alleged that during the summer camp of eight regiments of foot in the south of England in 1759, John Willan, a forage contractor, had, with the connivance of a number of officers, charged the public with a much greater number of rations than had been consumed by the battalions. The profit on the sale of the excess rations was split between the parties. A number of commanding officers fell in with the scheme but the young third Duke of Richmond and Lord George Lennox did not, and reported it. A Board of General Officers which met in June 1760 to examine the charges was charitably inclined towards the offenders and reported that those implicated had acted 'inadvertently'. The King retorted that such inadvertence was highly culpable in an officer and ordered that all those concerned be given a severe reprimand.[87]

Except for a privileged minority fortunate enough to serve in the household formations or the regiments of horse, the regimental officers of Georgian Britain often found it necessary to exercise what Lieutenant Nicholas Delacherois called '... a great deal of ye savonto ministerial word *oeconomy*' in the arrangement of their disbursements.[88] Their pay was little more than adequate and often not even that; in the case of the subalterns of infantry it was downright stingy; and there was no prospect of it being increased. Their access to service allowances and prize money was limited and the traditional proprietary advantages of the captains were being either restricted or withdrawn. Moreover, their prospects were materially worsened by the fact that although proprietary benefits were being interdicted, proprietary responsibilities were not lessened in proportion. Indeed, two decades of world-wide military activity caused the pressure of their public liabilities to grow inexorably.

Notes

1 R. A. Cumb. C44/260, Duroure to Col. Robert Napier, 15 Aug. 1752, *ibid.*, 273, Duroure to the Hon. Governor, Council and Assembly of the Isle of Antigua, 1 Sept. 1752, copy in 271, Duroure to Napier, 1 Sept. 1752. For the Dalzell affair, see below, pp. 151–2. Dalzell was cashiered in March 1750. His immediate successor was Col. Richard Phillips, but the latter's sudden death resulted in the colonelcy being transferred to Duroure in February 1751.

2 Critics of the army included Col. Henry Hawley, who wanted an equivalent of the naval examination for lieutenant, and examinations before a Board of General

Officers for promotion to higher grades; NAM. 7411–24–16. For the introduction of examinations and qualifying periods of sea service for promotion in the Royal Navy before the end of the seventeenth century see Baugh, *Naval Administration*, pp. 101–3, also Sir H. Richmond, 'The Navy' in Turbeville, *Johnson's England*, I, p. 57. However, for some trenchant criticism of the unprofessional attitude of naval officers, which has numerous parallels in military literature, see Admiral Sir Charles Knowles's *Essay on the Duty and Qualifications of a Sea Officer*, London, 1765, p. 71.

3 Coxe, *Pelham Administration*, I, pp. 192–5.

4 J. W. Hayes, 'Social and Professional Backgound', p. 64.

5 R. Reilly, *Wolfe of Quebec*, London, 1973, pp. 19–20.

6 Cuthbertson, *System*, pp. 1–2.

7 H. J. Habbakuk, 'Marriage Settlements in the Eighteenth Century', *TRHS*, XXII, 1950, p. 20; E. Hughes, 'The Professions in the Eighteenth Century', *Durham Univ. Hist. Jnl.*, XIIV, 1952, p. 46; L. Stone, *The Family, Sex and Marriage in England 1500–1800*, Penguin edn., Harmondsworth, 1979, p. 242.

8 BL. Add. MSS. 35, 354 f. 23, The Earl of Hardwicke to Ensign Joseph Yorke, 27 Dec. 1742.

9 In this analysis I follow evidence and conclusions presented by E. E. Curtis, *The Organization of the British Army in the American Revolution*, New Haven, Conn., 1926, pp. 27–8; Hayes, 'Social and Professional Background', pp. 64–7, 80–110, and his 'Scottish Officers in the British Army, 1714–1763', *Scottish Historical Review*, XXXVII, 1956, pp. 23–33; Houlding, *Fit for Service*, pp. 99–116, and G. Holmes, *Augustan England: Professions, State and Society*, pp. 262–74.

10 PRO. WO 71/3 f. 242, James Craggs the Younger to E. Hughes, 11 July 1717.

11 PRO. SP 41/5 f. 1.

12 PRO. WO26/16 f. 177. In this sketch of the early eighteenth-century purchase system I follow A. P. C. Bruce, *The Purchase System in the British Army 1660–1871*, London, 1980, pp. 19–31. The book is a rather drastically edited version of Bruce's 1973 University of Manchester D. Phil. thesis, 'The System of Purchase and Sale of Commissions in the British Army and the Campaign for its Abolition, 1660–1871', which, with its greater concentration on the eighteenth century, is a more useful guide. Additional valuable comments are made by Holmes, *Augustan England*, pp. 267–70.

13 BL. Add. MSS. 34,207 f. 11, Burrard to his brother Henry, 26 April 1741; *ibid.*, f. 15, same to same, 7 Dec. 1741. Out of eighty-six commissions authorised by John, Earl of Loudoun in North America between December 1756 and April 1757, only sixteen went by purchase; S. M. Pargellis, *Lord Loudoun in North America*, New Haven, Conn., 1933, p. 313.

14 Holmes, *op.cit.*, p. 270. Details of commission price inflation are provided by Bruce, 'System of Purchase and Sale', pp. 93–9.

15 Bruce, *Purchase System*, p. 37.

16 *Observations on the Prevailing Abuses in the British Army* 'by the Honourable ——, an Officer', attributed to Ensign Thomas Erskine, 1st Foot, London, 1775, p. 8.

17 NAM. 7805–63, Lt. Nicholas Delacherois, 9th Foot, to his brother Daniel, 17 July 1765.

18 PRO. WO 71/10 f. 239, Charles Gould, Judge Advocate General, to William Viscount Barrington, Secretary at War, 3 Feb. 1766.

19 PRO. WO 8/4 f. 19, Royal Warrant to the Lord Lieutenant of Ireland, 12 March 1752; *ibid.*, f. 31, Warrant from the Lord Lieutenant to the Muster Master General and Clerk of the Cheque, 12 March 1754; R. A. Cumb. C45/146, Lords Justices of Ireland to the Duke of Dorset, Lord Lieutenant, 4 March 1755. The amounts were: 1s per diem for quartermasters of dragoons (1752) and 6d per diem and 2d per diem for captains and subalterns of foot (1754).

20 P. Mathias, 'The Social Stucture in the Eighteenth Century: a Calculation by Joseph Massie', *Economic History Review*, Second Series, X, 1957, pp. 30–45, *passim*.

21 *A Treatise of Regimental Finance*, attributed to John Williamson, first edn., London, 1782, pp. 8–9.

22 R. Porter, *English Society in the Eighteenth Century*, Harmondsworth, 1982, p. 13.

23 Simes, *Military Medley*, pp. 197–8.

24 Simes, *Military Guide*, p. 372.

25 NAM. 7805–63, Nicholas Delacherois to his brother Daniel, 24 July 1757.

26 *Memoirs of the Life and Writings of Percival Stockdale*, 'written by Himself', London, 1809, I, pp. 383–5.

27 Simes, *Military Medley*, pp. 195–6; Stockdale, *Memoirs*, pp. 386–8.

28 Lister to his father, 6, 13 April 1771, B. A. Innes ed. 'Jeremy Lister, 10th Regiment, 1770–1783', *JSAHR*, XLI, 1963, pp. 32–4.

29 C. V. F. Townshend, *The Military Life of Field Marshal George, First Marquess Townshend 1724–1807*, London 1901, p. 8.

30 BL. Add. MSS. 24,207 f. 15, William to Henry Burrard, 7 Dec. 1741.

31 PRO. WO 4/36 f. 10, Circular to officers from Sir William Yonge, 19 June 1740.

32 Ensign James Wolfe to his mother, Mrs Henrietta Wolfe, 12 Feb. 1743; Ensign Edward Wolfe to his father, 12 April 1743; Wright, *Wolfe*, pp. 32–4.

33 PRO. WO 26/26 f. 74, Orders for reducing the regiments serving in Germany, 24 Dec. 1762.

34 PRO. WO 4/70 f. 21, Welbore Ellis, Secretary at War, to the Marquess of Granby, 24 Dec. 1762; PRO. WO 1/165 f. 263, Lt.-Gen. Henry Seymour Conway to Charles Townshend, Secretary at War, 22 Jan. 1763; Lord Harcourt, Lord Lieutenant of Ireland, to Charles Jenkinson, 21 Nov. 1762, N. S. Jucker ed., *The Jenkinson Papers*, London, 1949, p. 94.

35 Lt.-Col. Charles Russell, 1st Foot Guards, to his wife, 26 Feb. 1743, *Hist. Mss. Comm. Frankland Russell Astley*, p. 224; Cornet Philip Browne, 2nd Horse, to his brother Thomas, 18 June 1743, J. H. Leslie ed., 'Letters of Captain Philip Browne', *JSAHR*, V, 1926, p. 64.

36 Russell to his wife, 26 Feb. 1743, *Hist. Mss. Comm. Frankland Russell Astley*, p. 224.

37 Wolfe to his mother, 25 March 1749, 11 Feb, 1755, Wright, *Wolfe*, pp. 121, 202.

38 Same to same, 17 Jan. 1758, *ibid.*, p. 411.

39 JRL. B2.3.153, Bagshawe to William Bagshawe of Ford, 14 Dec. 1750; *ibid.*, 160, same to same, 9 June 1752; *ibid.* 163, same to same, 31 Oct. 1752; W. H. G. Bagshawe, *The Bagshawes of Ford*, London, 1886, pp. 192–3, 236.

40 GPL. Ellison. A18 Cuthbert to Henry, 13 July, 15 Aug. 1730; 19 Aug. 1733; 19 March 1734; 10 Feb., 25 Oct. 1735; 1 March, 29 Sept. 1739; see also E. Hughes, *North Country Life in the Eighteenth Century: The North East 1700–1750*, Oxford, 1952, pp. 83–8; J. W. Hayes, 'Two Soldier Brothers of the Eighteenth Century', *JSAHR*, XL 1962, pp. 150–61, *passim*.

41 *Observations on the Prevailing Abuses in the British Army*, p. 17.

42 Holmes, *Augustan England*, p. 265.

43 For a survey of the origins of half pay see Clode, *Military Forces of the Crown*, I, pp. 26, 69–70, 368–76.

44 The use of surplus half pay or other revenue was a stop-gap measure until a request for an equivalent sum could be inserted in a parliamentary vote of 'Extraordinaries'; BL. Add. MSS. 32,695 f. 5, Memorandum on payments from the contingencies, Jan. 1739.

45 PRO. WO 4/32 f. 230, Sir William Strickland to the Commissioners of the Royal Hospital, Chelsea, 9 Sept. 1731.

46 BL. Add. MSS. 32,708 f. 60, Petition of Ensign Abram Barber, Aug. 1746.

47 PRO. WO 71/5 f. 305, Report of a Board of General Officers, 8 March 1727.

48 PRO. WO 26/20 f. 262, Warrant for continuing the pay of Lt.-Col. Sir Sheffield Austin, 8th Dragoons, 9 July 1745.

49 PRO. WO 4/34 f. 208, Sir William Yonge to Maj.-Gen. William Barrell, 7 July 1736.

50 PRO. WO 4/42, Henry Fox to Lt.-Col. Charles Davenant, 30th Foot, 14 Oct. 1746.

51 Capt. Edmund Burt, *Letters from a Gentleman in the North of Scotland*, Edinburgh, 1822, II, p. 189; W. Taylor, *Military Roads in Scotland*, London, 1976, pp. 32–5. The allowance was made at the request of Major-General George Wade, the roadbuilder. Taylor regards it as 'one of his most remarkable achievements'.

52 JRL. B2.5.1 f. 36, Additional Allowances to the King's Forces in the East India Company's service, 2 March 1754; R. Callahan, *The East India Company and Army Reform 1783–1798*, Cambridge, Mass., 1972, p. 27. There were dozens of these allowances, presenting '. . . a tangled web to the investigator'. For a further discussion of their significance, see below, pp. 168–9.

53 These are the ration allowances for the Seven Years' War; BL. Add. MSS. 40,759, 'Francis Report', f. 243. For the allowances made during the War of the Austrian Succession, which were distinctly more generous, see *Committee Report* (1746), p. 99.

54 Charles to Hugh Whitefoord, 15 Dec. 1738; same to same, 26 Feb. 1739; Lt.-Col. Charles Whitefoord to Major John Irwin, 1752; Hewins, *Whitefoord Papers*, pp. 3–4, 9, 104.

55 R. A. Cumb. C44/260, Col. Alexander Duroure to Col. Robert Napier, 15 Aug. 1752.

56 I. F. Burton, A. N. Newman, 'Sir John Cope: Promotion in the Eighteenth Century Army', *EHR*, 78, 1963, p. 661.

57 Antigua has already been referred to. For alleged misdemeanours in Georgia see BL. Add. MSS. 32,709 f. 126, J. Hammerton, Secretary to the Council of South Carolina, to Andrew Stone, Private Secretary to the Duke of Newcastle, Oct. 1746.

58 S. M. Pargellis, 'The Four Independent Companies of New York', *Essays in Colonial History presented to Charles M. Andrews by his Students*, New Haven, 1931.

59 *Committee Report* (1746), pp. 122–7.

60 PRO. WO 27/3–6, Inspection Returns, 1754–59.

61 Some suspected the regimental agents of profiting from large non-effective balances lodged in their hands. (see note 9, p. 82 above). Deputy Paymasters serving with the armies abroad were other prime suspects. At the outbreak of the Seven Years' War, Peter Taylor, a Strand silversmith and acquaintance of Henry Fox and John Calcraft, was appointed as a Deputy Paymaster in Germany. He remained on the Continent for five years, and at the height of the war £150,000 a month was passing through his hands. He came home with a fortune and an unsavoury reputation; *House of Commons 1754–1790*, 'Taylor, Peter'. See also a thought-provoking article by T. H. McGuffie: 'A Deputy Paymaster's Fortune: the Case of George Durant, Deputy Paymaster to the Havana Expedition, 1762', *JSAHR*, XXXII, 1954, pp. 144–7. Durant went to Havana poor and came home a rich man. McGuffie speculates that he was in a good position to corner dead men's prize money. He was equally well placed to pocket their unclaimed subsistence.

62 Baugh, *Naval Administration*, p. 112.

63 An Order in Council of June 1698 which despatched three troops of dragoons to the Kent Coast laid down that this allowance was to be 2*d per diem* for each man, '. . . and in proportion to the officers, the whole not to exceed £200 *per annum*'. This money was irregularly and ungenerously paid. The allocation of prize money was revised in 1732; P. Muskett, 'Military Operations against Smuggling in Kent and Sussex, 1688–1750', *JSAHR*, LII, 1974, pp. 89–110.

64 JRL. B2.2.260, Hepburne to Major Samuel Bagshawe, 2 Feb. 1748.

65 Distribution of Prizes and Bounty for taking Ships of War, 19 June 1740, *Army List*

(1740); Distribution of Prizes, 7 July 1756, Beatson, *Naval and Military Memoirs*, III, pp. 104–6.

66 PRO. WO 40, 'America'.

67 JRL. B2.5.1/240, Bagshawe to his Uncle, William Bagshawe of Ford, 1755.

68 JRL. B2.5.1/18. For Boscawen's expedition, see Beatson, *op.cit.*, I, pp. 391–9.

69 M. Edwardes ed., Major John Corneille, *Journal of my Service in India*, Folio Society, London, 1966, p. 130.

70 Corneille, *Journal*, pp. 130–2; JRL. B2.6.177, Robert Clive to the Captains and Subalterns of the Army, 5 July 1757; Messrs Clive, Watts and Manningham to the Secret Committee, 25 July 1757, S. C. Hill ed., *Bengal 1756–1757: The Indian Records Series*, London, 1905, II, pp. 455–6.

71 One-eighth of the spoil was divided between Clive and Major Kirkpatrick of the company's forces and four-eighths between the captains, staff officers and subalterns; Corneille, *Journal*, pp. 133–8. In 1768 it was computed that Clive, in various military and company capacities, had received the equivalent of £234,000. Captain Grant's donative was believed to be £11,250; Hill, *op. cit.*, III, p. 395.

72 PRO. CO 117/1 f. 163, Albemarle to the Earl of Egremont, 11 Oct. 1762.

73 SRO. HA67.894.B.29, General Return, 18 Oct. 1762.

74 PRO. CO 117/1 f. 180, Amherst to Albemarle, 6 Sept. 1762.

75 Beatson *op.cit.*, II, pp. 407, 570; D. Syrett, *The Siege and Capture of Havana 1762: Navy Records Society*, London, 1970, pp. xiii–xxxv, *passim*. The charge was groundless, but Albemarle was certainly not the sort of general to seize the opportunity for a brilliant escalade. Although Havana revived the failing fortunes of the Keppel family, the Earl never enjoyed good health thereafter and he died 'of a mortification of the bowels' in 1772.

76 *Colonel Draper's Answer to the Spanish Arguments claiming the Galleon and refusing Payment of the Ransom Bills for preserving Manila from Pillage and Destruction*, London, 1764, p. 21; A. P. Thornton, 'The British in Manila 1762–1764', *History Today*, VII, 1957, pp. 44–53.

77 *Colonel Draper's Answer*, pp. 6–7; Cornish and Draper to the East India Company council at Fort St George, Madras, 28 July 1762; N. P. Cushner ed., *Documents Illustrating the British Conquest of Manila, 1762–3, Camden Series Four*, VIII, p. 36; *ibid.*, p. 123, note, pp. 125–6, 172; PRO. WO 1/319 f. 405, Draper to Charles Townshend, 2 Nov. 1762.

78 The pamphlets were the *Answer* and *A Plain Narrative of the Reduction of Manila*, London, 1764. See also *Woodfall's Junius*, London, n.d., letters III, IV, V, Feb.–April 1769.

79 JRL. B2.2.394, Sewell to Bagshawe, 20 May 1751. Sewell held the army rank of brevet lieutenant-colonel, but he only ranked as major in the regiment.

80 JRL. B2.2.186, Bagshawe to Capt. Francis Forde, 39th Foot, 25 Sept. 1750. Bagshawe strongly disapproved of this perquisite.

81 This practice continued at least up to the issuing of the Warrant for Regulating the Non-effective Funds of the Regiments in Infantry of 19 Feb. 1766, which expressly prohibited it; *A Collection of Regulations*, pp. 176–8.

82 J. Railton, *The Army's Regulator or the British Monitor*, London, 1738, has some sweeping indictments of this sort, see in particular pp. 128–9. 'Railton' claimed to have served in the House Grenadier Guards, the dragoons, the Foot Guards and the Royal Regiment of Artillery: he found scandalous malpractices everywhere but was abused and obstructed by his officers and even the Secretary at War when he tried to bring them to official attention. One of the two Bodleian Library copies of this work, Bod. 8°Rawl. 579, is particularly interesting, as it is heavily annotated by its one-time owner, obviously an officer or someone with extensive understanding of regimental affairs. The margins are peppered with splenetic comment, such as 'impudence',

'scandalous liball', 'malicious and groundless and a compilation of ignorance and impudence' or, frequently, long (and in this author's opinion, convincing) expositions of the bias and half-truths in Railton's account. Midway through the book, the former owner convinces himself that Railton is a Jesuit agitator! Of Railton's introduction of the term 'fagots', he retorts that it '... has not been made use of this fourty year in the army, nor no abuses under such denominations put in practise', p. 128. It is revealing that an alternative version of this work, also published in 1738, is entitled *The Army Regulator: or the Military Adventures of Mr John Railton*. I am very grateful to Mr Glenn Steppler for drawing Railton's book and the Bodleian copy of it to my attention.

83 See, for example, PRO. WO 71/34, General Court Martial of Matthew Draper, Captain of a Company of Invalids at Clifford's Fort, 2–16 May 1716; PRO. WO 7/123, Thomas Hillyard Esq. to Thomas Gore, Commissary General of the Musters, 18 Feb. 1758; *ibid.*, f. 290, John Hesse, First Clerk to Deputy Commissary Balderston, 2 March 1758; *ibid.*, f. 291, Balderston to Hesse, 8 March 1758.

84 Pargellis, 'The Four Independent Companies of New York', pp. 118–20.

85 PRO. WO 4/40 f. 40, Sir William Yonge to Lt. Gen. Charles Churchill, 3 Aug. 1744.

86 PRO. WO 4/42 f. 335, Sir William Yonge to Sir John Ligonier, 15 Nov. 1746. Railton, *op. cit.*, p. 12, alleges a similar type of fraud with dragoon horses hired out to '... the plow and cart'.

87 PRO. WO 71/10 f. 25, Barrington to the Judge Advocate General, 29 May 1760; *ibid.*, f. 27, Paper detailing the transaction; *ibid.*, f. 43, Report of a Board of General Officers, 20 June 1760; *ibid.*, f. 46, Barrington to the Judge Advocate General, 27 June 1760.

88 NAM. 7805–63, Lt. Nicholas Delacherois, 9th Foot, to his brother Daniel, 10 May 1768.

5

Undertakers under pressure

The public liabilities of field officers, captains and subalterns

'If we subsist chiefly by perquisite,' suggested Lieutenant-Colonel Campbell Dalrymple of the 3rd Dragoons, 'peace is the time to reap the sweets of it.'[1] Although in time of peace regimental establishments were sharply reduced, while the amount of money circulating in the corps declined in proportion, there were compensating factors working in favour of the junior proprietary officer. Charges against the non-effective fund dropped to the level of routine contingencies, recruiting became less frenetic and less expensive and drafting less frequent. Desertion slackened, there was less wastage of regimental equipment and hopes rose that any embargo on the division of non-effective balances would be lifted. But, in supposing that peace restored equable administrative conditions, we should note that this was only so in relation to the much more extreme nature of wartime demands. In no station was regimental administration entirely settled or straightforward and in many places it was only carried on with great difficulty. Even in Great Britain, soldiers were in constant motion between one quarter and another, quelling riots and suppressing smugglers and divided perforce into small detachments, which posed as great a threat to administrative efficiency as it did to tactical training.[2] Meanwhile, regiments on duty in the Scottish Highlands, where there was much greater activity after the crushing of the Forty-five, endured service conditions little better than those in Nova Scotia. 'When I am in Scotland,' complained James Wolfe, 'I look upon myself as an exile.' On his enforced return from leave in April 1753 he found his unit in as bad a state as if it had been quartered in the Leeward Isles, '... officers ruined, impoverished, desperate and without hopes of preferment ... an ensign struck speechless with the palsy and another that falls down in the most violent convulsions. Some of our people spit blood and others are begging to sell.'[3] Absenteeism from the forces in Scotland became a problem in the immediate aftermath of Culloden and all those who could get away did their best to do so.[4]

Ireland, though not loathed so intensely as the Highlands, was also disliked, which was unfortunate, for in peacetime nearly half the regiments, reduced to skeleton strengths, served there. The superficial objection was that, even in comparison with English country quarters where there was little to do off parade except read or saunter about, Irish billets were ineffably boring, with '.. nothing to divert a high spleen and melancholy engend'rd by a want of company and ye sulphureous vapours of a boggy situation'.[5] Other delights included 'The Limericks', an enteric complaint which commonly afflicted persons quartered there.[6] Fortunately, some officers found Irish quarters somewhat more appealing.[7]

Most to be pitied perhaps were the four regiments of horse which spent much of the century quartered in Ireland: after the reduction of three senior regiments of horse in England to dragoon guards in December 1746, they were the only regiments of horse remaining in the army apart from the Royal Regiment of Horse Guards, and were popularly known as the 1st to the 4th Irish Horse.[8] They were always dispersed in minuscule detachments. The regiments of foot were somewhat better off. A major concentration of four battalions was under command in Dublin, and the remainder participated in an annual rotation of quarters which after a year in isolated postings brought them into the garrison towns of Galway, Limerick, Cork, Waterford and Kinsale, but even in these places they were obliged to detach men on outpost service.[9] As Viscount Townshend observed in a retrospective survey of the management of the army in Ireland, gentlemen and corporations had sometimes pined so much for the sight of a red coat that a distribution of quarters had been sanctioned by Dublin Castle which made it impossible to discipline the regiments effectively.[10]

So beneath the surface objections to serving in Ireland lurked more threatening personal and administrative concerns. Personal pay was generally lower than on the British Establishment. There was a loss by exchange on any clearings and arrears owed to the regiment in Britain. There was a threat of incipient confusion in accounts passing between the British and Irish agents. Except in times of national emergency, Irish regiments were obliged to recruit in Great Britain, adding greatly to the cost of the exercise. Officers absent on leave or recruiting were subjected to a regime of swingeing fines to remove respites, imposed on them for the benefit of the Chief Secretary and the Clerk of the Cheque. All these factors help to explain why, only months after returning to Ireland at the end of the War of the Austrian Succession, Major Thomas Gage was complaining from Cork that he was '... already sick of this Establishment, which is worse than ever'.[11] Colonel Henry Hawley believed that officers serving in Ireland were '... banish'd from their friends and relations and all hopes of preferment'.[12] Ambitious men were ever on the lookout for ways of returning to England, with or without their regiments,[13] and cynics wondered how it was they had been sent to Ireland at all. Hawley and Colonel Joseph Yorke, both men with ample knowledge of the army and its governors, interpreted a posting to the sister kingdom as a mark of disfavour,[14] while John Calcraft, the regimental agent, varied the prejudice by suggesting that only a good interest at court would enable a regiment to get out again.[15]

These were mild irritations, however, compared to the tribulations afflicting regiments chosen for service in the Mediterranean, in Nova Scotia or the West Indies. Once there, they could not expect to return in the forseeable future: 'It would be inconvenient and so expensive to the public to give our army their turn of duty on such service,' declared the Earl of Hardwicke in 1742, '... that no man I believe will ever pretend it ought or can be done, and therefore it must be allowed as an establish'd maxim that ev'ry man that enlists in the army is patiently to submit to his lot and to serve in any part of the world where the regiment or company in which he engages is appointed to serve as long as the government shall think fit to continue in that place the regiment or company to which he belongs.'[16]

In the fortresses of Gibraltar and Minorca, military life was notorious for its tedium, seediness and general lack of elbow-room. So many officers absented themselves from their commands that it was sometimes difficult to carry out routine garrison duty. Others made themselves useless by over-indulgence, or drifted into senseless quarrels with each other or their superior officers. The regime in both places was sickly, the cost of living high, and the charge of shipping out recruits from England ruinously dear.[17] Regimental husbandry was made even more difficult by the fact that the rank and file, brimfull of cheap wine, took to comparing their lot with that of transported felons, and from Minorca in particular came serious reports of suicide, self-inflicted wounds and desertion attempts.[18]

One of the most significant achievements of Cumberland's captain-general-ship was his introduction of regular rotations for units in Gibralter and Minorca. In 1749 all the battalions serving there were relieved and, commencing in 1751, one battalion from each place was replaced by a unit from home. But this hope of eventual relief was denied to regiments serving in North America and the West Indies until the aftermath of the Seven Years' War, when Empire-wide rotations were, with great difficulty, instituted.[19] In the meantime, regiments exiled to Nova Scotia battled for months at a time with ferocious weather and marauding bands of French and Indians,[20] while those in Jamaica, Bermuda, the Leeward Isles and (from 1763) Florida succumbed to fevers, agues, lassitude and the kind of moral torpor that prompted even a keen soldier like Lieutenant Nicholas Delacherois of the 9th Foot to wonder whether by opting for a military career he had traded his liberty for a hat with a feather in it.[21] Moreover, it was in these 'remote corners of the world', as Delacherois termed them, that regiments were most vulnerable to frauds perpetrated on them from afar, or the disastrous consquences of agency failures, the first warning of which came months too late with the arrival from London of bundles of protested bills.[22]

What needs emphasising in this cursory sketch of conditions of service is that every officer of the infantry (excepting the Foot Guards and Invalids), and many officers of the cavalry, were confronted by the prospect of extended tours of duty outside Great Britain, often in circumstances which imposed a grievous burden on their personal and regimental finances. With the extension of the practice of imperial rotations after 1749 and 1764 the likelihood of this increased. Thus any account of the purchase system which stops short of exploring service conditions tells less than half the story of investing in command. Ultimately, any man who had bought a commission even in an 'old corps' in peacetime had not purchased the mere equivalent of an annuity. Instead of being able to sit back and wait for the dividend from his investment, he soon found that he had incurred '... the obligation of service and the slavery of subordination'.[23]

War, with its massive augmentations of men and flourishing growth of young corps, was welcomed as a means of escape from the half-pay list or a subordinate commission, but even this opportunity emphasised the essentially precarious character of the military investment. The Crown reserved the right to do as it chose with its regiments, and though it had drawn back from breaking Bragg's 28th Foot in 1748, it was capable of ruthless strokes against the oldest formations. In December 1746 the King disbanded the 3rd and 4th troops of his own Horse Guards in a move calculated to ease the passage of future army estimates through the House of Commons. Simultaneously, he ordered the downgrading of three senior regiments of horse, Honywood's, Montagu's and Wade's, to the status and remuneration of dragoons; the only sop to their pride and lineage was the appellation 'Dragoon Guards'. The whole measure saved an estimated £60,000 *per annum* and led to Henry Fox being '... reckon'd the devil of a Secretary at War'.[24]

As for any young regiments, it was understood that they would be unlikely to survive the inevitable peacetime reductions, and the main reason for venturing life and patrimony in raising and leading one was that by good conduct and good fortune the undertaker might eventually obtain a commission of a higher grade in an old corps. The merest hint of impending peace was sufficient to make a captaincy in an old corps a great deal more difficult to obtain than field rank in a young one.[25] From about midsummer 1759 to the eve of the Peace of Paris a vast amount of money and effort was lavished on these new units. Lured by the prospect of preferment, ambitious officers opened up fertile recruiting grounds in Ulster, Wales and the Scottish glens with the prodigal expenditure of private funds at double or more the customary rate of government levy money, £5 per man. They bedizened their recruiting parties with flamboyant uniforms, adorned wtih the legend 'Death or Glory' and the like, a cause of much disdain among the veteran regiments.[26] As an additional incentive they adopted extravagant titles: Barré's 106th Foot was known as 'The Black Musketeers', Beauclerk's 107th as 'The Queen's Own Royal Regiment of British Volunteers', Markham's 112th as 'The King's Royal Musketeers' and Deaken's 110th as 'The Queen's Royal Musketeers'.[27]

It was the ambition of these military projectors that once their units were complete, they would march with them to win imperishable glory in Germany (the most fashionable seat of war) under Prince Ferdinand of Brunswick. Government's view, however, was much more utilitarian, and its treatment of the young corps and their commanders was ruthless indeed. The fresh reserves of manpower were wrested from their inexperienced subalterns and noncommissioned officers and drafted into the impoverished old corps, whose recruiting had been greatly hindered by the open-handedness of the new. The officers of the young corps were disgusted to find themselves reduced to the level of perpetual recruiters.

The fate of Colonel Samuel Bagshawe's 93rd Foot, raised for rank in Ireland during 1760, is typical. Two swingeing drafts made in November 1760 and March 1761 left only 346 rank and file, sixty of them unfit for duty, out of an establishment of 630. As was the custom, only the best men were taken, and all the captains lost money by having men drafted who were still in debt to them for necessaries. After the second and heaviest draft, Edward Windus, Bagshawe's lieutenant-colonel, reported that the regiment had been torn to pieces, broken before its time. No hint had been given as to how or when the corps would be reimbursed for these drafts. Disconsolately the captains set about recruiting for the third time.[28]

Meanwhile, in England, Lieutenant-Colonel Commandant Charles Beauclerk (107th Foot) lost 300 recruits in one draft for Germany in March 1762. Seven other young corps lost between 100 and 150 men each on the same occasion. At the end of the month Colonel David Graeme (105th Foot) was ordered to draft 226 men for Germany. In April all these regiments, plus a number more, were drafted again for Germany and also for Portugal. So insistent was the demand for recruits that young corps were even gutted before their initial completion date, leading to predictable confusion as to what credit or time extension should be allowed them.[29] Only a vestigial respect for the proprietary claims of the undertakers restrained the War Office from breaking a number of young regiments even before the end of the war.[30] They, and the men who commanded them, were disposable commodities.

1. Public liabilities

Narrowing the scope of our enquiry to observe the regimental administrative machine in action is to discover that the public responsibilities of officers as trustees of public money and custodians of regimental equipment for government were, like their access to proprietary incomes, ill defined. If cash or equipment was lost on service, it was uncertain whether any relief would be granted, or if so, when and how much. For example, in 1741 Captain Matthew Swiney was shipwrecked on a mission from Cuba to Jamaica. He suffered a personal loss of £107 and £83 worth of company necessaries in his charge. Captain Killigrew, a companion in misfortune, was reimbursed the sum of £434 10s in 1743 (largely on account of shipwrecked company funds), but Swiney was still petitioning for relief in 1752. Henry Fox was sympathetic, but unwilling to draw up a warrant on Swiney's behalf; such a concession, he argued, would open the door to endless petitions from officers who had suffered similar disasters.[31]

A number of captains who lost considerable sums of regimental money at the battle of the Monongahela in 1755 (as much as £60 each) were forced to make good the deficits out of their personal pay. In May 1760 they were still petitioning for relief from the frozen non-effective balances of their regiments.[32]

The wish to avoid such financial embarrassments easily led to acts of calculated callousness. In February 1747 Lieutenant-Colonel Matthews Sewell (39th Foot) issued an order to discontinue paying subsistence to women whose husbands were away serving as Marines aboard the fleet. Any officer continuing to subsist the women would do so at his own risk, for the corps would not bear the loss which would result by a man's death two or three months before news reached home.[33]

It was dangerously easy for officers to become embroiled in the incompetence or crimes of others. There are a number of references to regimental paymasters being placed in detention or subjected to legal scrutiny as a result of errors or misappropriation and it was far from easy to obtain redress from these defaulters.[34] Government had a clear escape route: the captains had nominated the paymaster, so they were responsible for his actions and any deficits would be made good out of their pay.[35] It was very uncertain what the captains should do about prosecuting a defaulting paymaster, or what help, if any, they would receive from the War Office.

A case which graphically illustrates the difficulty arose in September or October 1749 when it came to the attention of Henry Fox that Lieutenant Israel Mitchell of Churchill's Marines, Lieutenant-Colonel Mitchell, his father (and surety), and Quartermaster Harris had gone into Ireland without coming to account. The regimental books were believed to be with the absconding parties. On 10 October Fox put a stop against their half pay until they settled with the captains. It was left entirely up to the latter, headed by Captain Robert Shafto, to find a way of bringing this about. In 1751 the elder Mitchell returned from Ireland, admitted to Shafto that it was impossible to make up a proper account and offered him £100 in lieu of what might be owed to him if he would use his influence with his brother captains to bring about the lifting of suspensions on his and his son's half-pay. Shafto agreed, and a memorial from him and three of the other captains led to the lifting of suspensions on the two Mitchells on 14 March 1751. At least two of the captains received money from Lieutenant-Colonel Mitchell, while in May Shafto accepted a bond with the knowledge, he later claimed, of Fox and William Pitt, Paymaster General.

At this point Mrs Joanna Harris, wife of the quartermaster, memorialised Fox to expedite the lifting of the suspension order on her deceased husband's half pay. With the memorial she sent papers alleging that a number of frauds had taken place in the regiment and an accusation that Shafto had offered to help her obtain benefit of the half pay in return for a covert bond of £150.

Fox pressed Shafto for his version of the proceedings and submitted it to a Board of General Officers which reported on 9 January 1753 that Shafto was 'unjustifyable' in demanding money for himself and some of the other captains merely as a consideration for their help in removing suspensions. The Board argued that a properly authenticated demand should have been submitted to authority by all Churchill's captains jointly. How long this might have taken to arrange, or how the matter could ever have been settled when even Lieutenant-Colonel Mitchell admitted the accounts were utterly perplexed, did not come under discussion. Shafto was struck off the half-pay list.

His only recourse was to prosecute Lieutenant-Colonel Mitchell in Chancery, where he was fortunate enough to obtain a ruling that '... no man could be unjustifyable for taking a sum which was offered by the party who had the accounts in his possession and therefore must be better able to judge what was due than the other who accepted what was offered', but the victory was hollow, for he was unable to overturn the generals' decision, despite lobbying on his behalf by friends and relations in Parliament. The only contribution made by government was to imply that if captains acted against defalcators, they should only do so in concert. Some public money had been saved by stoppages imposed on the offenders' half pay, but no assistance had been rendered to Shafto and his fellow creditors.[36]

A similar reluctance to become involved in relieving financial difficulties incurred by officers as a result of the defalcations of third parties was shown by the government's handling of regimental agency failures. A resolutely negative attitude may have been fair enough in the case of colonels who actually nominated the agent, and if a junior officer chose to use the agent as a personal banker and lost money as a result, then it was just a case of bad luck, but in a number of instances the insolvency of an agent seriously affected men who had no influence whatsoever in his appointment.

Agency failures were as likely to take place in peace as in wartime, as they usually came about either as a result of financial adventurism or sudden death, but the damage was worst in units on foreign service, subsisting on credit, where news of a bankruptcy took months to arrive. As a result of the death and insolvency of Alexander Stevenson, agent to the two independent companies in Jamaica in 1727, bills drawn on him in good faith by Lieutenant William Dodd, acting commander of one of them, were returned protested to the West Indies. Dodd's creditors sued him for £417 10s 1d and when he decamped to England in search of payment he was arrested for an additional debt of £200 and 'confin'd for some time 'till he found a friend to join with him in a bond for the same with interest'. Out of jail again he was 'daily threaten'd to be again arrested for the remainder'. He petitioned unsuccessfully for payment of the protested bills over a period of six years, notwithstanding the culpability of the War Office, which had nominated Stevenson in 1717 without taking security from him. In the meantime Dodd had been joined in his distress by Captain Joseph Delaunay of the second Jamaica company, who had overspent the sum of £356 maintaining it, and as a result expected to be thrown into jail at any moment. The main justification for delaying compensation was that legal action was in progress to extract sufficient funds from the agent's effects, and no public grant was made until 1736, by which time only £140 had been recovered.

Three years later, in the spring of 1739, a similar catastrophe overtook the affairs of six independent companies sent out from Gibraltar to Jamaica during 1734. They had suffered severely from the climate, and a vigorous programme of recruiting was carried out in 1738–39. This exhausted their non-effective funds and on the failure of their agent, Henry Popple, there were debts of £6,249 16s 4¾d owing to them, as well as £2,316 17s 2¾d to a company in New Providence and £650 to the 34th Foot, then serving in Scotland. Securities had once been provided by Popple, but they were totally inadequate to answer such a large debt. Popple absconded, and his effects become the object of complicated legal activity. At length the only proposal advanced by the Treasury was that the captains should petition Parliament for relief. This was not granted until July 1741, two years after the collapse.[37]

Although government grudgingly admitted responsibility in this instance, it was capable on other occasions of taking arbitrary action which penalised junior officers who could have taken no part in appointing the agent. In June 1716, for example, stoppages of pay amounting to £1,486 4s were imposed on officers of the 7th Foot after the failure of its agent. The commander, James, Lord Tyrawley, bore the brunt of this as colonel and captain but his share only amounted to £150. The balance was made up by the two field officers, who were obliged to part with £60 and £40 respectively (as well as an additional £50 as captains) by the captains, who were each stopped £50, the subalterns, who paid £25 each (those doubling as adjutant and quartermaster each paying another £20), the surgeon, who was stopped £20, and the chaplain, who paid £28 4s.[38]

2. Recruiting and remounting

Once a regiment had been raised or augmented by a grant of levy money, it was intended to be self-sufficient for all normal recruiting purposes. The primary function of the stock purse and non-effective funds was to provide a cash reserve for this operation. The provision of officers' dividends from the same source was always a secondary consideration; sufficient funds were carried forward to keep the troop or company complete with men and horses, and the captain's allowance of warrant men could be suspended if this was not done.

The actual duty of recruiting was devolved to the officers of the regiment. In wartime they were assisted by the local authorities, who implemented a limited press of the able-bodied poor,[39] but for the most part, in peace and war, it was the aim to fill the ranks with volunteers, and the method of obtaining them was to despatch small parties, consisting of a subaltern, sergeant and escort, to raise men by beat of drum in a locality authorised by the Secretary at War's beating order. The recruiting officers were supplied with explicit guidelines, drawn up by their commanding officers, which applied and interpreted current physical and other standards for recruits fixed by the War Office. These were commonly relaxed in wartime.[40]

In time of peace, regiments on the Irish Establishment were prohibited from entertaining even Protestant Irish recruits; all their recruiting had to be undertaken in Great Britain. This requirement, which may have had the long-term social and political benefits of buttressing the Protestant interest in Ireland, was very costly to the non-effective funds of Irish regiments in the short run. One way round it was to ship Ulster Protestants to Scotland, garnish them with bonnets and ferry them home again as *bona fide* Caledonians.[41]

During 1716–17, 1745–47 and 1757–63 shortages of manpower caused this restriction to be abandoned, but it was always forbidden to entertain Roman Catholics in the land forces. However, there is no denying that many papists did serve in the Irish army. Once any Irishmen were being accepted it became difficult to pick them out, and this is one reason why in peacetime urgent steps were taken to reduce Irishmen, of whatever creed, and replace them by recruits from Great Britain, preferably Englishmen. But some officers knowingly recruited Catholics, and their success or failure depended on the vigilance and probity of the field officer who examined the new arrivals at regimental headquarters.[42]

The best recruits were those enlisted in a neighbourhood where a good account of them could be obtained. Officially, they would be offered a bounty of no more than a guinea and a crown. They were entitled to claim this for themselves, but the careful recruiter would try to withold the guinea to supply the man with provisions for the march and his 'necessaries'—shirt, stockings and shoes—on joining the corps. The crown was to enable the man to drink King George's health. If he insisted on his full bounty, there was '. . . just reason to suspect him of being an idle, ill-designing fellow, and therefore he ought to be closely looked into or, what may answer better for the officer, turned about his business'. If he did succeed in haggling successfully for his bounty, the recruit would be put under heavy stoppages as soon as he joined the regiment.[43]

When a man made his initial undertaking to the recruiting officer, the latter had four days in which to take him before a Justice of the Peace to assent to or deny his enlistment. If he refused to serve, he was obliged to repay his bounty with an additional pound for the trouble he had caused. Failure to do so within a period of one day confirmed the enlistment.

The smooth operation of this procedure depended on the co-operation of the civil authority, but deeply entrenched opposition to recruiting in some localities, coupled with the cunning of bounty-jumpers, meant that the officer was unable to recover his money or obtain his man in all cases. He was held responsible for the loss. He was also responsible for getting his often unwilling charges back to regimental headquarters or to a secure lodging in the Savoy Hospital to await a passage overseas.[44] It was also necessary for his recruits to meet with the approval of the field officers. If the latter were honest men they would reject all recruits below the regimental size (unless they could be categorised as growing lads), and turn out any disabled men, papists or, in time of peace, Protestant Irish. The rejected men would be put to the charge of the recruiting officer. Losses sustained by men having died, sickened or deserted on their way to the regiment would also be put at his door. It was small wounder that even careful and sober officers were apprehensive when their turn came for the recruiting service.[45]

Cumberland preferred that only experienced officers should be sent recruiting, but the unpopularity of the duty meant that this was not always possible.[46] Even those men who were good at it objected to being sent out time after time instead of having their chance to win renown in the field.[47] If, on the other hand, a regiment spread the responsibility equally, by employing a roster, this meant that young and unreliable men would be sent with large sums of regimental money far beyond the supervision of their captains and field officers.[48] An alternative method of control involved placing an experienced officer at a point where he could co-ordinate the activity of a number of parties and so regulate their expenditure.[49]

Recruiting was always a potentially difficult and costly undertaking, and never more so than in time of war when, with old and young corps competing keenly for a shrinking pool of manpower, it was axiomatic that the greater the number of guineas employed, the greater would be the success of the recruiter. Every officer had his cautionary tale of some acquaintance who had bankrupted himself in this endeavour and had been forced to dispose of his commission to cover his debt to the regiment.

There were no government studs for breeding cavalry horses in Great Britain. Officers obtained the powerful black horses used for mounting the horse and dragoons, and the smaller roadsters used from 1756 in the light troops of the dragoon guards and dragoons, and in the regiments of light dragoons, on the open remount market.[50] They were provided with an imprest from the stock purse, a regulation of the size of horses and additional instructions, just as for human recruits. It was necessary for them to have expert knowledge of horseflesh, for although the animals would be unlikely to desert they were just as likely as men to fall sick. Officers who purchased horses not up to standard were obliged to bear the charge of their rejection. The sums involved were considerable; £15 for a troop horse in time of peace, rising to as much as £26 in wartime, and £12 for a dragoon horse, rising to £22 10s.[51] It was not unknown for a stock purse fund to be unable to bear even the cost of peacetime replacements, and the nicely computed allowances for remounts incorporated in the regulations of stock purses would not answer a season of inflated prices, losses in battle or decimation from infected stables. Such accidents effectively disposed of favourable stock purse balances, and it then became necessary to apply to Parliament for relief.[52] During the War of the Austrian Succession it was customary to allow between £15 and £20 for a troop horse and £12 to £15 for a dragoon horse against losses testified on oath, but only months in arrear, during which time the stock purses went into debt. It is a fair indication of the real extent of Cumberland's authority that when he was applied to for relief by his angry colonels of cavalry after the arduous campaign of 1745, all he was able to do was to send a trusted subordinate, the Earl of Rothes, to represent to Henry Pelham '... how necessary it was for the service that something should be speedily determined therein, and that the stock purses were only sufficient to purchases horses worn out or disabled by common accidents. But not for those lost by the enemy' (*sic*). Pelham told Rothes that until the matter was laid before the House no payments could be made, and that although 'the customary allowances would be made some time in the future, now was not a good time to protest too much', the Commons having recently set up their committee to investigate the condition of His Majesty's land forces and Marines. Rothes impotently reported this to the Duke.[53]

3. Drafts

Drafting was a procedure used to recruit regiments on service or reinforce those about to take the field. It involved transferring a cadre of experienced men or a batch of recruits from one regiment to another. It was a common feature of wartime military administration, hated by the men and resented by their officers, who, after seeing their fittest soldiers weeded out for somebody else's benefit, were obliged to re-recruit with no assurance of prompt reimbursement. An alternative scheme of forming depot companies for battalions serving in Europe during 1744–45 collapsed when it became necessary to embody them in impromptu regiments under field officers of Marines to combat the Jacobite rebellion, creating sublime confusion in the accounts of the parent regiments.[54]

Drafting seriously disrupted the finances of a proprietary command. It was usual for a large proportion of the men to be in debt to their captains for necessaries, especially if they had been only recently recruited, and it was not always possible to settle these debts.[55] Moreover, although it was assumed that regiments receiving drafts would reimburse the parent corps, heavy charges on their own non-effective funds in time of war might exhaust their ability to pay. In 1744 the price of drafts going to regiments which had suffered heavy casualties at the battle of Dettingen was fixed at £5 per man. The receiving regiments proved unable to pay this amount and it became necessary for a Board of General Officers to decide what should be done. The Board declared that the regiments could not pay more than £3 per head and that the balances must be made good either by allowing the parent corps to muster complete for a period or by payments from the Extraordinaries of the army. Some debts were still outstanding on this score in 1749.[56]

When officers were left in doubt as to how or when any debts to their commands would be answered, it is not surprising to find them resorting to acts of calculated callousness, stripping men of uniforms, accoutrements and necessaries, striking them off the regimental books and sending them half naked and without subsistence to their new units.[57] Alternatively, rather than disposing of their best men, the officers made every effort to pass off the worst, and from here it was only one step to recruiting low-grade personnel in the first instance.[58]

4. Desertion

Desertion was widespread at all times but especially so when regiments were ordered abroad. It was expedient to keep these movements secret up to the last moment and the men under close surveillance.[59] Bounty-jumpers, men who deserted in debt to their captains or those who absconded wearing their regimental 'necessaries', turned desertion from a straightforward disciplinary problem into a financial one, for money and equipment lost in this way were effectively written off. This provided additional justification for harsh and exemplary punishments, and made it necessary to track down the deserter wherever possible.

In the first place, this entailed expenditure on the printing of handbills and newspaper advertisements.[60] If a Justice of the Peace then apprehended a deserter, he contacted the Secretary at War, who notified the man's regiment. During his time in jail or the 'house of correction' the deserter was subsisted by the county or borough, but ultimately his company became liable for the fees of the jail and, it was argued, a gratuity to the keeper. Some officers disputed these charges, while others neglected to reclaim the men, allowing them to continue as a charge on the locality (possibly with an indigent wife and children) for an indefinite period. A rebuke from the Secretary at War was sometimes necessary to produce any action.[61] In such circumstances the officer might agree to pay the prison fees but ask the civil authority to release a man not worth sending after.[62] From 1742 the Mutiny Act fixed the rate of compensation to the jail keeper at full daily subsistence, but his claim to any other fee or reward was denied.

One method of lowering the risk of desertion was to levy the smallest possible stoppages, and these at a standard regimental rate. This prevented the men from thinking that they would be perpetually in debt to the captains, a powerful incentive to abscond.[63]

5. Weapons

The Board of Ordnance supplied a regiment with its firelocks and bayonets. The regiment was accountable to the Board for the weapons it had received and it was insisted upon that, when it was reduced, surplus firearms should be returned to store and the Ordnance value paid for those missing or ruined, the exceptions being weapons lost or damaged on active service for which proper vouchers could be submitted, and (in practice) those worn out by the passage of time. Under the Articles of War the captain was accountable to his colonel for any losses and damage other than by 'unavoidable accidents' or on active service. The routine repair of firelocks was chargeable to the non-effective fund.[64]

Great vigilance was required to keep the weapons in good repair and prevent them becoming too great a charge on troop and company finances. It was prudent to inspect them even before taking delivery, which entailed removing the locks and examining the screws, stocks and rammers, checking that the bayonets were straight and free from obvious flaws and testing the hooks, sling swivels and leatherwork. The assistance of a soldier skilled in gunsmithing was highly requisite, for no weapon would be exchanged once a receipt of delivery had been given. After a captain had taken charge of the weapons he would be wise to examine them once a week and order his subalterns to inspect them every day.[65] Even these precautions were futile, however, if third parties intervened. In November 1744 companies of the 39th Foot stationed at Portsmouth had returned to them *via* the carrier a quantity of firelocks carried up by drafts to London. Any care once taken of them in the regiment was now of no avail, 'they having been promiscuously thrown together in a storehouse in the Tower and many of them broke, both locks and stocks and bayonets, the scabbards of which are entirely unfit for use'. There were no new muskets available for issue at that juncture, so the cost of these extensive repairs was borne by the captains.[66]

6. Ten regiments of Marines, 1739–64

On October 19, 1739 England declared war on Spain. At the opening of Parliament on 15 November the King declared that 'as in the prosecution of the war a number of soldiers to serve on board the fleet may be requisite. I have judged it proper that a body of Marines should be raised'.

The levy consisted of six regiments of 815 rank and file. The colonels were experienced officers; all but one had served abroad in Queen Anne's war, as had the majority of the field officers. The captains were gentlemen of service from the half-pay list, the independent companies of Jamaica or deserving subalterns from the old corps. The lieutenants and second lieutenants were ensigns from the old corps, volunteers who had carried arms in the ranks in hopes of obtaining a free commission, and young gentlemen new to the service. Competition was keen. Lord Crighton, nephew to the Earl of Stair, arrived in London in December only to find that 'everything in the Marine regiments was given away before I came'.[67] On 1 January 1740 each regiment was augmented to 1,000 rank and file, and the first drafts joined the fleet at the end of April. In January 1741 four additional regiments were raised, each of 1,000 men, which brought the establishment of Marines up to 11,500, a figure which remained constant until all ten regiments were disbanded in November 1748.

None of the officers could have envisaged the extent of the financial confusion which would quickly engulf their new commands. Although the disaster is atypical, in that almost every implicit weakness of Georgian military administration was laid bare more or less simultaneously, the fate of the Marines sums up the way in which active service conditions upset delicately engineered regimental economies. Sixteen years were to pass between the breaking of the regiments and the final arbitrary and approximate clearing of their accounts.

To be fair to the military administrators of 1740, they were not unaware that sea service posed particular problems. Even though the Marines remained under the administrative authority of the War Office until February 1747, when they were transferred to the Admiralty,[68] an attempt was made from the start to equip them with a distinct bureaucratic organisation consisting of a Paymaster, Deputy Paymaster and Accountant, a Commissary General and Deputy Commissary General and from May 1742, a military Inspector General, Brigadier-General Edward Wolfe, colonel of the 1st Regiment of Marines.[69] Furthermore, specific 'Instructions for the Better Government of the Marine Forces' were promulgated in May 1740. On land, the Marines were to be mustered by deputy commissaries of the musters just as if they were regiments of foot. Aboard ship, the officer commanding a detachment was to make a two-monthly return to the Commissary General of Marines, signed by himself and another officer of Marines and attested to by the captain and purser of the vessel as being conformable to the number of effectives entered in the ship's books. Five copies of this precious paper were to be made: one for the ship's captain, one for the commander of the detachment and three for the Commissary General of Marines, to be sent home by separate conveyances. They were the authority for him to compile muster rolls in his office – a dubious expedient, but no more so than the current practice of allowing palpably weak regiments to be mustered as if complete. To avoid confusion, it was further ordered that not less than twenty-four Marines should be embarked as a detachment and that they should always be commanded by one of their own officers.[70] A further order, dated 21 May 1740, declared that ships of ninety guns or more should carry a captain, two lieutenants and 100 marines, and so on down through the rates to the humble twenty-gun vessel with its lieutenant and thirty Marines. These strictures were relaxed to the extent that sloops-of-war were permitted to embark fifteen Marines as supernumeraries. The hope was expressed that detachments would always consist of men from the same company.[71]

It was soon discovered that shipboard life frustrated these pious hopes. Firstly, a comparison between Marine returns sent home from sea and entries in the ship's books rarely produced an identical figure. Marine officers proved negligent or unlucky in their attempts to send returns home safely and the Commissary General of Marines was obliged to fall back on returns of effectives compiled in their headquarters at Portsmouth, Southampton, Plymouth and Chatham. These, not surprisingly, were often at variance with the limited information seeping home from the fleet. In March 1745 a return from the Marine headquarters declared that 8,517 men were then at sea, another 690 in quarters and that 1,255 were either recruiting, on furlough or sick. Returns from sea revealed only 6,578 Marines aboard the fleet, a deficiency of 1,939 with many discrepancies between numbers attributed to particular vessels.[72] Irritated by this confusion, the Admiralty ordered its captains to forward Marine returns direct for comparison with the ships' books, although it is uncertain how useful this exercise was, the clerks of the men-at-war often neglecting to enter the various ranks of Marines on board their ships, failing to distinguish the regiments to which they belonged, and omitting to take notice of occasions when men were embarked or when they were discharged, '... hereby cutting off all means of tracing them forwards or backwards'.[73]

It soon became impossible to compile adequate muster rolls. Respites, '... so dire in their consequence that they ought to be guarded against with all the care imaginable', could no longer be avoided. Knowing that the West Indies were a sickly station, and that it was administratively imperative to prevent heavy overpayments of subsistence being made to the captains, Sir William Yonge ordered the Paymster of Marines, Charles Hanbury-Williams, to detain the monthly subsistence of 200 men from each regiment, declaring, more in hope than expectation, that an adjustment could be made 'from time to time' as better information became available.[74] In the meantime the regiments could not be cleared and, despite the difficulty of their personal situation, the officers could not receive their arrears.

The muddle of returns, ships' book entries, presumed overpayments of subsistence and arbitrary respites brought the regimental economies of the Marines grinding to a standstill. In March 1752, more than three years after the Marine regiments had been disbanded, an analysis of their muster rolls revealed that although rolls for 1740 were cleared in 1742, those for 1741 were not complete until June–July 1747, while rolls for 1743 and 1744 were not submitted until September 1748 and September–October 1749 respectively. Rolls for 1745, 1746 and 1747 were only made up between April 1750 and May 1751, and rolls for 1748 had not yet been delivered to the Pay Office.[75] All these rolls were peppered with respites. Officers were being charged with overpayments which they denied or attributed to breakdowns in accounting for which they were blameless. The accounts of the agents of Marine regiments were at variance with those of the captains. Men were still arriving home who had long since been presumed dead and struck off the rolls. The contingent bills, never the easiest documents to audit, were in a state of wild confusion.

At the beginning of 1757 the officers of Marines with accounts still unsettled and arrears unpaid memorialised Lord Barrington that they and their families had been ruined by the delay. Barrington summoned a Board of General Officers which met in March and submitted reports in June and September. However, there were limits to what the Board could achieve and although agreeing that the officers (or, in many cases, their widows and executors) had a right to an equitable settlement, the best the generals could do was to suggest that the regimental papers be applied to once more.

The luckless wretch to whom this task was delegated was the former Deputy Paymaster and Accountant of Marines, Edmund Herbert of Whittleborough.[76] In February 1760 he informed Barrington that his attempts to examine the papers of the 1st Regiment had led to a mental collapse that had laid him low for nine months. Since his partial recovery he had continued the struggle against thousands of cash books, vouchers, journals and ledgers submitted by the agents, assisted only by a gaggle of agents' clerks who appeared when it suited them. Finding that in many cases the Marine accounts were 'utterly incapable of a separation', he complained of his 'great toil and vexation', and reported that threats had been uttered against him in the House of Commons.[77] Herbert eventually handed in the reports to the Treasury in June 1761 and January 1762. They were submitted to the War Office for consideration, and warrants for clearing the ten regiments were issued on 30 October 1764. The payments were still based on the spurious muster rolls and vouchers for contingent expenses, in so far as Herbert had been able to methodise them. £22,548 7s 5d was issued as clearings, subject to a drawback of £3,944 10s 6¾d on account of alleged overpayments. The accounts were now closed, twenty-four years after the regiments had been raised and sixteen years after their disbandment.[78]

Investing in a regimental commission was a highly speculative venture. Even leaving aside any consideration of the attendant hazards of exile, sickness, wounds and violent death, it was clear that in many instances, and particularly in the regiments of infantry, that the personal pay and declining incidental dividends were not proportional to the responsibilities incurred in managing the command. State assistance in carrying out these responsibilities was erratic and its administrative machinery, designed to prevent fraud rather than ease the passage of business, could effectively deprive the officer of a considerable part of his pay for an indefinite period. Only a privileged minority of proprietors, the colonels of regiments, were able to stand above this maelstrom, and, in marked contrast to the junior military undertakers, they ended the period with the most lucrative of their perquisites intact.

Notes

1 Dalrymple, *A Military Essay. Containing Reflections on the Raising, Arming, Cloathing, and Discipline of the British Infantry and Cavalry*, London, 1761, p. 141
2 For a masterly dissection of service conditions in Great Britain and abroad see Houlding, *Fit for Service*, pp. 1–90. Additional information on duties undertaken in support of the civil power is provided by Hayter, *The Army and the Crowd in Mid-Georgian England, passim*, and Muskett, 'Military Operations against Smugglers in Kent and Sussex'. The impressionistic survey of conditions of service contained in this chapter is concerned only with the impact on regimental administration.
3 Lt.-Col. James Wolfe, 20th Foot, to his father, 22 April 1753, Wright, *Wolfe*, p. 263. Wolfe served in Scotland as major and lieutenant-colonel of the 20th for much of the period March 1749–September 1753.
4 'Colonel Naizon wants to go to London,' complained Maj.-Gen. Humphrey Bland to the second Earl of Albemarle, Cumberland's successor in command of the army in Scotland, '... I presume two-thirds of your army here are teazing you for the same and having business of the utmost importance to transact, tho' the greatest part of them, like Colonel Waldegrave, only want to buy a hat or some trifle.' Bland to Albemarle, 22 Aug. 1746, C. Sandford Terry, ed., *The Albemarle Papers*, London, 1902, I, p. 151.

5 BL. Add. MSS. 39,189 f. 216, Ensign John Mackenzie, 19th Foot, to his brother William, 6 April 1739.

6 NAM. 7805–63, Ensign Nicholas Delacherois, 9th Foot, to his brother Daniel, 22 May 1757.

7 See the diverting account by Ferguson, 'The Army in Ireland', pp. 85–6.

8 G. A. Hayes-McCoy, 'The Irish Horse Regiments of the Eighteenth Century', *Irish Sword*, IX, 1969–70, pp. 127–34.

9 Houlding, *Fit for Service*, pp. 45–57.

10 NAM. 6806–41–7, George, Viscount Townshend, Lord Lieutenant of Ireland, to the Earl of Rochford, Secretary of State, 16 Oct. 1770; PRO. SP 63/432 f. 262, same to the Earl of Weymouth, Secretary of State, 20 Dec. 1770.

11 HUL. DDHO4, Major Thomas Gage, 44th Foot, to Charles Hotham, 20 Feb. 1749.

12 NAM. 7411–24–16, 'Some Remarks', *c.* 1725.

13 One of these was Capt. Cuthbert Ellison of the 3rd Dragoons, who complained from Lucas's Coffee House in Dublin that '. . . tho' our regiment is in this garrison, and we are distinguished as a very fine one, yet I am heartily sick of both and wish myself on the English Establishment'. GPL. Ellison A.18, Cuthbert to Henry Ellison, 8 Jan. 1730. 'I have desir'd my uncle to get me a change,' he revealed; '. . . his interest wou'd effect it, if he'd exert himself.' See also JRL. B2.1.231, David Roberts, clerk in the War Office, to Col. Samuel Bagshawe, 93rd Foot, 8 July 1761, expressing the hope that Bagshawe's election to the Irish House of Commons would serve as a lever to procure him an appointment in England.

14 NAM. 7411–24–16, 'Some Thoughts'; BL. Add. MSS. 35,357 f. 102, Col. Joseph Yorke, 9th Foot, to the Earl of Hardwicke, 4 March 1757.

15 BL. Add. MSS. 17,494 f. 56, Calcraft to Maj.-Gen. Edward Pole, 10th Foot, 23 Dec. 1758.

16 *Parl. Hist.*, XII, pp. 384–5.

17 See the various complaints of Capt. Charles Whitefoord, 18th Foot, from Minorca during 1738–39 in the *Whitefoord Papers, passim*, also PRO. WO 4/32 f. 343, Sir William Yonge to Maj.-Gen. Philip Anstruther, Governor of Minorca, 22 April 1740, and WO 1/294 f. 891, Anstruther to the Duke of Newcastle, Secretary of State, 3 July 1742. Lieutenant-General Humphrey Bland and Lieutenant-General Philip Anstruther, governors of Gibraltar and Minorca respectively, were two officers whose style of command was very irksome to some of their prickly subordinates, see Lt.-Col. James Wolfe to his father, 31 Jan. 1751, Wright, *Wolfe*, p. 143; *Seasonable and Affecting Observations*, p. 37, and, for a general comment, above, pp. 37–8.

18 PRO. WO 1/294 f. 715, Report by Brig.-Gen Thomas Paget, Lieutenant-Governor of Minorca, April 1740. Paget was a bitter critic of the Anstruther regime; this, and his apoplectic constitution (he died not long after this report was written), must cast some doubt on the judgment and accuracy of his reporting.

19 Houlding, *Fit for Service*, pp. 18–23; J. Shy, *Toward Lexington: The Role of the British Army in the Coming of the American Revolution*, Princeton, N. J., 1965, pp. 274–6. The extent of Cumberland's achievement in instituting the Mediterranean rotations can be appreciated by referring to the estimated cost to the public; £6,131 3s 6d to relieve a battalion in Minorca and £4,297 18s for Gibraltar, R. A. Cumb. C43/10. Popular rumour inflated the bill to £80,000! GPL. Ellison. A30, H. T. Carr to Henry Ellison, 4 July 1750.

20 See the graphic account by Commodore Charles Knowles, RN, Governor of the captured fortress of Louisbourg, of conditions in the garrison during winter 1746–47, quoted in H. C. Wylly, *History of the 1st and 2nd Battalions, the Sherwood Foresters, 1740–1914*, London, 1929, I, p. 10; also DRO. D86 X3, Col. the Hon. Edward Cornwallis, Governor of Nova Scotia, to Henry Fox, 27 Nov. 1750. James Wolfe's

assessment is typically bleak; '... the dirtiest and most unpleasant branch of military operations; no room for courage and skill to exert itself, no hope of ending it by a decisive blow and a perpetual danger of assassination. These circumstances discourage the firmest minds.' Wolfe to Capt. William Rickson, 9 June 1751, Wright, *Wolfe*, p. 168. This must have cheered poor Rickson up no end.

21 NAM. 7805–63, Delacherois to his brother Daniel, Bermuda, 20 March 1767.

22 See below, pp. 122–3.

23 *Observations on the Prevailing Abuses in the British Army*, p. 8.

24 Ilchester, *Henry Fox, First Lord Holland*, I, pp. 140–1.

25 PRO. WO 34/90 f. 29, Lt.-Col. Isaac Barré, commandant of the 106th Foot, to Maj.-Gen. Jeffery Amherst, 13 Feb. 1762.

26 *Memoirs of Sir James Campbell of Ardkinglass*, London, 1832, I, p. 113.

27 These outlandish titles are all printed in the *Army Lists*. Over sixty independent companies were raised for rank and over thirty regiments, into which some of the companies were subsequently drafted. The terms and conditions of service of these units are described in more detail in A. J. Guy, 'Drafts for Portugal, 1762: Recruiting for Rank at the End of the Seven Years' War', *ARNAM*, 1977–78, pp. 29–34. Biographical details of many of the unit commanders are provided by J. W. Hayes, 'Lieutenant Colonel and Major Commandants of the Seven Years' War', *JSAHR*, XXXVI, 1958, pp. 3–13, 38–9.

28 JRL. B2.1.161, Windus to Bagshawe, 23 Nov. 1760; *ibid.*, 165, Capt. Montgomery, regimental agent, to Bagshawe, 16 Dec. 1760; *ibid.*, 175, Windus to Bagshawe, 2 Jan. 1761; *ibid.*, 190, 193, same to same, 2, 17 March 1761; *ibid.*, 232, Montgomery to Bagshawe, 25 July 1761; *ibid.*, 203, Memorial of Col. Samuel Bagshawe to the Lords Justices of Ireland, 1761.

29 PRO. WO 4/68 f. 70, Circular to Beauclerk and other commandants, 11 March 1762; *ibid.*, f. 73. Charles Townshend to Graeme, 25 March 1762; *ibid.*, f. 76, Abstract of Drafts, 27 April 1762.

30 Proposals included drafting the whole of Craufurd's 85th Foot, and obliging the officers to re-raise it from scratch, reducing officers from heavily drafted units to half pay and breaking the 61st, 66th, 68th and 70th Foot, all of which were very weak; SRO. HA.174.1026.361, Proposals for Recruiting the Army in Germany, Feb. 1761.

31 PRO. WO 4/48 f. 247, Fox to Swiney, 17 March 1752.

32 PRO. WO 4/61 f. 265, Memorial and Affidavit of Major Ross, 46th Foot, May 1760

33 JRL. B2.2.221, Lt. Archibald Grant to Major Samuel Bagshawe, 26 Feb. 1747.

34 PRO. WO 26/21 f. 377, *London Gazette* advertisement offering 100 guineas' reward for apprehending Adjutant George Colley of Torrington's Marines, suspected of having absconded with £600 or £700 of the regimental funds, 2 Dec. 1748; SRO. HA.174.1026.38/3 Ensign B. Grier, 3rd Foot, to Gen. Peregrine Hopson, 19 Oct. 1758; PRO. WO 4/61 f. 487, Barrington to Henry Fox, Paymaster General, on the Grier case, 25 July 1760; PRO. WO 4/66 f. 446, Charles Townshend to Lt.-Col. Reade, 34th Foot, 15 Dec. 1761. Captains were also responsible for the actions of their other nominees, their paymaster-sergeants, clerks or other rank-and-file assistants. In July 1750 Sergeant Macartney of Captain Francis Forde's company (39th Foot) absconded with £28 of subsistence. Forde proposed that his new sergeant should serve on a corporal's pay and the corporal on a private man's to make up the deficit—Lt.-Col. Bagshawe held Forde responsible and thought he ought to find the money himself; JRL. B2.2.549, Lt.-Col. Matthews Sewell to Bagshawe, 25 July 1750.

35 See above, p. 62.

36 This convoluted affair can be followed in PRO. WO 4/46 f. 368, Fox to Pitt, 10 Oct. 1749; PRO. WO 4/48 f. 24, Memorial of four captains of Churchill's Marines; *ibid.*, f. 26, Warrant lifting suspensions of half pay belonging to the two Mitchells, 14 March

1751; SRO. HA 174.1206.36.293, 'Case of Captain Shafto and Additional Papers', *c.* 1759; PRO. WO 4/48, Fox to the Judge Advocate General, 22 July 1752; *ibid.*, f. 53, Fox to Shafto, 10 June 1752; *ibid.*, f. 77, Fox to the Judge Advocate General, 28 Feb 1753; *ibid.*, f. 93, Fox to Pitt, 5 March 1753. The younger Mitchell was brought before a general court-martial on 10 July 1753 accused of having 'misbehaved in several particulars' while paymaster, but the court confined itself to ascertaining whether he was telling the truth about his father's engagements with Shafto and the captains. This was scarcely of any help to the creditors; PRO. WO 4/48 f. 226, Fox to the Judge Advocate General, 17 July 1753. It will be recalled that Shafto was no stranger to controversy. He had made out a case for himself as a victim of the resentment of Major-General Edward Wolfe before the Commons committee of 1746, and this was later cited as an instance of arbitary behaviour of which Cumberland was thought to be chief exponent; see above, pp. 37–8.

37 These cases are examined in greater detail in Guy, 'Regimental Agency', *BJRL*, LXII, 1980, pp. 432–7.

38 *Ibid.*, p. 438.

39 The wartime Recruiting Acts of our period were: 17 Geo. II, cap. 44, 'An Act for the Speedy and Effectual Recruiting of His Majesty's Land Forces and Marines', 1744; this provided for a bounty of £4 to volunteers after which JPs and Commissioners of the Land Tax would press men not following lawful employment, with a reward to the parish for each man taken up. The bounties and rewards were advanced from receipts of the land tax and charged against non-effective funds: 18 Geo. II, cap. 10, 'An Act for the Speedy and Effectual Recruiting of HM's Regiments of Foot serving in Flanders, Minorca, Gibraltar and the Plantations and the Regiments of Marines', 1745, which made marginal amendments to the previous Act: 29 Geo. II, cap. 4, 'An Act for the Speedy and Effectual Recruiting of HM's Land Forces and Marines', 1756, which instituted a new press of the sturdy poor, paid for out of the non-effective funds and organised by local civilian commissioners, whose meetings officers were obliged to attend: 30 Geo. II, cap. 8, 'An Act for the Speedy and Effectual Recruiting of HM's Land Forces and Marines', 1757, which reintroduced a bounty (of £3) for volunteers, to be charged against the non-effective funds and followed by another press of the indigent. All these acts were to be suspended by Proclamation, Order in Council or notice in the *London Gazette* when regimental returns showed that current manpower targets had been reached.

40 In addition to the usual warnings against entertaining papists, foreigners, boys, old men, the ruptured and the crippled, instructions issued by Lt.-Col. Edward Windus of the 93rd Foot cautioned recruiting officers to be wary of '... strollers, vagabonds, tinkers, chimney-sweepers, colliers and saylors', JRL. B2.1.20, 1760.

41 'By enquiry and advice of several officers I am informed that it is constantly practised without any bad consequences'; NAM. 7805–63, Ensign Nicholas Delacherois, 9th Foot, to his brother Daniel, 22 Nov. 1757; see also J. C. Leask, H. M. McCance. *Regimental Records of the Royal Scots*, Dublin, 1915, p. 120.

42 The whole question of recruiting in Ireland is illuminated by Ferguson, 'The Army in Ireland', pp. 68–75. The temptation to enlist Roman Catholics was particularly great when officers raising men for rank were hurrying to meet their deadlines. Lt.-Col. Edward Windus of the 93rd Foot caught two of his subalterns at this game in 1760, but charitably attributed their indiscretion to the fact that they had been based on their home estates, '... where young gents. are apt to be little giddy and to mind their country diversions more than their recruiting'; JRL. B.2.1.46, Windus to Col. Samuel Bagshawe, 26 March 1760.

43 Cuthbertson, *System*, p. 76; B. Seton, 'Infantry Recruiting Instructions in England, 1767', *JSAHR*, IV, 1925, pp. 88–9.

44 The great dormitory, sisters' and porters' lodgings at the Savoy Hospital, London, were converted into barracks between 1679 and 1713. The accommodation was notoriously unhealthy, and recruits and drafts quartered there were kept under a virtual prison regime.

45 JRL.B2.3.77, Lt. Samuel Bagshawe, lst Foot, to his uncle, William Bagshawe of Ford, 12 Sept. 1740.

46 PRO. WO 4/48 f. 369, Henry Fox to Col. Henry Holmes, 31st Foot, 20 July 1752.

47 DRO. D86.X3, Fox to Col. Robert Napier, Adjutant General, 17 July 1749.

48 Cuthbertson, *System*, p. 66; PRO. WO 72/5, Statement by Gen. Sir Robert Rich, 4th Dragoons, cited during the general court-martial of Lt. James Boyd, 27 April 1762.

49 Cuthbertson, *System*, pp. 77–9.

50 The characteristics of these animals are described by G. Tylden, *Horses and Saddlery: An Account of the Animals used by British and Commonwealth Armies from the Seventeenth Century to the Present Day with a Description of their Equipment*, London, 1965, pp. 10–13. See also the Marquess of Anglesey, *A History of the British Cavalry, 1816 to 1919*, I, London, 1973, pp. 107–8.

51 PRO. WO 4/40 f. 237, Sir William Yonge to Lord Duncannon, 1 March 1745; WO 4/60 f. 305, Viscount Barrington to Richard Rigby, Chief Secretary, 18 March 1760. This letter implies that remount prices in Ireland were even higher.

52 PRO. WO 71/6 f. 360, Petition of Col. Sir Robert Rich to the Board of General Officers, 22 Feb. 1744; *Journals, H.O.C.*, XXIV, p. 613, Account of the number of Horses lost at Dettingen; *ibid.*, XXV, p. 136, Account of Extraordinary Expenses incurred on account of the Rebellion and for Horses lost at Sea; R. A. Cumb. C3/188, Abstract of Horses lost at Laffeldt, 22 Jan. 1748; PRO. WO 4/39 f. 160, Sir William Yonge to John Scrope Esq., 8 May 1744; PRO. SP 87/11 f. 104, Memorial of Sir Thomas Hay, 1 March 1743.

53 R. A. Cumb. C10/177, Rothes to Cumberland, 8 Feb. 1746. For payments eventually authorised in respect of these claims, see Sir Charles Whitworth, *Public Accounts of Service and Grants*, pp. 28, 32, 34.

54 R. A. Cumb C3/63, Sir Everard Fawkener to Newcastle 20 June 1745; *ibid.*, C3/126, Newcastle to Fawkener, 21 June 1745. There were thirty-four such companies in England and twelve in Scotland. In March 1746 their tangled affairs were referred to a committee headed by the Secretary at War, Paymaster-General and the Comptrollers of the Accounts of the Army. The only way out of the mess was to allow them to pass muster as if complete and unite them with their parent battalions; PRO. AO 17/37 f. 172, Report on the Finances of the Additional Companies, 5 May 1746.

55 'Our captains suffer greatly by giving these drafts ... all are obliged to send them complete in necessaries, even those which are greatly in debt, which is so much loss to each captain ...', JRL. B2.1.161, Lt.-Col. Edward Windus, 93rd Foot, to Col. Samuel Bagshawe, 23 Nov. 1760.

56 PRO. WO 71/1 f. 113, John, Earl of Stair to the Board of General Officers, 30 May 1744; *ibid.*, f. 117, Report of the Board, June 1744; *ibid.*, f. 136, Supplementary Report, 14 June 1744; PRO. WO 4/46 f. 13, Henry Fox to Lt.-Gen. Henry Skelton, 16 March 1749.

57 PRO. WO 1.609 f. 11, Robert Wilmot Esq. to Barrington, 5 Oct. 1757; *ibid.*, f. 13, Thomas Waite, Secretary to the Lords Justices of Ireland, to Wilmot, 29 Sept. 1757.

58 Guy, 'Drafts for Portugal', *passim*.

59 PRO. WO 4/36 f. 475, Sir William Yonge to Gen. Jasper Clayton, 11 July 1741; JRL. B2.2.371, Lt.-Col. Samuel Bagshawe, 39th Foot, to Lt.-Col. Matthews Sewell, 20 June 1749.

60 Examples of the latter can be found in *London Chronicle*, No. 636 (20–22 Jan. 1761)—an

advertisement for fourteen deserters from an independent company in Barnet; *ibid.*, No. 697, (11–14 June 1761)—an advertisement for five deserters from the 16th Foot. There are numerous other advertisements for one, two or more men.

61 PRO. WO 4/30 f. 148, Richard Arnold, Deputy Secretary at War, to Capt. John Pretty, 1 May 1729; WO 4/33 f. 141, Arnold to Capt. Middleton, 20 May 1735; WO 4/37 f. 41, Sir William Yonge to the Revd. Mr Vievor, 6 Oct. 1741; *ibid.*, f. 200, Yonge to T. Lister Esq., 20 March 1742.

62 PRO. WO 4/34 f. 193, Arnold to Thomas Vernon Esq., 3 June 1736; *ibid.*, f. 273, Arnold to the Lord Mayor of York, 15 Jan. 1737.

63 Cuthbertson, *System*, pp. 26–9.

64 BL. Add. MSS. 40,759, 'Francis Report', f. 248   See below, pp. 146–7.

65 Cuthbertson, *System*, pp. 108–9.

66 JRL. B2.2.324, Capt. Thomas Levett, regimental agent, to Capt. Samuel Bagshawe, 39th Foot, 13 Nov. 1744.

67 Crighton to Stair, 15 Jan. 1740, *Stair Annals*, II, p. 262.

68 PRO. WO 26/21 f. 58, 26 Feb. 1747.

69 PRO. WO 26/19 f. 444, Warrant instructing Wolfe to look into 'the condition, number etc. relating to the Marines now in Great Britain or serving on board the Fleet', 4 May 1742.

70 PRO. WO 26/19 f. 250, Rules and Instructions for the better Government of the Marine forces, 9 May 1740.

71 PRO. WO 26/19 f. 352, Warrant to Phillip Cavendish, Admiral of the Blue, 21 May 1741.

72 PRO. Adm 2/1150 f. 48, An Account of Marines on Board the Fleet, March 1746.

73 PRO. WO 71/7 f. 146, Report of a Board of General Officers, 24 Jan. 1746.

74 PRO. Adm 96/3 f. 417, Yonge to Hanbury-Williams, 23 March 1743.

75 PRO. Adm 96/3 f. 363, An Account of the Times when Marine Muster-Rolls were delivered to the Pay Office, 23 March 1752.

76 PRO. WO 95/2 f. 70, Report of a Board of General Officers on the Arrears of the Regiments of Marines, March–Sept. 1757.

77 PRO. Adm 96/375, Petition of Edmund Herbert, 29 Feb. 1760.

78 PRO. WO 26/27 f. 21, Warrant of 30 Oct. 1764, with statement of clearings annexed.

6

The colonel's advantage

Regimental proprietors and the profits of command

From the accession of George I to the end of the Seven Years' War, 374 colonels of regiments served in the army. At least 170 of them were owners of landed estates: they included fifty-seven peers, seventeen baronets, at least seventy untitled country gentlemen and twenty-five sons of peers or baronets who had acquired estates of their own. Thus two-thirds of all the proprietary colonels were men firmly established in the upper reaches of political society, exclusive of any distinction brought by high command. What was more, an average of fifty per cent serving at any one time sat in the two Houses of Parliament at Westminster, and others attended the Irish Parliament in Dublin.[1] It is true that the first two Georges succeeded in making some encroachments on their independence and customary emoluments, but it was inconceivable that these could be trifled with in the manner in which the proprietary captains' dividends had been. Moreover, besides being quantitatively superior, there was a qualitative difference in the nature of these emoluments. They were not usually subject to the vicissitudes of active service; neither did they depend on the management of limited numbers of men and horses or paltry sums of subsistence, but on contracts and gentlemen's agreements with agents, clothiers, sword cutlers and gunmakers.

1. Public liabilities and central regulation

Regardless of their social and political influence, the colonels were also deferred to by the Crown for purely military considerations. The most senior served as reviewing generals and members of the Board of General Officers, backbone of the military administrative structure. They were scarcely less important in their role as regimental proprietors, for they provided vitally important services that the tiny War Office bureaucracy was incapable of supplying. They appointed agents and determined the level of their securities; they contracted for clothing and some species of weapons, insured these items and even arranged their package and transport; they approved advances of money for recruiting and remounting from the regimental funds, reviewed the stock purses and often decided what balances should be paid to the captains; they nominated regimental staff officers, selected recruiters, vetted candidates for commissions and restrained purchase deals which threatened the harmony of the regiment. On them to a large extent depended the character and level of effectiveness of the regiments.[2]

The first two Georges believed that this degree of influence was incompatible with the right freely to dispose of colonelcies on the commission market, and they intervened more directly in the appointment of regimental proprietors than in any other promotions. They did not confront existing property-holders head-on by depriving them of the right to sell what they had bought (even the colonels broken for Jacobite sympathies in 1715 were permitted to dispose of their commissions), but whenever an opportunity arose of freely disposing of a regiment, they excluded the cash consideration and appointed officers with a long or otherwise distinguished service record. The Regulation of the Prices of the Commissions in all His Majesty's Land Forces of 27 February 1720 had stated a tariff of colonelcies—£9,000–£7,500 for regiments of horse, £7,000 for regiments of dragoons and £6,000 for marching regiments—but over a long period, as existing colonels died in harness and no sale was allowed to take place, the operation of purchase was greatly reduced. The sale of the 1st Dragoon Guards for £6,000 in 1762 was among the last transactions of its type, and no tariff of colonelcies was stated in the commission price regulations of 10 February 1766.[3]

Striking evidence of the Crown's success in asserting control over the disposal of colonelcies and its predilection for men of long service is seen in the fact that out of 290 colonels appointed between 1714 and 1763, over twenty had served for more than forty-five years, over sixty between thirty-five and forty-five years and the other ninety for more than fifteen years. The majority of those remaining had served for over a decade before obtaining command of a regiment.[4]

The paradox inherent in the purchase system as it was allowed to operate under the first two Georges was that the places really worth having in terms of interest and perquisites, the proprietary colonelcies, were precisely those that could no longer be freely acquired. What was more, this novel control of the market was paralleled by an attempt to make colonels more responsible in their persons and fortunes for the material condition of the units entrusted to their care. As Henry Fox insisted, government made them sufficient allowances to keep their regiments well appointed, and they or their executors were answerable for that trust.[5]

In extreme cases this meant cashiering. The dreadful condition of Lieutenant-General Thomas Ecklyn's 6th Dragoons was as much a cause of his dismissal in 1715 as his latent Jacobitism,[6] and Lord Hervey suggested that the breaking of Lord Bolton (1733) was partly owing to his corrupt management of the Royal Regiment of Horse Guards.[7] Other equally effective but less drastic measures were also developed by the Crown during the 1720s to keep lesser defaulters up to the mark. Three important cases, that of Lieutenant-General George Macartney, 21st Foot and 7th Horse (1727–30), Colonel Richard Lucas, 38th Foot (1728–31) and Colonel Richard Phillips, 40th Foot (1729–32), show the growth of administrative expertise in this area.

The colonel's advantage

Sir James Wood succeeded Macartney in the command of the 21st Foot in March 1727. Far from occupying a post of honour and profit, he soon found that £1,500 of regimental money had been misapplied by Macartney and the paymaster. Moreover, the unit had suffered 'divers injuries ... for want of arms and clothing, although a fund sufficient for this purpose has been provided'.

The Secretary at War, Henry Pelham, ordered the paymaster to come to account. It appeared in the course of this transaction that Macartney had allowed the captains to appoint the paymaster without consulting him, an astonishing abdication of responsibility. In what was to become standard practice, Macartney's defaults were referred to the Board of General Officers. The Board discovered that he had neglected to pay for a consignment of weapons, that he had failed to provide a full clothing in 1726, that he had gained £970 by the sale of a company in the regiment in 1717 (for which the captain was prosecuting him in Chancery), that he had engrossed £131 intended to provide the corps with tents, as well as another £184 15s that had been issued on account of contingencies seven years previously. Even his agent, Mr John Mulcaster, had joined in the plunder by pocketing £100 issued to the corps in 1723 on account of wear and tear to its camp equipage.

Macartney promised redress, and this, together with his distinguished military record, preserved him in the command of his new regiment, the 7th Horse, but before his death in 1730 he had reverted to his old tricks by robbing it of £500. When it became clear that his effects would not cover this amount, orders were issued to detain his arrears of pay as Governor of Portsmouth and lieutenant-general on the Irish staff.[8]

The case of Colonel Richard Lucas of the 38th Foot, which had already overtaken the Macartney affair, was tackled in a similar way. The regiment was then at the mid-point of its sixty-year exile in the Leeward Islands. Lucas, the major and many of the captains were absentees. The few officers remaining at their posts believed themselves to be the victims of fraud. By the time their complaints surfaced in the autumn of 1728 they had received no subsistence for over a year. Whatever money had arrived previously had been changed into local currency to their disadvantage. No bills sent to Lucas had ever been honoured and no abstracts of company accounts had been provided for years. It was already apparent that the corps was £3,000 in debt, and protested bills, carrying interest of up to twenty per cent, were arriving in Antigua on every ship.

Lucas got wind of the captains' petition and embarked for the Leeward Islands just before it arrived. Three days before the ship docked in Antigua, he died. When Lieutenant-Colonel Valentine Morris searched the corpse, there were only twenty-four guineas on it.

The 'voluminous matter' was at once submitted to the Board of General Officers. An examination of the accounts revealed that Lucas owed the 38th £7,089 17s 3¾d, besides clothing and weapons. The Pay Office declined to issue any arrears until the Board had apportioned blame.

Oeconomy and discipline

Much of the confusion could be traced to the fact that Lucas had tried to act as his own agent. He was absolutely incapable in this department and had sunk his regiment's funds in his own chaotic finances. Then, looking round for a way of extricating himself, he had fallen into the clutches of 'a very sharp man', John Mulcaster, the regimental agent, who had already played an unwholesome role in the swindling of the 21st Foot. Mulcaster offered Lucas a loan of £1,500 in return for the agency, but extorted interest of £400 *per annum*, as well as money to insure his new client's life. The only source of cash was the regimental fund. The Board of General Officers was horrified at this bargain struck with public money. Mulcaster was ordered to refund any balances in his hands (he had tried to withhold them as a substitute for his now vanished £1,500), while all Lucas's unpaid subsistence, clearings and off-reckonings were appropriated.[9]

For the future it was proposed that colonels of regiments serving in the Plantations should give securities to the Paymaster General to indemnify the public against misadventures of this sort, and a circular was issued to that effect on 15 February 1729, but it did not name any particular sum. The prosecution in 1750 of another colonel of 38th, Lieutenant-General Robert Dalzell, for similar offences suggests that the value of this initiative was limited.[10]

Meanwhile the Crown was attempting to recover funds from a living defal-cator, Colonel Richard Phillips (40th Foot). Like many other units on long-term foreign service the 40th's administrative record was dismal. The financial affairs of the independent companies in Annapolis Royal around which it had been formed in 1717 had been subjected to intensive scrutiny in 1718.[11] In 1729 one of Phillip's captains, Joseph Bennett, a veteran of thirty years' service, ten of them with the regiment in Nova Scotia, accused the colonel of failing to come to a proper account with him and withholding part of his personal pay in hands of the agent. The Secretary at War passed the complaint to the Board of General Officers, which heard similar accusations from a number of other serving or ex-captains of the regiment. On 28 April 1730 Phillips was given a twelvemonth to come to account, and at the year's end, substantial amounts still being unpaid, his personal pay was detained. The Board spent 'many weeks' on the matter again in the spring of 1732 before discharging Phillips.[12]

By the early 1730s therefore, without causing major affront to the colonels as an interest group, the Crown had developed three ways of regulating their be-haviour: the gradual interdiction of the custom of purchase and sale of regiments; dismissal for serious offences and the use of an enquiry before the Board of General Officers (in effect, a trial by one's peers), followed, if necessary, by distraint of pay, allowances and personal effects. No further dramatic encroach-ments on the independence of colonels were made in our period; indeed, they were not even attempted.

This discreet approach was warranted by the relatively low personal re-muneration attached to colonels' commissions. Even the full pay *per annum* of a colonel of horse, £748 5s (inclusive of his salary as captain of a troop but before deductions and arrears), though well up on Joseph Massie's 1759 estimate of the income of a prosperous merchant, was less than half-way up the scale of revenues of landed gentlemen. The salary of a colonel of dragoons was only £638 15s, and that of a colonel of foot £438. The latter's subsistence was 18s a day, only 5s more than his lieutenant-colonel.[13] Rather than taking the perilous step of asking the House of Commons for a more ample salary provision for these indispensable servants of the Crown, the alternative was chosen of allowing them to continue to receive a range of perquisites traditionally associated with the command of a regiment.[14] As by doing so the Crown and its ministers were in the ambivalent position of endorsing at one level of the army the sort of customary arrangements they were virtually eradicating at another, it is hardly surprising that whenever colonel's perquisites came under review, a marked indecisiveness of touch was evident. For their part, the colonels made good use of their interest in maintaining their prescriptive emoluments, some of which were not supported by any royal warrant, while others were of doubtful legality.

2. Vacant pay

As proprietors of troops or companies in their own regiments, colonels had the advantage of dividends on the stock purse and non-effective funds just like any other captain. In so far as payments from these sources were suppressed or reduced during the period, so was a proportion of their customary income. However, as it was standard practice to allow the captain-lieutenant to finger this dividend, he may have been the real loser by this reform.

Other sources of vacant pay were unaffected. From 11 August 1716 in Great Britain and 2 August 1740 in Ireland the colonel was credited with the equivalent of one man's subsistence per troop or company *per diem* as a perquisite and a contribution towards the cost of replacing clothing carried off by deserters. This allowance was stated on the regimental establishment in lieu of fictitious men and was an entirely legal *douceur*. The colonel was also credited with the balance of full pay *per diem* belonging to these 'colonel's men' in lieu of off-reckonings, also sums equivalent to the off-reckonings of the captains' two warrant men per troop or company and the one agent's man per troop or company.[15]

Claims to the vacant pay of other officers or men were of doubtful validity, although Captain Thomas Levett, the regimental agent, asserted that any pay not respited by a deputy commissary of the musters became a perquisite of the colonel. Levett was unable to cite a royal warrant to support his contention, but he was an experienced operator and, in an era of thoroughly ineffective mustering, we may infer that he had given his colonels credit on this head many times without being challenged. Furthermore, Mr John Winter, agent to the 6th Foot, testified to the Commons committee on the land forces and Marines of 1746 that during the regiment's service in the West Indies the colonel, John Guise, had been credited with the vacant pay of officers and men. Mr John Innes, until recently agent to Colonel Duncomb's regiment of Marines, believed that the vacant pay of officers belonged to the colonel not only by the custom of the army but also by royal warrant.[16]

This was certainly not the view of the War Office. In June 1746 an examination of the returns of Brigadier-General John Jefferys's regiment of Marines revealed that Lieutenant John Lister had been entered months after his transfer to Lieutenant-General Edward Wolfe's Marines. Jefferys, who had signed a recent return, was accused of false musters and of pocketing the vacant pay of the lieutenancy. His plea of 'an inadvertent want of recollection' was not admitted at his court-martial in August and he was cashiered.[17]

In February 1751 it was the turn of Lieutenant-General Edward Wolfe to cross swords with the War Office on the question of vacant pay when Henry Fox demanded repayment of £1,217 11s 9d overpaid to Wolfe's late regiment of Marines. Wolfe replied that as far as he was concerned the money was not subject to any drawback and was a perquisite of the colonel. Fox replied that it would be '... impossible for me ever to call vacant pay a perquisite of the colonels. The colonels have no right to it.' The enraged Wolfe fired off a highly abusive rejoinder, but Fox insisted that 'H. M does not think vacant pay a perquisite of the colonel'. The most he was prepared to offer was to meet Wolfe at the War Office and explain the policy on vacant pay to him.[18]

One quasi-legitimate allowance of vacant pay which enjoyed long continuance was the income derived from hautboys in the two troops of Horse Grenadier Guards and in each troop of the regiments of dragoons. The Commons committee of 1746 enquired into the status and duty of these elusive musicians and one colonel, the Hon. Richard Onslow, First Troop, Horse Grenadier Guards, actually exhibited George Wormington, one of his four hautboys, for interview. Wormington told the committee that he had been regularly enlisted and that he attended the troop at musters, reviews and other services as required. The distinct impression was registered that the latter were not very frequent. Moreover, it appeared from the examination of the troop's agent, Captain Alexander Wilson, that he accounted direct with Onslow for the hautboy's subsistence (£45 12s 6d per annum), but of this only between £6 and £9 was paid to Wormington. The general rule in regiments to which he was agent was for the colonels to be accounted with directly for hautboys in all the troops, and that as far as he was concerned, their subsistence was a *douceur* while their off-reckonings went into the clothing account.[19] Francis Grose, the military antiquary, tells a story '... current among some of the old standers in ... [the dragoon] ... service that the King (whether George I or II I know not) at a review asking General Churchill what was become of his hautboys, the general struck his hand on his breeches pocket, so as to make the money rattle and answered, "Here they are, please your majesty, don't you hear them?" Churchill being a favourite, the King laughed and made no further inquiry.'[20]

In 1768 a committee of the Irish House of Commons also looked into the employment of hautboys, and concluded that the perquisite amounted to £27 7s

6d (Irish) per hautboy *per annum*. The committee inveighed against the Muster-Master and Clerk of the Cheque in that kingdom for allowing the abuse to continue over so many years.[21]

3. The sale of commissions

The Crown was often forced to rely on colonels to vet young gentlemen seeking to obtain commissions, and it was usual for them to have a host of clients of their own to recommend. This was a potential source of profit, for it was understood in certain cases that if a recommendation was endorsed by the King, the colonel could sell the commission. Indeed, it was quite common for staff commissions to be sold in this way. Captain Wilson, the agent, recalled an adjutant's commission being sold by a colonel for £300, the chaplaincy of one old regiment for £400 and another for £500.[22] Lord Barrington tried to put a stop to this long-standing custom in January 1760 but the prohibition does not seem to have been particularly effective.[23]

Commissions in the line were potentially more valuable. Captain Wilson believed that a cornet's commission was worth up to £900 to a colonel and a subaltern commission in a marching regiment £450, but that, owing to the Crown's disapproval of such traffic, trade was slack. He thought that few colonels had the disposal of more than one commission a year or eighteen months and testified that one of his colonels had only sold one commission in eight years. Nevertheless, at several hundred pounds a time, the perquisite was a substantial one and the Crown would sometimes condone it as a reward for outstanding service, or to reimburse a colonel for heavy regimental expenditure. In July 1746 Cumberland gave permission for Lieutenant-General Humphrey Bland to sell a cornetcy in his 3rd Dragoons to compensate him for a loss of £1,400 on clothing and accoutrements. Bland was effusively grateful and hinted that mercenary engagements between colonels and their nominees were much more widespread than Captain Wilson had suggested: 'Had I followed the example of my brethren,' he fawned, 'I could have had a good many cornetcies in my pocket, but as I look upon this kind of traffic as contrary to His Majesty's intentions and detrimental to the service, I have hitherto had virtue enough to resist it.'[24]

4. The appointment of the agent

Although the War Office occasionally appointed interim agents pending the gazetting of a new colonel, it was usual for colonels to appoint their own agents and fix the level of their securities and allowances by private treaty. An attempt by Lord Barrington to interfere in these arrangements in 1760 was successfully warded off.

The extent to which colonels were free to choose their own men depended on their relationship to their patrons. When the young War Office clerk Leonard Morse applied to Lieutenant-Colonel Samuel Bagshawe for the agency of a battalion Bagshawe was believed to be about to be given, he was warned '... how

143

seldom the colonels have the power to name their agents'.[25] John Calcraft, who was also fishing for Bagshawe's agency, was told, 'Your merit, capacity and connections make it an honour to me to have such a person manage the affairs of the regiment, but I need not mention to you that these appointments are now reduced to a method and indeed it is very far from being unreasonable when a person by the credit of his patron and friend obtains promotion to accept a person whom his friends shall recommend. The D... of D...... is my patron, Sir Robert Wilmot has long been a disinterested friend. It will be my desire when I obtain a regiment that the agent may be agreable to them.'[26]

Other colonels, however, were not governed by such restraints and they appointed or swapped agents as they wished, sometimes in accordance with shifting political allegiances.[27] As relationships between colonels and agents were not constant, neither were the levels of the agents' allowances or securities, nor the benefit derived from them by the colonel.

There were two allowances payable to the agent. The first was a levy of 2d in the £ on the gross pay of the unit, deducted from the off-reckonings. The second was the subsistence of a warrant man per troop or company *per diem*, the 'agent's man'. The annual income from these sources fluctuated according to the number of troops or companies in the regiment and their internal strength, but in time of war it could rise to £420 for a regiment of horse, £370 for a regiment of dragoons and £240 for a marching regiment, salaries which compared very favourably with the pay of regimental officers.[28] However, a wide range of bargains were struck between colonels and agents as to how this money should be divided. Some agents received the two-pences but credited their agents' men to the colonel; other agents received the agents' men but credited the twopences to the colonel with the off-reckonings. Some agents enjoyed both allowances without deduction, others received part of both but made over the balance, some of it perhaps going to the regimental pay-master. Some agents were obliged to transfer everything to the colonel in return for a fixed stepend.[29]

There was a similar variety in the method of taking securities and their amount. Colonels who failed to demand adequate securities took grave risks with their regiment's and ultimately their own money. Bulk payments of subsistence, periodic issues of nett off-reckonings and clearings and the annual 'assignment' (an instrument of credit to finance the manufacture of regimental clothing)[30] were all tempting fare to a financially adventurous agent or worse, a man trying to stave off bankruptcy.[31] If this happened, or if the agent died suddenly, the consequences could be disastrous, for any regimental funds and personal balances passed into the hands of third parties and could not be recovered without many delays occasioned by legal process. Lieutenant-General Philip Anstruther (26th Foot) probably lost most of his personal fortune after the posthumous bankruptcy of Captain Alexander Wilson (1751), and Lord Mark Kerr (11th Dragoons) had a stop of £1,191 10s 3¾d put against his personal pay. In 1729 an agent had died £3,000 in debt to the 1st Dragoons and one anonymous colonel had lost over £2,000.[32]

Lord Barrington was concerned about the damaging effect of such failures and used the death and posthumous bankruptcy of the agent Maynard Guerin on the night of 5–6 May 1760 to initiate a debate in the Board of General Officers. To stimulate discussion he submitted a paper of his own, suggesting that agencies should be carried on in partnership, so that at the very least a surviving partner could prevent public money being engulfed in the deceased's effects.[33]

The Board gave only scant attention to Barrington's ideas and insisted that the only method of avoiding difficulties on this score was for a colonel to take adequate security, the informal system already in operation.[34] Undeterred, Barrington asked what sum an agent should deposit. The generals retorted that '... notwithstanding we have considered this matter with the utmost attention, so many difficulties have arisen from the different numbers of which a corps may at different times consist or from different issues of pay to the agent, which must vary according to the place where any corps is situated and the service on which it is employed, that it appears impracticable to fix any certain sum which may be adapted to the several circumstances which may occur ... the sum to be deposited cannot be properly determined by any person as by the colonel of each corps, whose interest as well as regard for the service must induce him to require sufficient security, which has always been the constant practice of the army.' In conclusion they had the effrontery to add that '... no instance occurs to us wherein the service has suffered or been impeded by the death or insolvency of an agent'.[35]

Barrington did not feel capable of pushing the generals any further, and he was obliged to content himself with submitting their observations to the King, who ordered him to pass them on to all colonels. This he did in a sharply worded circular of 10 July 1760 which stated, '... that if any of them have omitted to require sufficient security from their agents they may be apprized of the necessity of speedily taking that precaution as in the case of any accident, His Majesty must look to the colonel as the only person accountable, not only for the payment of the regiment, the regimental funds and any other money with which the agent is usually entrusted, but also any inconvenience which may arise to H.M.'s service from the death or failure of agents'.[36]

Although this was subsequently interpreted as a binding obligation on colonels,[37] it was obvious that Barrington's victory over their interest was very incomplete. Disregarding the actual and potential injuries inflicted on the service by agency failures, dangers which at least one member of the Board had actually experienced,[38] the generals opted for a situation in which it was left up to the colonel and his undertaker to haggle over the level of securities: whether they were to be regarded as non-refundable, whether there was to be a purchase price in addition to the security, who was to receive the benefit of any interest on the money, or whether the agent's customary allowances were to be appropriated by the colonel in lieu of a security or in addition to it. A glance at the amount of money involved makes it obvious why colonels were wary of government intervention; the purchase prices of agencies were between £500 and £850, and the usual security offered for a marching regiment was between £1,200 and £2,000.[39]

5. The provision of weapons

Administrative action taken by the Board of Ordnance in the early years of the new dynasty had the effect of greatly reducing the colonels' opportunities to make a profit from furnishing their men with muskets.[40]

Since the reign of Charles II[41] it had been the custom for the Board of Ordnance to provide a regiment of foot with muskets at its first raising, but only to replace without charge those weapons lost or damaged on active service. This rule was regularly restated,[42] although by the end of the period due allowance was also being made for unavoidable wear and tear.[43] All other loss or damage had to be made good out of company funds.[44] Rather than receiving weapons out of store, some colonels contracted for them privately and were credited with the Board of Ordnance value. The opportunities for personal profit inherent in this arrangement resulted in the manufacture of weapons of diverse pattern and variable quality, but the Board's lengthy campaign to standardise production and enforce more stringent quality control was directed less at the colonels than at the monopoly exerted over the supply of complete arms by the Worshipful Company of Gunmakers of London. Thanks to its excellent internal discipline, the company had been able to keep prices high and quality low. The Board fought back by instituting rigorous comparisons between the gunmakers' products and firearms made to its own specifications, issuing contracts for weapon components rather than complete arms, imposing stricter standards of viewing and proof, and drawing up a register of approved gunmakers. Components received at HM Tower of London were set up (assembled) there by Ordnance armourers or in the nearby Minories by setters-up working under further contracts, and the finished weapons were stored in and issued from the Tower. In July 1722 the Board declared that, in future, all muskets provided by the colonels should conform to a government pattern about to go into production under the supervision of its Master Furbisher, Richard Wooldridge, and be viewed and proved by the Board's inspectors.[45] Surviving examples of muskets furnished by the colonels after this date suggest that a suitably high quality of weapon was obtained as a result of this measure.

Privately contracted muskets were common in the infantry at least until the general rearming of all the regiments with government arms during 1740–41.[46]

In the cavalry, some privately designed and contracted pistols and carbines were used at least into the 1780s. Quality in this area seems to have been high, but there was still a need for vigilance when any private enterprise was at work, as demonstrated by the controversy over pistols suplied to Highland regiments by their colonels during the Seven Years' War. In May 1757 the Board of Ordnance allowed Colonel Archibald Montgomery to contract for 1,080 distinctive High-land pistols for his 62nd Foot, and similar concessions were granted in 1758 to Simon Fraser (63rd Foot) and Lord John Murray (42nd Foot). By the time of the raising of Colonel John Campbell's 88th foot in 1761 the suspicious Board was asking for proof that the weapons had actually been provided. Then, in 1762, it was discovered that although the Board had been allowing credit of £1 15s 7d a pair for Highland pistols, the colonels had been buying weapons '... of a very bad sort' in Birmingham for no more than 18s a pair.[47]

The colonels provided hangers for the infantry and swords for the cavalry out of the nett off-reckonings. During the War of the Spanish Succession they had also furnished the majority of bayonets. The Board of Ordnance, which had formerly supplied infantry regiments with a proportion of pikes, had been unwilling to bear the additional cost of supplying this novel weapon, and the Land Pattern arms of 1722 were the first to include the bayonet with the musket to form a complete 'stand of arms'.[48]

Colonels were free to employ cutlers of their choice. Early in the century, the majority of blades were of Solingen or Toledo origin; later, many of them came from Birmingham, while the hilts were manufactured in England, Ireland and Scotland. No regulation patterns of cavalry swords were authorised until 1788, and prior to that date, although there was general agreement on the type of weapon necessary for the service, regimental variants abounded. Blades were generally of fair to good quality, but the workmanship of the hilts was sometimes indifferent.[49]

6. The administration of the off-reckonings

The balance of the pay of the rank and file after subsistence had been issued was known as the 'gross off-reckonings'; the residue after deduction of 'poundage', the one day's pay for the up-keep of the Royal Hospital, Chelsea, the widows' pensions and the twopences for agency was known as the 'nett off-reckonings'.[50] The soldier was understood to have made over this portion of his pay to the colonel in return for his regimentals, accoutrements and some of his weapons; he rarely had the opportunity of fingering any part of it. Lieutenant-General (Cornelius?) Wood was believed to have made over any balances remaining after the clothing operation to his men, but this was exceptional,[51] for throughout the period and long after, the colonel obtained his most valuable perquisite from the off-reckonings account.

Scandalous deficiencies in this area of military supply had made government intervention necessary as early as January 1708. The Board of General Officers had formulated a scale of clothing requirements which was embodied in a royal pro-clamation of 19 January.[52] This established a cycle of clothing substantially the same as that operating in our period, ratified by the Regulation for Clothing His Majesty's Forces in Time of Peace, 20 November 1729 (Table 6.1),[53] and the Regulation for Clothing His Majesty's Horse and Dragoon Forces, 20 May 1736.[54]

Oeconomy and discipline

Table 6.1 *Regulations for the Cloathing of His Majesty's Forces in Time of Peace 20 Nov. 1729* (PRO. WO 26/17 f.307)

For a TROOPER.

A new Cloth Coat, well lined with Serge.
A new Waistcoat.
A new laced Hat.
A Pair of new large Buff Gloves, with stiff Tops, once in Two Years.
A Pair of new Boots, as they shall be wanting.
As it is difficult to fix a Period of Time for providing Saddles, it is to be left to the Judgment of the General Officer, who may be appointed to review them.
Housings, Caps, new Horse Furniture, Bitts, and Stirrup-irons; Cloaks faced with the Livery of the Regiment, entirely new; and new Buff or Buff coloured Cross-belts, to be provided as they shall be wanting.
The Second Mounting is to consist of new laced Hats, and Horse Collars.

For a DRAGOON.

A new Cloth Coat, well lined with Serge.
A new Waistcoat.
A Pair of new Breeches.
A new laced Hat.
A Pair of new large Buff-coloured Gloves with stiff Tops.
A Pair of new Boots, as they shall be wanting.
Saddles to be left to the Judgment of the General Officer who may be appointed to review them.
Housings, Caps, new Horse Furniture, Bitts, and Stirrup-irons; and Cloaks faced with the Livery of the Regiment, entirely new, as they shall be wanting.
New Buff or Buff-coloured Accoutrements; viz. A shoulder-belt, with a Pouch, a Waist-belt, sufficient to carry the Sword, with a Place to receive the Bayonet and Sling for the Arms, such as the General Officers, appointed to inspect the Cloathing, shall approve of, as they shall be wanting.
The Second Mounting is to consist of new-laced Hats, Gloves, and Horse Collars.

For a FOOT SOLDIER.

A good full-bodied Cloth Coat, well lined, which may serve for the Waistcoat the Second Year.
A Waistcoat.
A Pair of good Kersey Breeches.
A Pair of good strong Stockings.
A Pair of good strong Shoes.
Two good Shirts, and Two good Neckcloths.
A good strong Hat, well laced.

For the SECOND YEAR.

A good Cloth Coat well lined, as the First Year.
A Waistcoat made of the former Year's Coat.
A Pair of new Kersey Breeches.
A Pair of good strong Stockings.
A Pair of good strong Shoes.
A good Shirt, and a Neckcloth.
A good strong Hat, well laced.
For the Fusilier Regiment, Caps once in Two Years.

The new Waistcoat in the First Year, is only to be given to Regiments new-raised, and to additional Men; who are likewise to be furnished with Two Pair of Stockings, and Two Shirts.

And whereas it has been found, that Abuses in the Cloathing have been chiefly committed by Regiments in the Service Abroad; his Majesty therefore requires, That the Governor, or Commanding Officer of the Garison of each Place, as well as the Commanding Officer of each Regiment, shall see the Cloathing and Accoutrements that shall be sent abroad to such Regiments, delivered out to Soldiers, in the several Species, according to these Regulations: And that the said Governor and Commanding Officer shall certify the Delivery of every such Cloathing and Accoutrements with the State and Condition the same is in, to the Board of General Officers, to be entered by the Judge Advocate general, in the Books of his Office; and to be transmitted by him to the Cloathing-board for the ensuing Year: Which General Officers are not to pass any Contract for the

148

Table 6.1—*continued*

said Regiments, if it does appear to them by the said Certificate, that the Cloathing and
Accoutrements have not been delivered according to the before-mentioned Regulations; which will
prevent the like Abuses for the future.

As to the Cloathing of the Regiments in Great Britain and Ireland, which are under the Inspection of
such General Officers, as his Majesty shall think fit to appoint for their Review, his Majesty requires,
that the said General Officers do particularly inspect the Cloathing and Accoutrements of the said
Regiments, and see that they are cloathed and accoutred according to the foregoing Regulation: And
if any Deficiency shall be found, either in Quantity or Quality of the said Cloathing, they are to report
the same to his Majesty, in order to receive further Orders therein.

The Board of General officers was involved in the inspection and certification
of clothing from the outset. It was necessary for a colonel to produce patterns of
his clothier's work to its sub-committee, the Clothing Board, which examined
them and rejected them if they were below standard. George I was frequently
present at these inspections.[55] When the full clothing was ready, one of the Board
members was deputed to inspect the work at the clothier's premises before it was
despatched to the regiment. At regimental headquarters, 'all the taylors of the
companies' made final alterations to render it fit to be worn, prior to distribution
in the presence of a field officer.[56] George II insisted that his soldiers should put
on their new regimentals on 11 June, to celebrate the anniversary of his accession.
No excuse was admitted for failing to comply with this order, even in foreign
garrisons where it was difficult to carry out.[57]

Refinements of this process under the early Hanoverians were made at two
levels: the promulgation of dress regulations and a requirement for certificates of
delivery.

The introduction of army dress regulations is a landmark for students of
military uniform. It was prefigured in a book of hand-coloured etched plates,
depicting all the regiments of the army, that appeared in 1742 and has since been
referred to as the 'Cloathing Book' or 'Cumberland Book'[58] as well as in a draft
warrant regulating the clothing of the infantry drawn up in 1747 and submitted
to the Clothing Board in 1749 by Robert Napier.[59] On 1 July 1751 appeared the
Warrant for Regulating the Colours, Clothing, etc., of the Marching Regiments,
which governed the production of all uniforms except those of the household
formations. Deviations from the patterns established by this regulation were
prohibited, unless by express approbation of the Captain General. A side-swipe
at the long-standing pretensions of the colonels denied them the privilege of
putting their personal crests, arms, devices or livery on any of the appointments
of their regiments.[60]

Of greater administrative significance, however, is the sequence of regulations
governing the certification of delivery, formulated between 1721 and 1736. A
report submitted by the Board of General Officers in March 1721 proposed that
commanders of forts and garrisons overseas should send annual returns of the
quantity of clothing received, while, at home, certificates should be provided
annually by the commanding officers of foot and every two years by commanding

officers of horse and dragoons, whose clothing cycle was longer. These certificates were intended to be lodged with the Clothing Board to enable it to decide whether a subsequent assignment of off-reckonings should be granted.[61]

The plan was apparently not adopted at this juncture, but the proposals as applied to units overseas were incorporated in the clothing warrant of 20 November 1729. Responsibility for checking the number and quality of suits issued at home was given to reviewing generals.[62] The warrant of 20 May 1736 extended certification to all regiments in the service. The colonel of every corps was instructed to sign a paper to the effect that he had contracted for clothing and that he intended to have it delivered before the royal deadline of 11 June, while each commanding officer was ordered to return a certificate to the effect that he had issued the clothing at regimental headquarters. The Secretary at War was to produce these certificates to the King.[63]

By the late 1730s a comprehensive framework for monitoring the clothing process was under construction, consisting of regular cycles of issue, the inspection of pattern clothing and finished workmanship, and certificates of delivery, without which future assignments would not be passed. None of these measures contested the colonel's right to a dividend on the operation; instead, the objective was to make sure that the poor soldier had the 'King's cloathing' put on his back.

Unfortunately for the poor soldier, however, these developing instruments of control proved to be less powerful than the colonels' interest in maximising their surpluses on the clothing account. It will be remembered that when a colonel dealt with a clothier, the first step was for the latter to produce a complete regulation clothing for the soldier, which was then submitted to the Clothing Board. If the members approved the pattern, which they usually did, for he would have been at pains to present a good one, his colonel was authorised to assign the off-reckonings. However, unless the colonel was in the fortunate position of being able to pay for the clothing out of his own pocket it was usually impossible for him to put down ready money on the contractor's table. The full amount of nett off-reckonings for a regiment of foot would not accrue for a twelvemonth, and in the horse and dragoons the payment cycle took up to three years to complete. Furthermore, in time of war, pressure on the British and Irish exchequers sometimes made it impossible to issue funds to a colonel or his assigns within a twelvemonth of their becoming due. This meant that for periods of several years, assignments circulated as paper securities (capable of being used for speculation), with interest payable on them from the time the clothier delivered the uniforms until the day he was paid.

This meant that the real haggling between colonel and contractor only began *after* the Board had sealed the pattern. If the colonel had ready money and could pay the clothier promptly, he was in a position to drive down the latter's price, boosting his eventual profit when off-reckonings were paid. For his part, the clothier made thrifty contracts for labour and materials in order to preserve his own profit margins. These transactions led inevitably to loss of quality in the finished consignment or, worse, tempted the parties not to provide any clothing at all.

The inspection of the finished work by a member of the Clothing Board at the contractor's warehouse was supposed to prevent these frauds from taking place. As soon as the clothing was ready, the clothier notified the Board, which chose one of its number to compare the finished workmanship with the sealed pattern. It was alleged that in many instances the inspecting officer, who as a proprietary colonel was likely to be involved in such traffic himself, rather than turning out the whole consignment, only examined three or four specimens and left after a nominal review. Once the goods were shipped to the regiment, there was little hope of redressing this neglect, especially if the corps was serving overseas. The precious certificates of delivery signed by a commanding officer might well have been worthless, for the system was undermined by sending copies out to the regimental headquarters for signature and having them returned, undated, for use at home as convenient.[64]

The shabby affair of Dalzell's 38th Foot (1745–55) exposed all these administrative deficiencies to clear view. Lieutenant-General Robert Dalzell was a veteran of Queen Anne's war and had been commissioned colonel of the 38th, now going through a period of relative calm after the depredations of Colonel Richard Lucas, on 7 November 1739. He was no administrative dunce, for he had a parallel career in the Sun Insurance Office, first as treasurer and later as chairman of the board of directors.

On 23 March 1745 the Governor of the Leeward Islands, William Mathew, complained of the state of the 38th to the Secretary of State, the Duke of Newcastle; 'I have five companies, which instead of seventy don't round forty fit for service ... the colonel by the clothing (which is very bad as it always is, never exceeds forty a company) to be sure means they should never exceed that number, and from the distance between one clothing and another, which amounts at most to three clothings in four years, the men now, instead of being tolerably clothed are in rags, most of them bear-headed (*sic*), recruits in ragged sea frocks, trousers and not a cartouch box among the latter, as some of the others, not a sword in the whole regiment ...'[65]

Newcastle transmitted this garbled denunciation to the Secretary at War, Sir William Yonge, who referred it to a Board of General Officers. At its meeting on 6 June, Dalzell succeeded in mounting a vigorous defence. Certainly, he admitted, the mortality of the station had been a cause of heavy wastage in the regiment, but he had spent £6,606 17s 3½d on recruiting it, and had sent out 961 men since he became colonel. One hundred and sixteen men were on their way at that very moment. His agent, Captain Alexander Wilson, then submitted a number of delivery certificates for clothing signed by the lieutenant-colonel. He also reminded the Board that each consignment had been viewed by an officer from the Clothing Board and stated that more suits had reached the unit each year than the number of men returned effective. Cartouch boxes had been issued soon after

Dalzell had become colonel and had been receipted by the commanding officer. There was no requirement for the 38th to be armed with swords. The unit was in credit, and the non-effective account tallied with the muster rolls.

Governor Mathew having failed to support his original charges with the 'quire of proofs under oath' and 'forty enormities' that he had promised to send home, Dalzell was honourably acquitted, and in the following year he successfully fought off renewed allegations of fraud brought before the House of Commons committee on the land forces and Marines.[66] However, in the early spring of 1750 information reached the War Office that clothing due in 1748 had not been sent. Henry Fox referred the charge to a Board of General Officers, which discovered that notwithstanding that an assignment for 1748 had been passed, Mr Lancelot Craven, a tailor and subcontractor to Roberts, Dalzell's clothier, had made, at most, 300 suits for an establishment of 500 men and that none of them had been sent to the West Indies until 1749. John Hawkins, who had packed clothing for Dalzell for several years, also stated that no clothing had been sent in 1748.

An embarrassing revelation now followed, for it was a matter of record that Lieutenant-General John Campbell had viewed the clothing in Craven's warehouse. Campbell shamefacedly admitted that he had inspected, at most, fifty or sixty suits, that many more were not yet made up, and that although he had noticed that the quantity of material seemed insufficient for a battalion, when a certificate of inspection had been put in front of him a few days later he had signed it.[67]

This time the Board came down heavily against Dalzell, and he was superseded on 8 March 1750.[68] A prosecution was begun against him for £1,089 10s 5d on account of the off-reckonings for 1748 as well as £2,806 13s 7½d, which, in the aftermath of Captain Wilson's bankruptcy, it was found he had lifted from the regiment's non-effective fund. By decree of the Court of Exchequer (January 1755) he was ordered to refund this money to the public.[69] Meanwhile his lieutenant-colonel, Sherrington Talbot, was summoned home to explain the origin of the delivery certificates Dalzell had vainly produced in his defence.[70]

As long as colonels were given the opportunity of fingering the off-reckonings, especially colonels of regiments in distant outposts or on active service, there was a danger that these abuses would recur, and it became all the more likely when a warrant of 9 July 1756 empowered the Clothing Board to pass assignments for regiments serving abroad in the current war, whether certificates of delivery had been presented or not. A deliberate choice was made in favour of easing the passage of business and indulging regiments on active service at the expense of frugal administration. War Office officials, noting the tattered state of veterans coming home from America at the end of the war, thought that this abandonment of central control had led inexorably to profiteering at the expense of the soldier and the public purse.[71]

Dividends on the off-reckonings arose from the simple fact that the allowance was calculated on the full regimental establishment of rank and file inclusive of

Table 6.2

Payments for Cloathing provided for Lord Mark Kerr's 13th Foot, consisting of 10 Companies, each Company, 3 Serjeants, 3 Corporals, 2 Drums, and Fifty private Men, for the Years 1730 and 1731 (*Report of a Committee appointed to consider the state of His Majesty's Land Forces and Marines*, 1746, p. 170)

To Cash paid for a Set of Colours		£11 9s 0d	
To Cash paid for 580 Pair of Shoes, at 3s 6d per Pair		£101 10s 0d	£101 10s 0d
To paid for 45 Dozen and 9 Pair of Centinels Hose, at 12s 6d per Dozen	£28 11s 10½d		
And for 2 Dozen and 7 Pair of Serjeants, at 3s 6d per Pair	£4 13s 0d		
		£33 4s 10½d	£33 4s 10½d
To paid for 30 Serjeants Belts, with Silver Lace, at 18s 6d each, and a Box		£27 17s 6d	
To paid for 133 Swords, at 6s each, and for a large Box		£40 6s 6d	
To paid Mr. Wm. Wilson, Clothier, his Bill for the several Species of Cloathing, delivered the First June 1730, for this Year's Cloathing, excepting the Particulars charged above		£1206 11s 9d	£1176 15s 0d
To Cash paid for the Carriage of the Regiment's Cloathing from London to Bristol		£12 14s 9d	£7 1s 6d
To paid for turning 550 old Coats into waistcoats, at 1s each		£27 10s 0d	£27 10s 0d
		£1461 4s 4½d	£1346 1s 4½d
18 Months Interest on the foregoing Payments		£109 11s 10d	£100 19s 2d
		£1570 16s 2½d	£1447 0s 6½d
	Savings	£142 9s 4½d	£226 5s 0½d
One Year, or 365 Days, net Off-reckonings, for 30 Serjeants, 30 Corporals, 20 Drums, and 540 Men		£1713 5s 7d	£1713 5s 7d
Assignment of One Year's net Off-reckonings, from 25th April 1730, to 24th April 1731		£1713 5s 7d	
Assignment of One Year's net Off-reckonings, from 25th April 1731, to 24th April 1732		£1713 5s 7d	

warrant men, contingent men and real non-effectives. Credit of off-reckonings was not affected by respites on subsistence.[72] Any surplus accrued to the colonel's advantage and the more defective the regiment in point of numbers the greater the potential profit.

What was the dividend actually worth? Payments for clothing delivered to Lord Mark Kerr's 13th Foot on a low peacetime establishment (1730–31) show modest profits of £142 9s 4½d and £266 5s 0½d respectively (Table 6.2) The haul would have been greater had Kerr not been obliged to pay swingeing interest as a consequence of an eighteen-month delay in the issue of off-reckonings, a good example of how much profit margins could be reduced if a man lacked independent capital.[73] In 1741 Colonel Roger Handasyde's clothing account for the 16th Foot showed a profit of £354 0s 0½d, although his agent pointed out that 'out of the balance the colonel finds all sorts of clothing and accoutrements that are lost by desertion and many other accidental charges that in some years is considerable'.[74]

In the horse and dragoons more substantial profits could be realised. Dividends from Lieutenant-General Campbell's 2nd Dragoons averaged £641 8s 5d per annum from 1733 to 1745.[75] Estimates in the Cumberland papers suggest that a regiment of dragoons generated up to £650 per annum and the Royal Regiment of Horse Guards as much as £908 0s 6d.[76]

However, it should not be thought that a dividend from off-reckonings offered an automatic passport to high living. William, Earl of Home's annual income of £550 from clothing the 25th Foot was merely the one stable element in his otherwise chaotic finances,[77] while the detailed clothing accounts of Colonel Samuel Bagshawe's 93rd Foot reveal that an anxious year passed before the young regiment showed any profit at all. Bagshawe did not live long to enjoy it, for a disease of the liver culminated in 'the total breaking up of his constitution' and he died at Bath on 16 August 1762[78] (Table 6.3). The value of a colonel's perquisites could only be adequately realised when combined with money from other sources; an average £753 per annum obtained from various colonelcies held by Sir John Griffin Griffin between 1763 and 1797 is a relatively insignificant sector in a total emolument drawn from investments, an estate and home farm at Audley End, out-country properties and 'miscellaneous sources'.[79]

The importance of some extra-regimental income was emphasised by the fact that although the colonel's dividends were greater than those of the junior proprietors, his public obligations were greater still. He was expected to maintain the dignity of his rank with a proper standard of dress, equipage and entertainment, to be the patron of his impecunious subalterns, a philanthropist to the poor soldier and chief contributor to the band of regimental music or the excellence of its horseflesh.[80]

The Duke of Cumberland set standards in these informal aspects of a colonel's duty by bestowing his entire income from the off-reckonings of the 1st Foot Guards on gratuities and benefactions to the regiment and picking up a bill of

Table 6.3 Colonel Samuel Bagshawe's Clothing Account (93rd Foot) with Captain William Montgomery, regimental agent, Dublin, 1760 (JRL. B2.1.72)

Dr.				Cr.			
To Mr Nixon, Clothiers,	£1193	9s	5½d	By 365 Days Offreckonings			
To Mr Ford, Lacemans,	£147	0s	½d	from 5th Jany 1760 to 4th			
To Mr Page, Hatters,	£91	0s	3d	Jany 1761	£2021	1s	11d
To Mr Battiers, do, for				Balance	£133	12s	9d
Accoutrements, etc.	£545	16s	0d				
To p^d Mr Wills on acct of							
Swords,	£122	16s	0d				
To p^d fees of Offices on y^r							
Clothing Warr^t for 1 year							
to 4th Jany 1761	£28	8s	9d				
To Mr Irvine, Laceman	£26	2s	7½d				
	£2154	14s	8d		£2154	14s	8d

Dublin, 9 April 1762

Colonel Samuel Bagshawe's Clothing Acc^{ot}, 1761 (JRL. B2.1.286)

1762 Dr.				Cr.			
April 1 Paid Messrs Nixons				March 27th By 182 Days			
on Accot,	£700	0s	0d	Offreckonings from 5th			
April 16 To paid Mr Ford,				July 1761	£1007	15s	7d
Laceman	£50	0s	0d				
April 21 To paid Mr Page,				Septr 29th By 183 Days D^o			
Hatter	£40	0s	0d	6th July 1761 to 4th			
April 29 To paid Mr Ford,				Janry 1762	£1013	6s	4d
Laceman	£20	0s	0d		£2021	1s	11d
May 27 To paid Mr Irvine,				Deduct Fees of Offices	£28	8s	9d
Laceman	£18	1s	6d				
August 17 To paid Mr Ford,							
Laceman	£30	0s	0d				
May 23 To paid Mr Page,							
Hatter	£47	4s	10d				
Octr 11 To paid Mr Nixon the							
Ballance due on the Accot,	£369	2s	9d				
Octr 11 To paid Mr Ford the							
Ballance of his Accot,	£18	15s	½d				
To Ballance of Clothing Accot							
for 1760,	£133	12s	9d				
Ballance	£565	16s	3½d				
	£1992	13s	2d		£1992	13s	2d

Dublin, 12th October 1762

continued

Table 6.3—*continued*

Colonel Samuel Bagshawe, his Clothing Accompt, 1763 (JRL. B2.1.397)

	Dr				*Cr*			
1763					*1763*			
	To Credit Col° Windus's Ac for Janry 1763 for making of Clothing as p Accompt				March 18th By 182 Days Offrecks from 5th Janry to 5th July 1762			
		£15	6s	9d		£1007	15s	7d
1762								
Dec 24th	To Paid Col° Windus's Acct of 21st Dec to Christr Weldon on acco. and to compleat the small mountg of the Regt.				Ballance	£30	11s	9d
		£212	14s	9d				
1763								
March 22nd	To Paid Messrs Nixons in part of their Accot of Clothing for 1763,							
	£953 0s 1d,	£500	0s	0d				
25th	To Paid Mr Irvine for silver Lace	£19	2s	9½d				
26th	To Paid Mr Page his Accot of Hatts	£89	19s	6d				
29th	To Paid Mr Ford, Laceman,	£110	13s	7d				
	To credit the Janr^y Abstract 1763 on Accot of small mounting	£90	0s	0d				
		£1038	7s	4½d		£1038	7s	4½d

Dublin, 28 Jun 1763
Errors excepted

Col° Bagshaw's Clothing Accompt (JRL. B2.1.399.)

1763

July 21st By 183 Days Offrecks from 6th July 1762 to 4th Janry 1763		£1013	6s	4d
Deducted for Fees of Offices for one year to 4th Janry 1763		£28	8s	9d
		£984	17s	7d
To Ballance of the Prededing Acco^tt		£30	11s	9½d
July 21st To Messrs Nixons Ballance due on their Accot of Clothing for 1762		£437	15s	4d
To Paid Do. 120 ds interest on Do. from 22nd March to 21st July 1763		£7	3s	10d
Aug 8th To credited Private Accot, Ballance		£509	6s	7½d
		£984	17s	7d

Dublin, 9th August 1763, Errors excepted

£650 16s *per annum* for a band of fifes and hautboys,[81] and while it may not have been difficult for a king's son to behave in this manner, much poorer men felt obliged to make similar sacrifices. In raising a fine young regiment of dragoons in 1715, Colonel Richard Molesworth '... laid out above what was allowed him above £600, poor and in debt as he is, so well he loves the service ... honest Dick never took a penny to prefer any officer, whereas that is but too common elsewhere, as well as having three men short in each troop for the colonel's advantage.'[82]

Colonel Samuel Bagshawe was believed to have spent over £3,000 of his own funds raising the 93rd Foot in Ireland in 1760,[83] while his brother-in-law, the proud Sir James Caldwell of Castle Caldwell, Co. Fermanagh, declined to accept any money for commissions in his 20th (Light) Dragoons.[84] It was easy for such public-spiritedness to end in personal humiliation. Colonel Edward Richbell of the 39th Foot died in such poverty after his decades of service that within a few years his widow was petitioning Lieutenant-Colonel Samuel Bagshawe, a former subordinate, to intercede with Sir John Ligonier for the gift of a humble cadetship in the Royal Regiment of Artillery for her son.[85] (Richbell's agent, Captain Thomas Levett had died worth £40,000.)[86] Likewise, Colonel William Haviland of the 45th Foot, a 'kind father' to his regiment, after a lifetime 'overlooking many opportunities of emolument but none of benevolence' died leaving his family in narrow circumstances.[87] From this perspective, a proprietary colonelcy without independent means to sustain it was a prize of startlingly little consequence.

Notes

1 Statistics from Hayes, 'Social and Professional Background', pp. 68–76. Hayes excludes from the reckoning twenty colonels broken for Jacobite sympathies within a year of George I's accession (these included no fewer than nine peers and one baronet), and the lieutenant-colonel and major commandants of regiments raised for rank during the Seven Years' War.
2 Dalrymple, *A Military Essay*, p. 47.
3 Bruce, *The Purchase System*, pp. 27–8; Hayes, 'The Purchase of Colonelcies in the Army, 1714–1763', *JSAHR*, XXXIV, 1961, pp. 3–10
4 Hayes, *art. cit.*; 'Social and Professional Background', pp. 111–37.
5 PRO. WO 4/48 f. 27, Fox to the executors of Lt.-Gen. William Barrell, 4th Foot, 13 March 1751.
6 PRO. WO 4/17 f. 102, William Pulteney, Secretary at War, to Ecklyn, 26 May 1715.
7 Hervey, *Memoirs*, I, p. 176
8 PRO. WO 4/28 f. 317, Pelham to Capt. James Ogilvie, paymaster, 21st Foot, 8 June 1727; WO 4/29 f. 37, same to the Judge Advocate General, 24 Aug. 1927; WO 71/6 f. 35, Report of a Board of General Officers, 31 Oct. 1727; WO 4/29 f. 69, Pelham to Macartney, 3 Nov. 1727; *loc. cit.*, Pelham to the Judge Advocate General, 3 Nov. 1727; WO 4/32 f. 64, Sir William Strickland, Secretary at War, to Henry Pelham, Paymaster General, 6 Aug. 1730; *ibid.*, f. 74, Strickland to the Duke of Dorset, Lord Lieutenant, 25 May 1730.
9 PRO. WO 71/6 f. 60, Petition of the captains, 11 Dec. 1728; *ibid.*, f. 89, Morris to Wilmington, 4 Dec. 1728; *ibid.*, f. 150, Observations on the case by the Judge Advocate General, 10 Nov. 1729; *ibid.*, f. 166, Report of a Board of General Officers,

23 Dec. 1729; *ibid.*, f. 262, Examination of Lt.-Col. Morris, 8 Dec. 1730; *ibid.*, f. 305, Report of a Board of General Officers, 18 Feb. 1731.

10 PRO. WO 4/30 f. 23, Circular to agents of regiments serving in the Plantations, 15 Feb. 1729. For the Dalzell affair, see below. pp. 151–2.

11 PRO. WO 26/15 f. 98, Warrant to Major Lawrence Armstrong, 40th Foot, 26 Aug. 1718.

12 PRO. WO 71/6 f. 140, Reports of a Board of General Officers, 13–20 May, 10 Nov. 1729; *ibid.*, f. 213, Method by which Col. Phillips is to come to account, 28 April 1730; *ibid.*, f. 216, f. 245, f. 216, f. 335, Reports of a Board of General Officers, 5 May, 11 Nov., 8 Dec. 1730, 23 March 1732; WO 4/32 f. 323, Sir William Strickland to Henry Pelham, Paymaster General, 10 May 1732.

13 Massie estimated merchants' incomes between £200 and £600 *per annum*; the range of gentlemen's incomes was between £200 and £2,000. The full pay of the colonel of foot, £438 *per annum*, was only just above Massie's top rate of £400 for tradesmen; P. Mathias, 'The Social Structure in the Eighteenth Century: a Calculation by Joseph Massie', *Economic History Review*, Second Series, X, 1957, pp. 30–45.

14 The decision to continue screening the colonels' proprietary incomes, together with most of the other customary arrangements of regimental finance, was inherent in the suppression of fictitious names on the British Establishment (11 Aug. 1716) in favour of allowances of 'warrant men'. This administrative reform was not calculated to furnish MPs with a candid statement of the pay and allowances obtained by the colonel and regimental officers, and for that reason it was sharply criticised by Archibald Hutcheson, MP, in *Abstracts of the Number and Yearly Pay of the Land Forces*, pp. 3–7. However, the implication of Hutcheson's attack was that if these items had been unambiguously stated, they would have been objected to by the House of Commons.

15 See above, pp. 56–7

16 *Committee Report* (1746), p. 94.

17 PRO. WO 4/42 f. 89, Fox to Jefferys, 30 June 1746; *ibid.*, f. 148, Fox to the Judge Advocate General, 21 July 1746; WO 71/18 f. 511, Report of a Board of General Officers, 25 July 1746; WO 71/19 f. 180, General Court Martial of Brig.-Gen. John Jefferys, 21 Aug. 1746; WO 4/42 f. 207, Fox to the Judge Advocate General, 25 Aug. 1746

18 PRO. WO 4/47 Fox to Wolfe, 5 Feb. 1751; *ibid.*, f. 407, same to same, 7 Feb. 1751.

19 *Committee Report* (1746), p. 109. After 1747 it seems to have been the practice on the British Establishment for deputy commissaries to respite the hautboys; PRO. WO 25/3211, Abstracts of Musters, 1748–49; AO 16/4, 5, Computations of Musters, 1754–5.

20 Grose, *Military Antiquities*, II, p. 249.

21 R. A. Cumb. C vol. 9/1, Irish Committee Report 1768.

22 *Committee Report* (1746), pp. 93–4.

23 PRO. WO 4/59 f. 578, Barrington to John Calcraft, regimental agent, 24 Jan. 1760; Bruce, The *Purchase System*, pp. 28–9.

24 R. A. Cumb. C17/445, Bland to Sir Everard Fawkener, 29 July 1746; *Committee Report* (1746), p. 94.

25 JRL. B2.2.445, Bagshawe to Morse, July 1757.

26 JRL. B2.2.448, Bagshawe to Calcraft, 25 April 1758. Bagshawe's principal patron was the Duke of Devonshire; *Bagshawes of Ford*, pp. 248–50

27 See Guy, 'Regimental Agency', *BJRL*, LXII, 1980, pp. 452–3

28 *Ibid.*, pp. 443–4

29 *Committee Report* (1746), p. 96; *Abstracts of the Number and Yearly Pay of the Land Forces*, pp. 3–5.

30 See below, p. 151–2.

31 Capt. Alexander Wilson, the regimental agent, made systematic use of clothing assignments to obtain loans from the Sun Insurance Office; P. G. M Dickson, *The Sun Insurance Office 1710–1960*, London, 1960, pp. 242–5.

32 Guy, *art. cit.* p. 432; *Committe Report* (1746), pp. 95–7, PRO. WO 4/48 f. 401, Fox to Anthony Stuart, regimental agent, 15 Feb. 1752.

33 PRO. WO 71/10 f. 17, Barrington to the Judge Advocate General, 24 May 1760.

34 PRO. WO 71/10 f. 19, Report of a Board of General Officers, 12 June 1760.

35 PRO. WO 71/10 f. 22, Barrington to the Judge Advocate General, 20 June 1761; *ibid.*, f. 23, Report of a Board of General Officers, 27 June 1760.

36 PRO. WO 4/61 f. 367.

37 PRO. WO 4/71 f. 372, Report of a Board of General Officers, 5 May 1775.

38 The president of the Board, James, Lord Tyrawley, Colonel of the Coldstream Foot Guards, had lost £150 as a result of an agency failure in 1716 and his officers had suffered heavy stoppages from their personal pay; see above, p. 123.

39 *Committee Report* (1746), pp. 95–6; *Abstracts of the Number and Yearly Pay of the Land Forces*, pp. 3–5; BL. Add. MSS. 17,495 (no folio), John Calcraft, regimental agent, to Col. George Cary (?), 64th Foot, n.d (1760?).

40 I am very grateful to Mr DeWitt Bailey for sharing with me the results of his important research into the activities of the eighteenth-century Board of Ordnance and for allowing me to study the text of his unpublished lecture, 'The Board of Ordnance and the Production of British Military Small Arms, 1700–1783', given before the Arms and Armour Society at HM Tower of London, 7 May 1981. Mr Michael Baldwin of the Department of Weapons, National Army Museum, London, made some additional very helpful suggestions.

41 PRO. WO 55/344, Board of Ordnance minute, 26 Aug. 1706.

42 PRO. WO 55/342, Minute of 23 June 1702; WO 47/36 f. 152, Minute of 14 Sept. 1750.

43 BL. Add. MSS. 40,759, 'Francis Report', f. 248.

44 See above, pp. 127–8.

45 PRO. WO 47/201, Minute of 28 July 1722. Wooldridge set in motion the production of 2,000 muskets and bayonets on 8 Oct. 1722, *loc. cit.* The weapon was an early version of the familiar Long Land Pattern Musket with its 46 in. barrel and brass furniture. The development of this musket is comprehensively described and illustrated by H. L. Blackmore, *British Military Firearms 1650–1850*, London, 1961, and D. W. Bailey, *British Military Longarms 1715–1815*, London, 1971.

46 PRO. WO 47/36 f. 152, Board of Ordnance Minute, 14 Sept. 1750.

47 PRO. WO 47/59 f. 30, Minute of 4 Jan. 1762; *ibid.*, f. 345, Minute of 22 April 1726; Blackmore, *op. cit.*, pp. 65–6. The distinctive Highland pistols are described and illustrated by A. D. Darling, 'Weapons of the Highland Regiments, 1740 to 1780', *Canadian Journal of Arms Collecting*, VIII, 1970, pp. 76–85.

48 PRO. WO 55/344, Minute of 8 June 1706, 13, 17 June 1706; WO 55/355, Minute of 12 May 1711; WO 47/20(B), Warrant of 28 July 1722. The only bayonets regularly issued by the Board during the War of the Spanish Succession were to grenadier companies.

49 As yet there is no scholarly treatment of the swords of the British army prior to the introduction of regulation patterns, for which see B. Robson, *Swords of the British Army: The Regulation Patterns 1788–1914*, London, 1975, pp. 14–21. Houlding, *Fit for Service*, pp. 149–51, makes some interesting comments. An illustrated outline of edged weapons provided by the colonels during the period can be found in A. D. Darling, 'The British Basket-hilted Cavalry Sword', *Canadian Journal of Arms Collecting*, VIII, 1970, pp. 75–95, and 'The British Infantry Hangers', *ibid.*, pp. 124–36. I am grateful for the advice of

my colleague, Mr Peter Hayes, Keeper of Weapons, National Army Museum, for his advice in preparing this section.

50 See above, p. 58.

51 *Abstracts of the Number and Yearly Pay of the Land Forces*, p. 4. The identification of Cornelius Wood with 'Lieutenant-General Wood, deceased' is tentative.

52 Scouller, *Armies of Queen Anne*, pp. 149–53.

53 PRO. WO 26/17 f. 307.

54 PRO. WO 26/19 f. 34.

55 Scouller, *op. cit.*, p. 159.

56 Cuthbertson, *System*, pp. 81–3, JRL. B2.1.22, Regulation of Clothing for Col. Samuel Bagshawe's 93rd Foot, 1760.

57 PRO. WO 4/32 f. 135, Circular to colonels of regiments of foot serving in Gibraltar and Minorca, 16 Feb. 1731.

58 C. C. P. Lawson, *A History of the Uniforms of the British Army*, II, London, 1941, p. 6.

59 PRO. WO 7/25 f. 123, 11 Nov. 1749.

60 PRO. WO 26/21 f. 502; P. Sumner, 'Arms and Crests of the Colonels of Regiments to the Year 1743', *JSAHR*, XIII 1934, pp. 23–7. A so-called clothing warrant of 1743, discussed by Lawson, *op. cit.*, p. 11, and published in *The Rudiments of War: Comprising the Principles of Military Duty, in a Series of Orders issued by Commanders in the English Army*, London, 1777, is now believed to be spurious; N. P. Dawnay, 'The Clothing Warrant of 1743', *JSAHR*, XLVI, 1968, pp. 87–90.

61 PRO. WO 71/5 f. 128, Report of a Board of General Officers, 15 March 1721.

62 PRO. WO 26/17 f. 307; see above, p. 000.

63 PRO. WO 26/19 f. 34.

64 Analysis based on PRO. SP 41/48 f. 396, anonymous undated critique of the method of clothing the army, *temp.* George II; *Committee Report* (1746), pp. 79–93; BL. Add. MSS. 40,759, 'Francis Report', f. 238; PRO. WO 30/105, 'Custom and Practice of the Army concerning Off-reckonings', 25 April 1772. For the practice of fabricating delivery certificates in advance see BL. Add. MSS. 36, 592 f. 10, Col. Charles Cadogan, 6th Dragoons, to Cornet Hugh Whitefoord, 20 March 1739.

65 PRO. WO 4/40 f. 336, Sir William Yonge to the Judge Advocate General, 20 May 1745.

66 PRO. WO 71/8 f. 16, Report of a Board of General Officers, 6–12 March 1745; *Committee Report* (1746), pp. 110–12; *DNB*, 'Dalzell, Robert'.

67 PRO. WO 71/9 f. 101, Report of a Board of General Officers, 5–8 March 1750.

68 *Loc. cit.* Henry Fox to William Pitt, Paymaster General, 8 March 1750.

69 PRO. SP 41/40, Memorial of Lt.-Gen. Robert Dalzell; WO 4/48 f. 134, Fox to Col. Alexander Duroure, 38th Foot, 30 July 1751; WO 4/50 f. 144, same to James West, Secretary to the Treasury, 28 Jan. 1755.

70 Talbot must have acquitted himself satisfactorily, for he continued his military career and died a major-general in 1766.

71 BL. Add. MSS. 40,759, 'Francis Report', f. 238, f. 249.

72 It should be noted that evidence on this point is contradictory. In 1746 Captain Alexander Wilson the regimental agent, stated that respites were '... charged back and deducted out of subsistence'; *Committee Report* (1746), p. 128: BL. Add. MSS. 40,759, 'Francis Report', f. 232, also states precisely that respites were '... stoppages on the subsistence of officers and men not mustered'. The original wording '... whole pay' was struck through by Philip Francis and he, as First Clerk in the War Office,

should have been familiar with the procedure. On the other hand, in PRO. AO 16/4,5, Computations of Musters, 1754–55, the 'value of respitts' is calculated on full pay. In practice, ineffective mustering prior to 1747, and the habitual recommendation by reviewing generals thereafter that respites should be lifted, left credit of off-reckonings unaffected.

73 *Committee Report* (1746), p. 170.
74 *Ibid.*, p. 172.
75 *Ibid.*, p. 175.
76 R. A. Cumb. C44/149, 150.
77 BL. Add. MSS. 17,494 f. 31, John Calcraft, regimental agent, to James Pringle, 30 Sept. 1758.
78 JRL. B2.3.401, M. Crane to Sir James Caldwell, Bagshawe's brother-in-law, 5 Aug. 1762.
79 J. D. Williams, 'The Finances of an Eighteenth Century English Nobleman: Sir John Griffin Griffin', *Essex Archaeology and History*, IX, 1977, pp. 113–28.
80 Whitworth, *Ligonier*, pp. 48–51. 'J. Railton' in *The Army's Regulator* records an anecdote '. . . that a certain nobleman when first presented to a regiment of horse, which he found very much out of repair; out of his own honour and generosity, disburs'd a large sum of money for cloathing, and such other necessaries as were requisite, and I am told by his own domesticks, that his Grace was pleased to wear a coat of the same sort of cloth of which he had cloth'd the whole regiment', p. 115. The officer-owner of the Bodleian copy of this book warns, however, that by this stage in the argument the author's 'praise or dispraise' of individuals should have little weight with the reader; see note 82, p. 114 above.
81 *Committee Report* (1746), p. 176.
82 Robert Molesworth to the Hon. Mrs Molesworth, 17 Oct. 1715, *Hist. Mss. Comm. Report on Manuscripts in Various Collections*, VIII, 1913, p. 268; *DNB*, 'Molesworth, Richard, Viscount'.
83 *Bagshawes of Ford*, p. 263.
84 JRL. B3.10 (v), I, p. 34, Memorial of Sir James Caldwell, 7 Nov. 1759; *ibid.*, p. 161, Lady Abigail Denny to Lady Caldwell, 29 Dec. 1759.
85 JRL. B2.2.166, Theophilius Debrisay, regimental agent, to Bagshawe, 23 June 1752; B2.2.508, Mrs Richbell to same, 4 Oct. 1757; Richbell had died in 1752.
86 Guy, 'Regimental Agency', p. 447.
87 *Gents. Mag.*, LIV, 1784, Part Two, pp. 118–19; *DNB*, 'Haviland, William'.

Conclusion

1. Reforming the regimental economy, 1714–83

It has been argued in this study that in the period between the accession of George I and the issue of the Warrants for Regulating the Stock Purse Funds of the Regiments of Dragoon Guards, Dragoons and Light Dragoons and the Non-effective Funds of the Regiments of Infantry (19 February 1766) the traditional character of proprietary soldiering in Great Britain at troop and company level was fundamentally changed. The transformation was achieved not as a result of any sustained critique of the regimental economy developed by Parliament or the Crown, but *via* royal and bureaucratic initiatives, widely spaced in time and often concentrating on seemingly limited objectives, yet which had the effect of sharply restricting sectors of the regimental economy where captains had formerly managed public funds for private advantage. These measures included, it will be remembered, the suppression of fictitious names on the muster rolls (1716, 1740 [Ireland], 1747 [Horse and Horse Grenadier Guards]); the regulation of stoppages (1717, 1721, 1732, 1749); the reform of musters, and their integration with a more effective reviewing circuit (1747); the exact statement of services allowable in regimental contingent bills (1765–66), and restrictions on the amount and method of dividing surplus cash in the stock purse and non-effective accounts (1749, 1761 and 1766). In spite of inherent shortcomings in the administrative machinery at the Crown's disposal, this degree of intervention and control contrasted very favourably with the position elsewhere in Europe, notably in Austria, where drastic reform of the regimental economy did not begun until 1769[1] and, most strikingly, in Prussia, where the extensive powers exercised by the junker officers over their soldier vassals and associated facilities for *Kompanie-Wirtschaft* greater than anything seen in Great Britain since Tudor times led to an increase in speculative activity and corruption during the period.[2]

Having successfully asserted its authority, there was little incentive for the Crown to go further in dismantling financial machinery which was still capable of generating funds for routine regimental services virtually independent of parliamentary scrutiny. Of equal significance in the years immediately after the Peace of Paris was the pervasive sense of satisfaction with institutions that had just helped Britain to win a world war.[3]

When progress towards the reform of the regimental economy was resumed in 1780, this mood of complacency had been completely shattered. Great Britain faced humiliation in America at the hands of the rebel colonists and their French allies, and a Franco-Spanish fleet had sailed virtually unopposed in the English Channel the previous summer. Renewed military effort abroad was accompanied by outspoken parliamentary calls for 'economical reform' at home—a purge of

Conclusion

placemen, sinecurists and public servants who obtained their emoluments from fees or by handling large balances of public treasure, and a demand that in future all public accounts should be drawn up in a simple, expeditious and intelligible fashion and the state's servants maintained by known and equitable salaries. As parliamentary pressure for reform built up on the Prime Minister, the hapless Lord North, he attempted to regain the initiative by appointing commissioners to take and state the public accounts of the kingdom (February 1781).

Six of the commissioners' fifteen reports were wholly or partly concerned with army finance.[4] Their conclusions, as expressed in two important legislative instruments, the Act for the better Regulation of the Office of Paymaster General of 2 July 1781[5] and the more comprehensive Pay Office Amending Act of 3 June 1783,[6] revealed that the initiative for the reform of military accounting had passed from the Crown to Parliament, and proclaimed the apparent destruction of the gothic apparatus of regimental finance described in this book.

The principles which guided the commissioners in their thinking and the full details of their suggested military reforms have recently been explored by Dr Torrance and Dr Pimlott,[7] so it is necessary only to summarise the main features of subsequent legislation and draw attention to some of its more significant shortcomings.

The immediate objective of the reforms was to end the extensive freedom hitherto enjoyed by the Paymaster General in respect of his custody of unused annual balances of supply. From now on, these were to be lodged in the Bank of England, and any future issues of money were to conform strictly to specific military services. This measure had considerable implications for the operation of the regimental economy, for it became the responsibility of the Secretary at War, acting as a kind of controller of military finance, to authorise expenditure and produce much more explicit estimates of it to Parliament than before. The deductions of 'poundage' and 'one day's pay' made by the Paymaster from the gross pay of the regiment were abolished, to be replaced by annual estimates of the cost of the services to which this money had been applied, likewise the allowance to the widows. Annual estimates of the allowance to the regimental agents were annexed to the regimental establishments and the 'agent's men' abolished. The 'colonel's men' were also abolished and an equivalent allowance added to their personal pay. The warrant and contingent men were abolished and replaced by an annual allowance to the captain, governed by the current establishment of his command. Captains of cavalry continued to receive their annual contingent allowance of £30, but instead of this being entered as a charge on the stock purse, it was inserted in the establishment. Separate estimates were made of the allowances to surgeons, riding masters, rough-riders and the regimental paymaster. Contingent expenses and the cost of recruiting were estimated annually, and issues of funds only authorised on the basis of a detailed memorial from the regimental agent.

The main sources of income to the stock purse and non-effective funds having

Conclusion

been cut off and their functions covered by separate extimates, they were now abolished and the existing accounts wound up. At regimental level, the reforms were reinforced by the introduction of a muster roll incorporating details of every troop or company in one document, with the contents certified correct against entries in the regimental books.

These were important reforms, but they were far from being comprehensive. The household units (the troops of Horse and Horse Grenadier Guards, the three regiments of Foot Guards and the Royal Regiment of Horse Guards) were not subject to the new legislation and continued to operate the old accounting system up to the outbreak of war with France in 1793. This anomaly echoed the perverse survival of fictitious names in the Horse and Horse Grenadier Guards from 1716 to 1747.[8] Moreover, regiments on the Irish Establishment remained innocent of the new administrative procedures until the provisions of the Pay Office Acts were extended to them in April 1788. During this time the problems of recruiting and adjusting accounts between the Establishments, touched on elsewhere in this study, were aggravated as the agents operated both financial systems in conjunction.[9]

A more glaring deficiency was the failure to extend the principle of equating specific services to exact estimates into the area of the provision of regimental clothing. The commissioners would certainly have liked to have done so, for in their ninth report (31 March 1783), although drawing back from direct criticism of the colonels, they lodged a fundamental objection to the current method of managing off-reckonings to generate a perquisite:

'Off-reckonings being calculated on the full establishment, including the non-effectives, contingent men and warrant men, and clothing being provided for the effectives only, a surplus must accrue from the fund to the colonel, and the more defective the regiment, the greater will be that surplus and therefore different in different regiments. We do not mean to convey the least reason to imagine that undue advantage has been taken of this mode of clothing the army by any person whatsoever, but we are well grounded in suggesting a reform where an usage is open to abuse.

'The principles upon which our regulations proceed led us to reduce this vague emolument to certainty and equality. From the produce of a given number of years an average may be obtained of the profit accruing to the colonel, a compensation for which may be made in his pay, and increase either his subsistence or his arrears in the establishment or both, in such proportions as may be consistent with the regulations in use.

'A special fund upon estimate annually may then be voted for clothing and the Clothing Board may contract for the price. A distinct account for clothing the army may then be kept at the Pay Office.'[10]

It is revealing of the balance of power which still prevailed in the army that unlike the other proposals made by the commissioners for simplifying and regulating regimental finance, this suggestion vanished from the legislative programme. The colonels kept control of their covert bargains and flexible dividends until as late as June 1854, when the responsibility for clothing their men was withdrawn in return for a fixed allowance.[11]

Moreover, while the reforms of 1780–83 fell short of a revolution in military finance in these areas, so in another the commissioners' declared hostility to public servants receiving gratuities, dividends and allowances had long since been anticipated by the Crown as far as it applied to the junior proprietors of the army. The incidental income of the captain was not suddenly withdrawn in 1783, rather it had undergone progressive levelling in 1749, 1761 and 1766. As far as the concept of mercenary soldiering was concerned, the final dismantling of the traditional regimental economy post-1780 resembled the destruction of a temple from which the god had long since fled.

2. Officership and administration

Although the administrative reforms of the first two Georges outlined in this book had successfully reduced the heterodox regimental economies of the early eighteenth century to a degree of uniformity and, in so doing, had greatly reduced opportunites for officers to speculate with their troop or company funds, the extent to which this assisted the transformation of officership in Great Britain from a trade into a profession is highly debatable. Indeed, it could be argued that the removal of the captains' mercenary incentive, without the necessary compensating augmentation of personal pay, had, in conjunction with external factors, precisely the reverse effect. Restraints on customary dividends bore most heavily on those men with little or no personal fortunes, the backbone of the mid-Georgian officer corps. From the late 1750s these restrictions coincided with an accelerating cost of living and a more extravagant gentlemanly life style. 'What figure can a subaltern, nay, a captain, make upon his pay among the fashionable ornaments and amusements of the present time?' demanded Major Samuel Bever. 'Their dress, company and expenses are not regulated by their purse but by their spirit, by which means they are often utterly distressed on leaving quarters and reduced to borrow money or dispose of their commissions and become in both ways a burden to their friends and relations' (1756).[12]

Captain Thomas Simes likewise had a proper '. . . regard for the honour of the army. I am sensible how necessary is a proper appearance to support its character, and how inadequate the emoluments of the gentlemen employed in it are to the figure they should maintain' (1768).[13] For Ensign Thomas Erskine this was a matter of personal survival, for '. . . butcher's meat and bread are at present four times the prices they were when the pay was first established and every absolute necessity of life in proportion' (1775).[14]

The inflationary torrent could be ridden with confidence only by men who already enjoyed access to a private income from the burgeoning returns on landed estates, mineral wealth and urban property. Although during wartime

Conclusion

emergencies the category 'gentleman' was still capable of being stretched to include candidates whose main qualification for the King's commission was the ability to read and write,[15] the army became dominated in time of peace by representatives of the landed interest. Associated with their growing preponderance was an adverse change in the character of officership.

Up to the 1780s, officers from a wide spectrum of educated society had mingled on equal terms by virtue of the King's commission. Even if a man was not a member of polite society, his commission gave him entry to it. Officers serving in the household units sometimes indulged an embryonic caste superiority at the expense of their less fortunate cousins in the marching regiments (who gave as good as they got by accusing the Guardsmen of shirking service), but in their messes, social nonentities still mingled with the sons of peers. But during the decades from the Regency to the outbreak of the Crimean War, the officer corps became charged with snobbery and elitism founded on the criteria of wealth and ostentation rather than military merit. The phenomenon of the 'crack regiment' appeared, especially among the cavalry. (Probably the only equivalent in the mid-eighteenth century was 'Gentleman Johnny' Burgoyne's 16th (Light) Dragoons, whose social life was the acme of courtesy and propriety.) Uniforms, equipment and horseflesh, never cheap, became so expensive that their loss or damage involved a man in the expenditure of hundreds rather than ten of pounds. Grossly inflated over-regulation prices were paid for commissions, with the tacit approval of government which continued to see in the institution of commission traffic a buttress of the consitution and salvation from the obligation of providing adequate pensions.[16]

Within the regiment, a decline in the attention given to the drudgery attendant upon daily command was evident by the late 1780s and was to have an alarming impact on the Duke of York's campaign in Flanders, 1793–94.[17] A whole range of duties, which in European armies were the province of subalterns, were delegated to non-commissioned officers while the young gentlemen searched, often in vain, for diversion. Among the many tasks now entrusted to the non-commissioned officers was the care of the regimental accounts. In the era of proprietary command this would have been almost inconceivable, for as the anonymous author of the *Souldiour's Accompt* admitted (1647), personal profit was '... one of the chief ends why men undertake the military profession'.[18] Two hundred years later, when men received '... but little for their service beside the honour of serving the King',[19] a private income was absolutely requisite and such mundane husbandry was beneath a gentleman's notice.

In the last quarter of the eighteenth century Parliament was spared the trouble of debating the problem of the indigent junior officer by the paradox that although the army was still unpopular as an institution, officership was not, and in a calling increasingly dominated by market forces 'men without interest' discovered that although their swords had preserved the kingdom and magnified its commerce, they would not obtain an ample share of the 'luxuries and delicacies' of Empire by lingering in the royal army.[20] In the land forces of the East India Company, however, service was still a career rather than a gentlemanly avocation.[21] Promotion, although deadly slow, was determined by seniority rather than depth of purse, and a man blessed with a robust constitution and the fortitude to endure perpetual exile could surround himself with a cohort of servants and enjoy a generous supply of victuals within the narrow compass of his personal pay. More important, he also had access to a riot of allowances, perquisites, gratuities and dividends which flourished in India, and particularly in the Presidency of Bengal, at the very time they were being interdicted at home. These included the ubiquitous 'batta', bonus payments originally made as a compensation for the discomfort, expense and hazards of field service, but now become almost perpetual and often paid at 'double batta' rate; 'bazar'—duties levied on the trade of the native bazars which supplied the army with most of its provisions; 'revenue money', a percentage deduction from the revenues of the presidency and 'off-reckonings' which, in the company's service, were not restricted to colonels but divided between the field officers and captains as far down the seniority list as they would stretch. There were scores of additional, minor allowances, particularly in Bengal.[22] The growing divergence of character and interest between the company's forces and the King's army at home resulted in the former being prepared to fight for their customary emoluments. The first batta mutiny in the Bengal army took place as early as 1751. During 1795–96 a proposal to break through the established promotion regime and suppress the network of customary allowances induced such a hostile reaction in the Bengal army that it was hastily and shamefacedly abandoned.[23] The institution of mercenary soldiering had certainly not come to a termination; rather, it had been transported to a distant and more friendly environment.

As a substitute for his waning proprietary interest, the regular officer developed a more exalted ethic of service and personal sacrifice. He awaited the order to march '. . . with chearful expectation and pleasure, being ready to risque . . . [his] . . . life when the King's service and the public good requires it', courting danger and hardship abroad rather than safety and ease at home.[24] In distant outposts, exiled from family and friends, in constant danger of sickness and violent death, his mind dwelt upon eternal realities, his self-knowledge became acute, he tested the extent of his personal courage and understood how love of honour and dread of shame were superior to the love of life.[25] As for the suggestion that he should convert his commission into government stocks, this was a mean-spirited option. The true soldier always aimed at preferment in the line of duty, either by long and meritorious service or by the chances of war.[26] Even when, in the sickly garrisons of St Augustine and Bermuda, Lieutenant Nicholas Delacherois of the 9th Foot lamented that he was spending the noon of his life in the solitude of a hermit, he still felt morally superior to his younger brother Samuel, busy at home in Lisburn in the family linen manufacture. Naturally, he was pleased to hear that Sam was growing tall and, '. . . so clever an

Conclusion

expert in business, in which I hope you'll soon gain a fortune, while I am only endeavouring to gain empty titles at the risque of my life and separation from all my friends',[27] but he was positively delighted by the news that his brother was throwing in the business of 'rag picker' to become a '... rag carrier ... the common military appellation for an ensign', in the 24th Foot.[28] Nicholas soon had the sublime pleasure of preaching Sam on '... the inducements and temptations he would meet with as to expenses in the military life, and what oeconomy it would require to make his pay answer.'[29] It was but a small step to the gallant gentlemen who achieved their personal apotheoses by standing all day to be shot at on the field of Waterloo, and measured their achievement not in pay and perquisites, but in wounds borne without flinching or retreating,[30] a foretaste of the romantic ethos of Alfred de Vigny's *Servitude et Grandeur Militaires*.

Notes

1 C. Duffy, *The Army of Maria Theresa*, London, 1977, pp. 31–3. The chief beneficiaries of the Austrian company economy were not the captains but the proprietary colonel (*Obrist Inhaber*) and officials of the Commissariat.

2 Corvisier, *Armies and Societies in Europe*, pp. 89–95; Duffy, *Army of Frederick the Great*, pp. 30·4. The Prussian captain was in a much more influential position as middleman between the state and the soldier than his Austrian or British counterpart. He provided uniforms and equipment (naturally economising on them as much as possible), regarded the company's weapons as his stock-in-trade, extorting a swingeing fee for their use from his successor, demanded fees from his men for permission to marry or go on leave and pocketed large sums of subsistence during their prolonged absences.

3 Baker, 'Changing Attitudes to Government', *passim*.

4 Fourth Report, 9 April 1781, *Journals, H.O.C.*, XXXVIII, pp. 380–94; Fifth Report, 28 Nov. 1781, *ibid.*, pp. 572–92; Sixth Report, 11 Feb. 1782, *ibid.*, pp. 702–28; Seventh Report, 19 June 1782, *ibid.*, pp. 1066–111; Ninth Report, 31 March 1783, *ibid.*, XXXIX, pp. 325–44; Tenth Report, 2 July 1783, *ibid.*, pp. 522–73.

5 22 Geo. III, cap. 81.

6 23 Geo. III, cap. 50.

7 J. Torrance, 'Social Class and Bureaucratic Innovation: the Commissioners for Examining the Public Accounts, 1780–1787', *Past and Present*, No. 78, 1978, pp. 56–81; Pimlott, 'The Administration of the British Army, 1783–1793', pp. 121–208.

8 *Ibid.*, pp. 197–8.

9 *Ibid.*, pp. 198–9.

10 *Journals, H.O.C.*, XXXIX, pp. 371–2.

11 Clode, *Military Forces of the Crown*, II, p. 569; Pimlott, *op. cit.*, pp. 194–5.

12 Bever, *Cadet*, pp. 135–6.

13 Simes, *Military Medley*, p. 199.

14 *Observations on the Prevailing Abuses in the British Army*, p. 22.

15 M. Glover, 'Purchase, Patronage and Promotion in the Army at the time of the Peninsular War', *Army Quarterly*, CIII, 1972–73, pp. 211–15.

16 For the subtle change in the mores of the officer corps after 1763 and its more objectionable consequences, see Hayes, 'Social and Professional Background', pp. 101–10, and P. E. Razzell, 'Social Origins of Officers in the Indian and British Home Army, 1758–1962', *British Journal of Sociology*, XIV, 1963. Burgoyne's code of conduct for the 16th (Light) Dragoons is outlined by Fonblanque, *Life and Correspon-*

Conclusion

dence, pp. 15–20. The elitism of the nineteenth-century army, particularly among the cavalrymen, is explored by E. M. Spiers, *The Army in Society, 1815–1914*, London, 1980, pp. 22–4, and the Marquess of Anglesey, *A History of the British Cavalry, 1816–1850*, pp. 152–75.

17 R. Glover, *Peninsular Preparation: The Reform of the British Army, 1795–1809*, Cambridge, 1963, p. 3.

18 *The Souldiour's Accompt*, London, 1647(?), quoted by Scouller, *The Armies of Queen Anne*, p. 127.

19 A remark made by the Duke of Wellington, quoted by Anglesey, *op. cit.*, p. 168.

20 *Observations on the Prevailing Abuses in the British Army, passim*.

21 F. and M. Wickwire, *Cornwallis: The Imperial Years*, Chapel Hill, N.C., 1980, p. 105.

22 Callahan, *The East India Company and Army Reform*, pp. 27–32.

23 *Ibid., passim*, Wickwire and Wickwire, *op. cit.*, pp. 98–116.

24 Cornet Philip Browne to his brother Thomas, 3 June 1741, J. H. Leslie ed., 'Letters of Captain Philip Browne, 1737–1746', *JSAHR*, V, 1926, pp. 56–7.

25 Lt.-Col. James Wolfe to his father, 25 March 1749, Wright, *Wolfe*, pp. 125–6.

26 NAM. 7805–63, Nicholas to Daniel Delacherois, 17 July 1765.

27 NAM. 7805–63, Nicholas to Samuel Delacherois, 5 Feb. 1766; same to Daniel, 20 March 1767.

28 Sam served in the 24th from 1769 to 1774 and then re-entered the family business; S. G. P. Ward, 'The Letters of Captain Nicholas Delacherois, 9th Regiment', *JSAHR*, LI, 1973, pp. 5–14.

29 NAM. 7805–63, Nicholas to Daniel Delacherois, 13 May 1771.

30 See the illuminating remarks by J. Keegan, *The Face of Battle*, London, 1976, pp. 186–92.

Appendices

Appendix one. *Secretaries at War, 1714–63*

William Pulteney	MP for Hedon, 1705–34	Sept. 1714–April 1717
James Craggs (the Younger)	MP for Tregony, 1713–21	April 1717–March 1718
Christopher Wandesford (Lord Castlecomer)	MP for Ripon, 1715–19, wrongly listed as Secretary in Williams, '*Whig Supremacy*', p. 473. Wandesford was named for office, but did not take it on hearing that he might lose Ripon in the inevitable election contest	(March–May 1718)
Robert Pringle	Not a member of the House	May–Dec. 1718
George Treby	MP for Plymouth Erle, 1708–27	Dec. 1718–April 1724
The Hon. Henry Pelham	MP for Sussex, 1722–54	April 1724–May 1730
Sir William Strickland	MP for Scarborough, 1722–35	May 1730–May 1735
Sir William Yonge	MP for Honiton, 1715–54	May 1735–July 1746
Henry Fox	MP for Windsor, 1741–61	July 1746–Nov. 1755
William, Viscount Barrington	MP for Plymouth, 1754–1778	Nov. 1755–Nov. 1761
The Hon. Charles Townshend	MP for Saltash, 1756–61, and Harwich, 1761–64	March 1761–Dec. 1762
Welbore Ellis	MP for Aylesbury, 1761–68	Dec. 1762

Appendices

Appendix two. Irish military papers destroyed

The Public Record Office in Dublin was occupied by insurgents during the rising of 1916 and for a second time in June 1922 during the civil war. On this occasion, munitions were manufactured in the building and there was a strong suspicion that a mine was being prepared. Government forces attacked with light artillery which detonated the mine, blew up part of the building and started a conflagration which burnt for a considerable time and destroyed most of the documents.[1] Among them were a number of important military series, this loss of which can never be made good by historians of the army and its administration in eighteenth century Ireland. They included:

Chief Secretary's Office, Military Department:

   (i) Clothing, Letters and Papers (1710–1823).
  (ii) Establishments (1662–1778).
 (iii) Establishments (Letters and Papers) (1751–1818)
 (iv) Out-letter Books, (1760–1835).
  (v) Entry Books of Warrants (1697–1837).
 (vi) Military Memorials (1752–1815).
(vii) Military Papers and particular cases bearing on Military Administration, (1765–1831).
(viii) Muster Rolls (1741–95).
 (ix) Correspondence of General and other officers, including reports of the Irish Board of General Officers, reports of Courts Martial etc, (1686–1776).
  (x) Notification of absent officers, applications for leave (1702–1767).
 (xi) Order Books, Minutes of Proceedings of the Irish Board of General Officers, Reports to the Lord Lieutenant, Documents, etc. (1697–1782).
 (xii) Petition Books (1752–1809).
(xiii) Returns (1723–61).

The loss of the Board of General Officers' proceedings and reports, the muster rolls and the Entry Books and Warrants, 'an important collection'[2] is to be particularly regretted and has had a depressing effect on Irish military studies.[3]

Notes

1 S. C. Ratcliffe, 'Destruction of the Public Records in Dublin', *BIHR* 11, 1924, pp. 8–9.
2 H. Wood, *Guide to the Records Deposited in the Public Record Office of Ireland*, Dublin, 1919, pp. 215–22.
3 S. H. F. Johnston, 'The Irish Establishment', *The Irish Sword* 1, 1949, pp. 33–6. For additional comment see A. J. Guy, 'A Whole Army Absolutely Ruined in Ireland', *ARNAM* 1978–9, pp. 30–1.

Appendix three. *Pay and subsistence per diem of the noncommissioned officers of His Majesty's land forces (Army List, 1740)*

| | British Establishment | | | | | | | | Irish Establishment | | | | | |
| | Horse | | Dragoon Guards, Dragoons, Light Dragoons | | Foot Guards | | Foot and Marines | | Horse | | Dragoons | | Foot | |
	Pay £ s d	*Subce* £ s d	*Pay* £ s d	*Subce* £ s d	*Pay* £ s d	*Subce* £ s d	*Pay* £ s d	*Subce* £ s d	*Pay* £ s d	*Subce* £ s d	*Pay* £ s d	*Subce* £ s d	*Pay* £ s d	*Subce* £ s d
Kettle Drummer	3 0	2 6	–	–	–	–	–	–	2 6	2 4	–	–	–	–
Drummer	–	–	2 3	1 9	1 0	8	1 0	8	–	–	1 6	1 0	1 0	8
Drum Major	–	–	–	–	1 6	1 0	–	–	–	–	–	–	2 0	1 6
Trumpet	2 6	2 0	–	–	–	–	–	–	2 6	1 11	–	–	–	–
Sergeant	–	–	2 9	2 3	1 10	1 4	1 6	1 0	–	–	2 6	1 7	1 6	1 0
Corporal	3 0	2 6	2 3	1 9	1 2	10	1 0	8	2 6	1 11	1 8	1 1	1 0	9
Hautboy	–	–	2 0	1 6	1 6	1 0	–	–	–	–	1 6	1 0	–	–
Private Man	2 6	2 0	1 9	1 5	10	6	8	6	1 10	1 4	1 4	11	7	5

Bibliography

Manuscript sources

(i) British Library: Additional Manuscripts
17, 493–6, Letter Books of John Calcraft, regimental agent (1756–65).
20, 005, Entry Book of orders by John, Earl of Stair, Commander in Chief, South Britain (1743–44).
22, 537–8, Military correspondence of John, Earl of Carteret (1742–44).
23, 636, Irish military papers of James, Lord Tyrawley (1716–29).
23, 678, Remarks on the siege of Havana in the Isle of Cuba, by Admiral Sir Charles Knowles.
28, 188, Army list (1728), Establishments and Abstracts.
28, 551–3, Journal of the campaigns in Germany; various letters and accounts (1760–62).
28, 855, Standing Orders for the campaign in Germany (1760–61).
33, 046–8, Military Papers of Thomas Pelham Holles, Duke of Newcastle (seventeenth to late eighteenth centuries).
34, 207, Letters of Col. William Burrard (1740–46).
35, 354, Correspondence of Philip, Earl of Hardwicke with Ensign, subsequently Col. Joseph Yorke (1742–48).
35, 357–8, Correspondence of Col. Joseph Yorke and the Earl of Hardwicke (1756–64).
35, 431, Military correspondence of Joseph Yorke (1742–48).
35, 893–4, Military papers of the Earl of Hardwicke (1713–94).
36, 250, Private Diary of Joseph Yorke (1744).
36, 592 Papers of Col. Charles Whitefoord (1738–52).
39, 189–90, Correspondence of Ensign John Mackenzie of Suddie (1730–41).
40, 759, Manuscript report on the organisation of the army with additions in the hand of Philip Francis, First Clerk at the War Office (*c.* 1764).
41, 144–50, Orderly Books of the English Forces in Germany and Flanders (1742–45).
41, 151, Orderly Book of the 6th Dragoons (1742–44).
51, 398–9, Correspondence and Accounts of John Calcraft with Henry Fox (1745–71).
(ii) Public Record Office
Admiralty Series
Adm 2/1150–51, Marines, Out Letters (1744–54).
Adm 96/3, Marine Pay Office, In-Letters (1740–90).
Adm 96/62–70, 74–86, Regimental Accounts (1742–48).
Adm 96/125–44, Vouchers (1740–48).

Audit Office Series
AO 16/3, Computations of Musters (1745).
AO 16/4–5, Computations of Musters, (1754–55).

Chatham Papers
30/8/75–76, Miscellaneous Military Papers.
30/8/84, Ireland

Bibliography

Colonial Office Series
CO 117/1–2, Havana Expedition (1762–64).

State Papers Domestic (Military Series)
SP41/6–25, Secretary at War (1714–72).
SP41/41–4, Miscellaneous Commissions.
SP41/45–7, Applications for Commissions (1714–27).
SP41/48, Undated Petitions and Military Papers (1727–60).

State Papers, Foreign Military Expeditions
SP87/18–48, Flanders and Germany (1742–63).

State Papers, Ireland
SP63/374–436, Out-Letters, Lord Lieutenant and Chief Secretary (1716–72).

War Office Series
WO 1/1, In-Letters, North America (1756–63).
WO 1/165, In-Letters, Belleisle, Germany, Portugal (1761–63).
WO 1/286, In-Letters, Gibraltar (1755–87).
WO 1/294, In-Letters, Minorca (1732–44).
WO 1/609, In-Letters, Ireland (1757–63).
WO 1/613–5, In-Letters, North Britain (1757–63).
WO 3/1–3, Out-Letters, Commander-in-Chief (1767–72).
WO 4/16–86, Out-Letters (General), Secretary at War (1714–70).
WO 4/313, Out-Letters (Mediterranean), Secretary at War (1730–34).
WO 4/981–2, Out-Letters (Private) (1759–65).
WO 4/1044, Letter-Book of Col. Edward Harvey, Adjutant General (1763–67).
WO 7/24–26, Out-Letters, Board of General Officers (Clothing) (1715–67).
WO 7/122–24, Out-Letters, Commissary General of the Musters (1716–79).
WO 8/1–5, Out-Letters, Ireland (1710–69).
WO12/(various), General Muster Books and Pay Lists (1732–1875).
WO 17/(various), Monthly Returns.
WO 24/(various), Establishments.
WO 25/3209, Estimates of the Land Forces (1714–59).
WO 25/3211, Abstracts of Musters (1748–49).
WO 26/14–28, Entry-Books of Warrants and Precedents (1712–74).
WO27/1–6, Inspection Returns (1750–60).
WO 30/105, Custom and Practice of the Army concerning Off-Reckonings (1772).
WO 34/71–99, Papers of Major-General Jeffery Amherst (various correspondents) (1753–65).
WO 71/1–10, Proceedings of the Board of General Officers (1706–55).
WO 71/14–26, General Courts Martial (1710–67).
WO 71/34–60, General Courts Martial (Home and Foreign Stations) (1715–67).
WO 71/65–67, Courts Martial Proceedings (Marching Regiments) (1756–58).
WO 72/2, Rules and Articles of War.
WO 81/1–11, Letter Books, Judge Advocate General (1715–68).
WO 93/2, Minute-Book of the Board of General Officers (1754–58).
WO 109/100-101, Paymaster General, Letters of Attorney (1719–31).
WO 109/102, Establishments (1720-21).
WO 109/103, Miscellaneous Estimates, Accounts etc. (1722–29).
WO 164/30, Prize Acts (1765–1868).

(iii) *Royal Archives, Windsor Castle*
RA. Cumb C/ (various); Papers of HRH William Augustus, Duke of Cumberland, 1744–*c*.

Bibliography

1768: 103 boxes of microfilm, *British Library Lending Division*, Boston Spa (Public Correspondence of the Duke with Ministers of State, British and Foreign Officers, Diplomats, etc.: Miscellaneous Memoranda, Draft Orders and Instructions).

(iv) National Army Museum, London

NAM.6707–11–18, *Aide Mémoire* belonging to 'Lieutenant Hamilton'.

NAM.6806–41–1, Townshend Papers, Services of George, Marquess Townshend.

NAM.6806–41–2, Townshend Papers, War of Austrian Succession (1742–48).

NAM.6806–41–3–4, Townshend Papers, Canada (1755–60).

NAM.6806–41–5, Townshend Papers, Germany (1761).

NAM.6806–41–6, Townshend Papers, Portugal (1762).

NAM.6806–41–7, Townshend Papers, Ireland (1767–70).

NAM.7406–50–47, 'An Establishment [of] Our Army, Ordinance [*sic*] and other Officers ... for Our Kingdom of Ireland' (1717).

NAM.7411–24–15, Hawley Papers; Manuscript Life of Lt-Gen. Henry Hawley.

NAM.7411–24–16, Hawley Papers, Various Papers and Correspondence (1719–65).

NAM.7411–24–29, Hawley Papers, 'Entry Book of Divers things' (1745–49).

NAM.7411–24–33, Hawley Papers, Extracts of Orders by H.R.H the Duke, Captain General and Commander-in-Chief (1755).

NAM.7805.63, Typescript of Letters of Capt. Nicholas Delacherois, 9th Foot (1757–74).

(v) Dorset Record Office, County Hall, Dorchester

D.86.XI, Out-letter book of Sir William Yonge (1741–45).

D.86.X3, Out-letter book of Henry Fox (1746–48).

D.86.X4, Out-letter book of Henry Fox, 'Private Letter Book' (1748–54).

D.86.X5, Out-letter book of Henry Fox (1745–55).

D.86.X6, Letters from Col. Robert Napier and others to Henry Fox (1748–51).

D.86.X8, Copies of out-letters of Henry Fox (1750–54).

D.86.X9–11, Account books of John Calcraft (1755–64).

D.86.X12, Bills and financial memoranda.

D.86.X13, Articles of co-partnership between John Calcraft and James Meyrick in the business of agents to regiments (1764).

(vi) Gateshead Public Library, Ellison of Hebburn Papers

Ellison A1, Letters of Henry Ellison to his father, Henry Ellison senior (1755–61).

Ellison A4–5, Various papers relating to the military services of Col. Robert Ellison (1729–55).

Ellison A6–7, Letters of Jane Ellison to her brother Henry Ellison senior (1728–60).

Ellison A18–21, Various papers relating to the military services of Gen. Cuthbert Ellison (1728–65).

Ellison A30, Letters of Henry Thomas Carr.

(vii) University of Hull, Brynmor Jones Library

DDHO3.34, Sir Charles Hotham, fifth Bt., Military Order Book.

DDHO4.1·34, Correspondence of Sir Charles Hotham-Thompson, eighth Bt. (1738–67).

DDHO4.142, Orders by Lord Albemarle relating to the Non-effective Fund of the Foot Guards, n.d. (*c.*1747–8?).

DDHO4.149, Circular from the Commissary General's office on the method of forming muster rolls (1754).

DDHO4.188, Paper on the Non-effective Fund of the Foot Guards, n.d (*c.*1747–48?).

DDHO4.231, 'Regiments proposed to be drafted' (1762).

DDHO4.233, 'Drafts for Germany' (1762).

DDHO4.277, Military notebook (*c.*1738–48).

DDHO4.285, *Standing Orders to be observed by His Majesty's Forces in Ireland*, Cork, 1764.

(viii) John Rylands University Library of Manchester, Bagshawe Papers

B2.1.1–303, Correspondence of Col. Samuel Bagshawe with officers and agents, concerning the 93rd Foot (1759–62).

B2.2.1–824, Other military correspondence of Col. Samuel Bagshawe (1747–62).

B2.3.1–881, Correspondence; Personal (1738–62).

B2.4.1–751, Miscellaneous Military Papers, Returns, Muster-Rolls, Accounts and Receipts.

B2.5.1–2, 6–294, Two bound volumes and two bundles of correspondence, papers and accounts relating to Bagshawe's service in India (1754–57).

B3.10.1–626, Letter books of Sir James Caldwell, fourth Bt., Captain Commandant, 20th (Light) Dragoons (1760–63).

(ix) Suffolk Record Office, Ipswich

HA 67.421, Correspondence, Memoranda, Orderly-Books, etc., of the Second and Third Earls of Albemarle (1718–1764), including Havana Papers (1762–64).

HA 174.112, Correspondence of William Viscount Barrington, with Fox, Granby, Amherst, Ligonier, Pitt, Bute, etc.; Memoranda and Applications for regiments (1755–61).

Unpublished theses and papers

Bailey, D. W., 'The Board of Ordnance and the Production of British Military Small Arms, 1700–1783' (typescript of a lecture given before the Arms and Armour Society at HM Tower of London), May 1981.

Bruce, A. P. C., 'The System of Purchase and Sale of Commissions in the British Army and the Campaign for its Abolition 1660–1871' (University of Manchester Ph.D. thesis), 1973.

Burton, I. F., 'The Secretary at War and the Administration of the War of the Spanish Succession' (University of London D.Phil. thesis), 1960.

Ferguson, K. P., 'The Army in Ireland from the Restoration to the Act of Union' (Trinity College, Dublin, Ph.D. thesis), 1980.

Hayes, J. W., 'The Social and Professional Background of the Officers of the British Army 1714–1763' (University of London M.A. thesis), 1956.

Pimlott, J. L., 'The Administration of the British Army 1783–1793' (University of Leicester Ph.D. thesis) 1975.

Printed sources: official publications and works of reference

Army List, Printed by Order of the House of Commons (1740).

Army Lists, First to Twelfth Editions, published by John Millan, '. . . by permission of the Right Honourable the Secretary at War' (1754 –Nov. 1763).

Beatson, R., *Naval and Military Memoirs of Great Britain 1727–1783*, London, 1804.

Clode, C. M., *The Military Forces of the Crown, their Administration and Government*, london, 1869.

A Collection of Regulations, Orders and Instructions formed and issued for the Use of the Army in consequence of the Pay Office Act, London, 1788.

Court and City Register, 1745–1764.

Dalton, C., *George the First's Army, 1714–1727*, London, 1914.

Dictionary of National Biography

Fortescue, Sir John, *A History of the British Army* I, II, London, 1899.

Frederick, J. B. M., *Lineage Book of the British Army 1660–1968*, Cornwallville, (N.Y), 1969.

Journals of the House of Commons, XVIII-XXIX, (1727–63).

Journals of the House of Commons of Ireland, III-VII, (1757–63).

Lawson, C. C. P., *A History of the Uniforms of the British Army*, I, II, London, 1940, 1949.

Namier, L. H., Brooke, J., *The History of Parliament: The Commons 1754–90*, London, 1964.

Report of the Committee Appointed to consider the State of His Majesty's Land Forces and Marines,

Bibliography

6 June 1746; *Reports from Committees of the House of Commons*, II, pp. 75–211.

Fourth, Fifth, Sixth, Seventh, Ninth and Tenth 'Reports of the Commissioners appointed to examine, to take and state the Public Accounts of the Kingdom' 1781–3; *Journals of the House of Commons*, XXXVIII, pp. 380–94, 572–92, 702–28, 1066–111; XXXIX, pp. 325–44, 522–73.

Rules and Articles for the Better Government of Our Horse and Foot Guards and all our Forces in Great Britain, Ireland and Dominions Beyond the Seas, London, 1718.

Sedgwick, R., *The History of Parliament: The Commons 1714–54*, London, 1971.

Standing Orders to be Observed by His Majesty's Forces in Ireland, Cork, 1764.

The Succession of Colonels to all His Majestie's Land Forces from their Rise to 1742, London, 1742.

Walton, C., *History of the British Standing Army 1660–1700*, London, 1894.

Whitworth, Sir Charles, *Public Accounts of Services and Grants 1720–1770*, London, 1771.

Contemporary military textbooks

Advice from a Father to a Son just enter'd in the Army and about to go Abroad into Action, London, 1776.

Bever, Major Samuel, *The Cadet: A Military Treatise*, Dublin, 1756.

Bland, Lt.-Col. Humphrey, *Treatise of Military Discipline* London, 1727.

Cuthbertson, Capt. Bennett, *A System for the Compleat Interior Management and Economy of a Battalion of Infantry*, Dublin, 1768.

Dalrymple, Lt.-Col. Campbell, *A Military Essay*, London, 1761.

Hamilton, R. (M.D.), *The Duties of a Regimental Surgeon*, Dublin, 1781.

Hinde, Capt. Robert, *The Discipline of the Light Horse*, London 1778.

Knowles, Admiral Sir Charles, *An Essay on the Duties and Qualifications of a Sea Officer*, London, 1765.

Letter to the Gentlemen of the Army, London, 1757.

Molesworth, Richard Viscount. *A Short Course of Standing Rules for the Government and Conduct of an Army*, 'by a Lieutenant-General of His Majesty's Service', London, 1744.

Pembroke, Henry Earl of, *Military Equitation, or a Method of Breaking Horses and Training soldiers to ride designed for the Use of the Army*, London 1761.

Pringle, John, *Observations on the Diseases of the Army*, London, 1752.

Rudiments of War, London, 1777.

Simes, Capt. Thomas, *The Military Medley: Containing the most necessary Rules and Directions for attaining a competent Knowledge of the Art ...*', London, 1768.

—*A Military Guide for Young Officers*, London, 1772.

—*A Military Course for the Government and Conduct of a Battalion*, London, 1777.

—*The Regulator: or Instructions to Form the Officer and Complete the Soldier*, London, 1780.

System of Camp Discipline collected by a Gentleman of the Army to which is added Kane's Discipline for a Battalion upon Action and Kane's Campaigns of King William and The Duke of Marlborough continued by an impartial Hand, London, 1757.

A Treatise of Military Finance, (attributed to John Williamson), London, 1782.

General Wolfe's Instructions to Young Officers, London 1768.

Contemporary journal and pamphlet literature

The Antient and Present State of the Military Law in Great Britain consider'd, London, 1749.

An Attempt towards an Apology for His R ... H ... the D ..., London, 1751.

Colonel Draper's Answer to the Spanish Arguments claiming the Galleon and refusing Payment of the Ransom Bills for preserving Manila from Pillage and Destruction, London, 1764.

Bibliography

A Dialogue between Thomas Jones, a Life-guard man and John Smith, late a Serjeant in the First Regiment of Foot Guards, just returned from Flanders, London, 1749.

Erskine, Lt. Thomas, *Observations on the Prevailing Abuses in the British Army*, London, 1775.

Hutcheson, Archibald, *Abstracts of the Numbers and Yearly Pay of the Land forces of Horse, Foot and Dragoons in Great Britain for the Year 1718 . . . with some Remarks relating to the same.* 'By a Member of Parliament', London, 1718.

A Letter to a Member of Parliament in relation to the Bill for punishing Mutiny and Desertion, London, 1749.

A Modest Defence of the Army by a Soldier, London, 1753.

A Plain Narrative of the Reduction of Manila and the Phillippine Islands, London, 1764.

'Railton, J.', *The Army's Regulator; or The Soldier's Monitor*, London, 1738.

Seasonable and Affecting Observations on the Mutiny Bill, London, 1750

A Seasonable Letter to the Author of Seasonable and Affecting Observations on the Mutiny Bill, London, 1751.

A Succinct and Impartial History of all the Regencies, Protectorships, Minorities and Princes of England . . . with a Proper Dedication to the Great Duke, London, 1751.

Reports of the Royal Commission on Historical Manuscripts, London

Frankland Russell Astley, 1900
Stopford Sackville, I, 1904.
Townshend, 1887.
Twelfth Report, Appendix; Part V: Rutland, 1889.
Various Collections, VIII, 1913.

Memoirs, journals, collections of contemporary correspondence

Albemarle, William, second Earl of, *The Albemarle Papers: Correspondence of William Anne, 2nd Earl of Albemarle*, ed C. Sandford Terry,   Aberdeen, 1902.

Argyll, John Second Duke of, *Life of John, 2nd Duke of Argyll and Greenwich*, Belfast, 1745.

Atkinson, C. T. ed., 'The Army under the Early Hanoverians: Gleanings from WO 4 and other Sources in the Public Record Office', *JSAHR*, XXI, 1942, pp. 138–47.

—'The Chequers Court Manuscripts: Some Extracts relating to the Foot Guards, 1742–48', *JSAHR*, XXIII, 1945, pp. 114–18.

—'Jenkins' Ear, the Austrian Succession and the 'Forty-five: More Gleanings . . .', *JSAHR*, XXII, 1943–44, pp. .280–98.

Bagshawe, W. H. G. ed., *The Bagshawes of Ford*, London 1886.

Barrington, Shute, *The Political Life of William Wildman Viscount Barrington*, London, 1814.

Browne, Capt. Philip, 'Letters of Captain Philip Browne 1737–46', J. H. Leslie ed., *JSAHR*, V, 1926, pp. 49–65.

Burgoyne, Col. the Hon. John, *Political and Military Episodes in the latter Half of the Eighteenth Century described from the Life and Correspondence of the Right Honourable John Burgoyne*, J. B. de Fonblanque ed., London, 1876.

Campbell, Sir James, *Memoirs of Sir James Campbell of Ardkinglass*, London, 1832.

Chesterfield, Philip, Earl of, *Letters of Philip Dormer Stanhope, Earl of Chesterfield*, J. Bradshaw ed., London, 1812.

Corneille, Major John, *Journal of my Service in India*, M. Edwardes ed., London, Folio Society, 1966.

Cumberland, William Augustus Duke of, *Historical Memoirs of His late Royal Highness, William Augustus Duke of Cumberland*, London, 1767.

—*William Augustus Duke of Cumberland*, A. M. Campbell-Maclachlan ed., London, 1876.

Cushner, N. P. ed., *Documents Illustrating the British Conquest of Manila, 1762–3*, London, Camden Fourth Series, VIII, 1971.

Bibliography

Davenport, Major Richard, 'To Mr Davenport: Letters of Major Richard Davenport 1742–60', C. W. Frearson ed., *JSAHR*, Special Publication No. 9, London, 1968.

Ellison, Col. Robert, 'The Correspondence of Colonel Robert Ellison of Hebburn, 1733–48', *Archaeologia Aeliana*, Fourth Series, XXXI, 1953, pp. 1–21.

Fox, Henry, *Henry Fox, First Lord Holland*, Earl of Ilchester ed., London, 1920.

—*Letters to Henry Fox*, Earl of Ilchester ed., London, Roxburghe Club, 1915.

Francis, Sir Philip, *Memoirs of Sir Philip Francis*, J. Parkes, H. Merivale ed., London, 1867.

Gardiner, Col. James, *Some Remarkable Passages in the Life of Colonel James Gardiner*, by Phillip Doddridge, DD, London, 1747.

George III, *Letters from George III to Lord Bute 1756–66*, R. Sedgwick ed., London, 1939.

Glover, Richard, *Memoirs of a Celebrated Literary and Political Character 1742–57*, London, 1813.

Hamilton, C. ed., *Braddock's Defeat: Three Eye-witness Accounts*, Norman, Oklahoma, 1959.

Hardwicke, Philip, Earl of, *The Life of Lord Chancellor Hardwicke*, P. C. Yorke ed., London 1913.

Hervey, Capt. Augustus, RN, *Augustus Hervey's Journal 1746–1759*, D. Erskine ed., London, 1953.

Hervey, John Lord, *Some Materials towards Memoirs of the Reign of King George II*, R. Sedgwick ed., London, 1931.

Hill, S. C. ed., *Bengal 1756–1757: The Indian Records Series*, London, 1905.

Lister, Lt. Jeremy, 'Jeremy, Lister, 10th Regiment 1770–1783', R. A. Innes ed., *JSAHR*, XLI, 1963, pp. 31–41, 59–73.

Marchmont, Hugh Earl of, *Selections from the Papers of the Earls of Marchmont*, G. H. Rose ed., London, 1831.

Murray, Col. Alexander, 'The Letters of Colonel Alexander Murray 1742–59', *Regimental Annual, The Sherwood Foresters, Nottinghamshire and Derbyshire Regiment*, 1926, pp. 181–220.

Pargellis, S. M. ed., *Military Affairs in North America, 1748–1765: Selected Documents from the Cumberland Papers in Windsor Castle*, New Haven, Conn., 1936.

Pelham, Henry, *The Administration of the Right Honourable Henry Pelham*, W. Coxe, London, 1829.

Richmond, Charles, second Duke of, *A Duke and his Friends: The Life and Letters of Charles, Second Duke of Richmond*, Earl of March ed., London, 1911

Shelburne, William Earl of, *The Life of William Earl of Shelburne*, Lord E. Fitzmaurice, London, 1875.

Stair, John, Earl of, *The Annals of Stair*, J. Murray-Graham ed., Edinburgh and London, 1899.

Stockdale, Ensign Percival, *Memoirs of the Life and Writings of Percival Stockdale, written by Himself*, London, 1809.

Townshend, George, first Marquess, *Military Life of Field Marshal George, First Marquess Townshend*, C. V. Townshend ed, London, 1901.

Walpole, Horace, *Memoirs of the Reign of George II*, Lord Holland ed., London, 1846.

Whitefoord, Col. Charles, *The Whitefoord Papers: Correspondence and other Manuscripts of Col. Charles Whitefoord*, W. S. Hewins ed., Oxford, 1898.

Wolfe, Maj.-Gen. James, *Life and Letters of James Wolfe*, B. Willson, London, 1909.

—*The Life of Major General James Wolfe, illustrated by his Correspondence*, R. Wright ed., London, 1864.

—'Some Unpublished Wolfe Letters 1755–58', R. H. Whitworth ed., *JSAHR*, LIII, 1975, pp. 65–86.

Secondary printed sources: books

Atkinson, C. T. *The History of the Royal Dragoons, 1661–1934*, Glasgow, n.d.

—*The Dorsetshire Regiment*, I, Oxford, 1952.

Bibliography

—*The Royal Hampshire Regiment*, Glasgow, 1952.

Bailey, D. W., *British Military Longarms 1715–1815*, London, 1971.

Baines, J., *The Jacobite Rising of 1715*, London, 1970.

Barnett, C., *Britain and Her Army: A Military, Political and Social Survey*, London, 1970.

Baugh, D. A., *Naval Administration in the Age of Walpole*, Princeton, N.J., 1965.

Beckett, J. C., *The Making of Modern Ireland 1603–1923*, London, 1969.

Blackmore, H. L., *British Military Firearms 1650–1850*, London, 1961.

Bruce, A. P. C., *The Purchase System in the British Army 1660–1871*, London, 1980.

Burton, I. F., *The Captain General: The Military Career of John Churchill Duke of Marlborough 1702–1711*, London, 1968.

Callahan, R., *The East India Company and Army Reform 1763–98*, Cambridge, Mass., 1972.

Charteris, E., *William Augustus, Duke of Cumberland: His Early Life and Times, 1721–1748*, London, 1913.

—*William Augustus, Duke of Cumberland and the Seven Years' War*, London, 1925.

Childs, J. *The Army of Charles II*, London, 1976.

—*The Army, James II and the Glorious Revolution*, Manchester, 1980.

—*Armies and Warfare in Europe, 1648–1789*, Manchester, 1982.

Colley, L., *In Defiance of Oligarchy: The Tory Party, 1714–60*, Cambridge, 1982.

Corvisier, A., *Armies and Societies in Europe, 1494–1789*, Bloomington, Ind., and London, 1979.

Cowper, L., *The King's Own: The Story of a Royal Regiment*, I, Oxford, 1939.

Cruickshank, C. G., *Elizabeth's Army*, second edition, Oxford, 1966.

Curtis, E. E., *The Organization of the British Army in the American Revolution*, New Haven, Conn., 1926.

Dickinson, H. T., *Liberty and Property: Political Ideology in Eighteenth Century Britain*, London, University Paperback edition, 1979.

Dickson, P. G. M., *The Sun Insurance Office, 1710–1960*, London, 1960.

Duffy, C., *The Army of Frederick the Great*, Newton Abbot, 1974.

—*The Army of Maria Theresa*, London, 1977.

Ettinger, A. A., *James Edward Oglethorpe, Imperial Idealist*, Oxford, 1936.

Field, C., *Britain's Sea Soldiers*, Liverpool, 1924.

Firth, Sir Charles, *Cromwell's Army*, London, 1962.

Foord, A. S., *His Majesty's Opposition, 1714–1830*, Oxford, 1964.

Fortescue, Sir John, *The British Army, 1783–1802*, London, 1905.

Glover, M., *Wellington's Army in the Peninsula, 1808–1814*, Newton Abbot, 1977.

Glover, R., *Peninsular Preparation: the Reform of the British Army, 1795–1809*, Cambridge, 1963.

Hatton, R., *George I – Elector and King*, London, 1978.

Hayter, T., *The Army and the Crowd in Mid-Georgian England*, London, 1978.

Hill, C., *The World Turned Upside Down: Radical Ideas during the English Revolution*, Penguin edition, Harmondsworth, 1975.

Holmes, G., *Augustan England, Professions, State and Society, 1680–1730*, London, 1982.

Holzman, J., *The Nabobs in England: a Study of the Returned Anglo-Indian 1760–1785*, New York, 1926.

Houlding, J. A., *Fit for Service: the Training of the British Army 1715–1795*, Oxford, 1980.

Hughes, E., *North Country Life in the Eighteenth Century: the North East 1700–1750*, Oxford, 1952.

Ivers, L. E., *British Drums on the Southern Frontier: the Military Conquest of Georgia*, Chapel Hill, N.C., 1974.

James, F.G., *Ireland in the Empire 1688–1770*, Cambridge, Mass., 1973.

Jarvis, R. C., *Collected Papers on the Jacobite Risings*, I, Manchester, 1971.

Keegan, J., *The Face of Battle*, London, 1976.

Kennet, L., *The French Armies in the Seven Years' War*, Durham, N.C, 1967.

Bibliography

Leask, J. C., McCance, H. M., *Regimental Records of the Royal Scots*, Dublin, 1915.

Lenman, B., *The Jacobite Risings in Britain, 1689–1746*, London, 1980.

Lindsay, Lord, *The Lives of the Lindsays: a Memoir of the House of Crawford and Balcarres*, Wigan, 1840.

McCardell, L., *Ill-starred General: Braddock of the Coldstream Guards*, Pittsburgh, 1958.

Maitland, F. W., *The Constitutional History of England*, Cambridge, 1908.

Manners, W. E.., *John Manners, Marquis of Granby*, London, 1899.

Marshall, P.G., *East Indian Fortunes: the British in Bengal in the Eighteenth Century*, Oxford, 1978.

Newhall, R. A., *Muster and Review: a Problem of English Military Administration 1420–1440*, Cambridge, Mass., 1940.

Niemeyer, J., Ortenburg, G., *The Hanoverian Army during the Seven Years' War*, Copenhagen, 1977.

Orr, M., *Dettingen, 1743*, London, 1972.

Owen, J. B., *The Rise of the Pelhams*, London, 1957.

Packenham, T., *The Year of Liberty: The Story of the Great Irish Rebellion of 1798*, London, 1969.

Pares, Sir Richard, *War and Trade in the West Indies, 1739–1763*, Oxford, 1936.

Pargellis, S. M., *Lord Loudoun in North America*, New Haven, Conn., 1933.

Plumb, J. H., *Sir Robert Walpole, I: The Making of a Statesman*, London 1956.

—*Sir Robert Walpole, II: The King's Minister*, London, 1960.

Porter, R., *English Society in the Eighteenth Century*, Harmondsworth, 1982.

Reilly, R., *Wolfe of Quebec*, London, 1973.

Robson, B., *Swords of the British Army: The Regulation Patterns, 1788–1914*, London, 1975.

Salmond, J. B., *Wade in Scotland*, London and Edinburgh, 1934.

Savory, R. H., *His Britannic Majesty's Army in Germany during the Seven Years' War*, Oxford, 1966.

Schwoerer, L. G., *No Standing Armies! The Anti-army Ideology in Seventeenth Century England*, Baltimore and London, 1974.

Scouller, R. E., *The Armies of Queen Anne*, Oxford, 1966.

Shy, J., *Toward Lexington: the Role of the British Army in the Coming of the American Revolution*, Princeton, N.J., 1965.

Skrine, F. H., *Fontenoy and Great Britain's Share in the War of the Austrian Succession, 1741–48*, London, 1906.

Raymond–Smythies, R. H., *Historical Records of the 40th (2nd Somersetshire) Regiment*, Devonport, 1894.

Speck, W. A., *The Butcher: The Duke of Cumberland and the Suppression of the '45*, Oxford, 1981.

Spiers, E. M., *The Army and Society, 1815–1914*, London, 1980

Stone, L., *The Family, Sex and Marriage in England, 1500–1800*, Penguin edition, Harmondsworth, 1979.

Taylor, W., *The Military Roads in Scotland*, Newton Abbot, 1976.

Tomasson, K., Buist, F., *Battles of the '45*, London 1962.

Tylden, G., *Horses and Saddlery*, London, 1965.

Vale, W. L., *The History of the South Staffordshire Regiment*, Aldershot, 1969.

Valentine, A., *Lord George Germain*, Oxford, 1961.

Ward, W.R., *Georgian Oxford: University Politics in the Eighteenth Century*, Oxford, 1958.

Webb, H. J., *Elizabethan Military Science*, Madison, Wis., and London, 1965.

Western, J. R., *The English Militia in the Eighteenth Century*, London, 1965.

Whitworth, R. H. *Field Marshal Lord Ligonier: The British Army, 1702–1770*, Oxford, 1958.

Wickwire, F. and M., *Cornwallis: The Imperial Years*, Chapel Hill, N.C., 1980.

Williams, B., *The Life of William Pitt*, London, 1913.

—*The Whig Supremacy*, second edition, Oxford, 1965.

Wylly, H. C., *History of the 1st and Second Battalions, the Sherwood Foresters*, London, 1929.

Bibliography

—*The Loyal North Lancashire Regiment*, London, 1933.

Secondary printed sources: articles

Anderson. O., 'The Constitutional Position of the Secretary at War 1642–1855', *JSAHR*, XXXVI, 1958, pp. 165–69

Baker, N., 'Changing Attitudes toward Government in Eighteenth Century Britain', A. Whiteman *et al.*, *Statesmen Scholars and Merchants*, Oxford, 1973, pp. 202–19.

Bartlett, T., 'The Augmentation of the Army in Ireland, 1767–1769', *EHR*, 96, 1981, pp. 540–59.

Burton, I. F., Newman, A.N., 'Sir John Cope: Promotion in the Eighteenth Century', *EHR*, 78, 1963, pp. 655–68.

Burton, I. F., 'The Committee of Council at the War Office: An Experiment in Cabinet Government under Queen Anne', *Historical Journal*, IV, 1961, pp. 78–84.

Cadell, Sir Patrick, 'Caroline Frederick Scott', *Army Quarterly*, LXVII, 1953–54, pp. 223–44.

Christie, I. R., 'The Personality of George I', *History Today*, V, 1955, pp. 516–28.

Darling, A.D., 'The British Basket-hilted Cavalry Sword', *Canadian Journal of Arms Collecting*, VII, 1969, pp. 79–96.

—'Weapons of the Highland Regiments, 1740–1780', *CJAC*, VIII, 1970, pp. 75–95.

—'The British Infantry Hangers', *CJAC*, VIII, 1970, pp. 124–36.

Dawnay, N. P., 'The Clothing Warrant of 1743', *JSAHR*, XLVI, 1968, pp. 87–90.

Duffy, M., 'The Foundations of British Naval Power', M. Duffy ed., *The Military Revolution and the State*, Exeter, 1980, pp. 49–85.

Ferguson, K. P., 'Military Manuscripts in the Public Record Office of Ireland', *The Irish Sword*, XV, 1982, pp. 112–15.

Fortescue, Sir John, 'The Army', A. S. Turbeville ed., *Johnson's England*, Oxford, 1933, I, pp. 66–87.

Glover, M., 'Purchase, Patronage and Promotion in the Army at the Time of the Peninsular War', *Army Quarterly*, CIII, 1972–73, pp. 211–15, 355–62.

Guy, A. J., 'Reinforcements for Portugal 1762: Recruiting for Rank at the End of the Seven Years' War', *ARNAM*, 1977–78, pp. 29–34.

—'A Whole Army Absolutely Ruined in Ireland: Aspects of the Irish Establishment', *ARNAM*, 1978–79, pp. 30–43.

—'Regimental Agency in the British Standing Army 1715–1763: a Study in Georgian Military Administration', *BJRL*, LXII, 1980, pp. 423–53, LXIII, 1980, pp. 31–57.

Habakkuk, H. J., 'Marriage Settlements in the Eighteenth Century', *Transactions of the Royal Historical Society*, XXXII, 1950.

Hayes, J., 'The Military Papers of Colonel Samuel Bagshawe 1713–1762', *BJRL*, XXXIX, 1956–57, pp. 356–89.

—'Scottish Officers in the British Army 1714–63', *Scottish Historical Review*, XXXVII, 1958, pp. 25–57.

—'The Royal House of Hanover and the British Army', *BJRL*, XL, 1957–58, pp. 328–57.

—'Lieutenant Colonel and Major Commandants of the Seven Years' War', *JSAHR*, XXXVI, 1958, pp. 3–13, 38–9

—'The Purchase of Colonelcies in the Army 1714–1763', *JSAHR*, XXXIX, 1961, pp. 3–10.

—'Two Soldier Brothers of the Eighteenth Century', *JSAHR*, XL, 1962, pp. 150–61.

Hintze, O., 'The Commissary, and his Influence in General Administrative History', F. Gilbert ed., *The Historical Essays of Otto Hintze*, New York, 1975, pp. 268–301.

Hughes, E., 'The Professions in the Eighteenth Century', *Durham University Historical Journal*, 44, 1952.

Johnson, S. H. F., 'The Irish Establishment', *The Irish Sword*, I, 1949–53, pp. 33–6.

Bibliography

Jones, C., 'The Military Revolution and the Professionalization of the French Army under the Ancien Regime', M. Duffy ed., *The Military Revolution and the State*, Exeter, 1980, pp. 29–48.

Jones, K. R., 'Richard Cox, Army Agent and Banker', *JSAHR*, XXXIV, 1956, pp. 178–86.

Hayes-McCoy, G. A., 'The Government Forces which opposed the Irish Insurgents of 1798', *The Irish Sword*, IV 1959, pp. 16–28.

—'The Irish Horse Regiments of the Eighteenth Century', *The Irish Sword*, IX, 1969, pp. 127–34.

McCracken, J. L., 'The Irish Viceroyalty 1760–1773', H.A. Cronne *et al.*, *Essays in British and Irish History in Honour of James Eadie Todd*, London, 1949.

McGuffie, T. H., 'A Deputy-Paymaster's Fortune: the Case of George Durant, Deputy-Paymaster to the Havana Expedition, 1762', *JSAHR*, XXXII, 1954, pp. 144–7.

Marini, A. J., 'Parliament and the Marine Regiments, 1739', *Mariners Mirror*, LXII, 1976, pp. 55–65.

Mathias, P., 'The Social Structure in the Eighteenth Century; A Calculation by Joseph Massie', *The Economic History Review*, Second Series, X, 1957, pp. 30–45.

Musket, P., 'Military Operations Against Smugglers in Kent and Sussex, 1698–1750', *JSAHR*, LII, 1974, pp. 89–110.

Newman, A. N., 'Leicester House Politics 1748–51', *EHR*, 76, 1961, pp. 577–89.

Owen, J. B., 'George II Reconsidered', A. Whiteman *et al.*, *Statesmen, Scholars and Merchants*, Oxford, 1973, pp. 113–34.

Pargellis, S. M., 'The Four Independent Companies of New York', *Essays in Colonial History Presented to Charles M. Andrews by his Students*, New Haven, Conn., 1931.

Pimlott, J. L., 'The Reformation of the Life Guards, 1788', *JSAHR*, LIII, 1975, pp. 194–209.

Razzell, P. E., 'Social Origins of Officers in the Indian and British Home Army, 1758–1962', *British Journal of Sociology*, XIV, 1963, pp. 248–60.

Rogers, N., 'Popular Protest in Early Hanoverian London', *Past and Present*, No 79, 1978, pp. 70–100.

Roots, I., 'Swordsmen and Decimators: Cromwell's Major-Generals' R. H. Parry, ed., *The English Civil War and After*, London, 1970, pp. 78–92.

Roy, I., 'The English Civil War and English Society', B. Bond, I. Roy eds., *War and Society*, London, 1975, pp. 24–43.

—'The Army and its Critics in Seventeenth Century England', B. Bond, I. Roy eds., *War and Society*, London, 1976, pp. 231–59.

Sutherland, L. S., Binney, J., 'Henry Fox as Paymaster to the Forces', R. Mitchison ed., *Essays in Eighteenth Century History*, London, 1966, pp. 231–59.

Thornton, A. P., 'The British in Manila, 1762–64', *History Today*, VII, 1957, pp. 44–53.

Torrance, J., 'Social Class and Bureaucratic Innovation: the Commisioners for Examining the Public Accounts 1780–87', *Past and Present*, No. 78, 1979, pp. 56–81.

Ward S. G. P., 'The Letters of Captain Nicholas Delacherois, 9th Regiment.' *JSAHR*, LI, 1973, pp. 5–14.

Whitworth, R. H. 'William Augustus, Duke of Cumberland', *History Today*, XXVII, 1977, pp. 82–91.

Index

Index

Index

Index

Index